The Nanjing Massacre in History and Historiography

ASIA

Local Studies / Global Themes

Jeffrey N. Wasserstrom, Rubie S. Watson,
and Hue-Tam Ho Tai, Editors

1. *Bicycle Citizens: The Political World of the Japanese Housewife,* by Robin M. LeBlanc
2. *The Nanjing Massacre in History and Historiography,* edited by Joshua A. Fogel
3. *The Country of Memory: Remaking the Past in Late Socialist Vietnam,* by Hue-Tam Ho Tai
4. *Chinese Femininities/Chinese Masculinities: A Reader,* edited by Susan Brownell and Jeffrey Wasserstrom

The Nanjing Massacre in History and Historiography

EDITED BY

Joshua A. Fogel

FOREWORD BY

Charles S. Maier

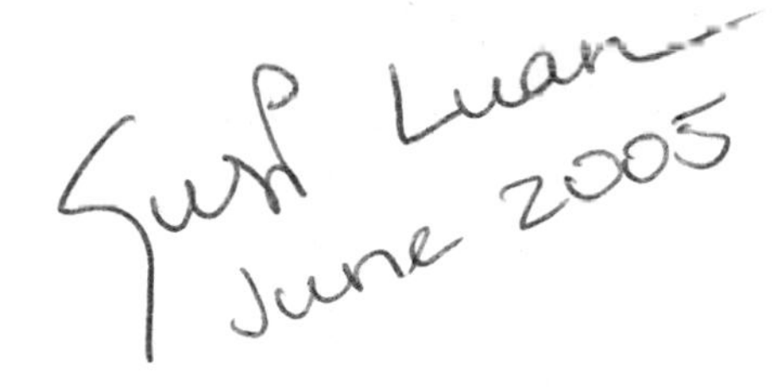

UNIVERSITY OF CALIFORNIA PRESS
BERKELEY · LOS ANGELES · LONDON

University of California Press
Berkeley and Los Angeles, California

University of California Press, Ltd.
London, England

Library of Congress Cataloging-in-Publication Data

The Nanjing Massacre in history and historiography /
edited by Joshua A. Fogel.
p. cm.
Includes bibliographical references and index.
ISBN 0-520-22006-4 (alk. paper).—ISBN 0-520-22007-2
(alk. paper)
1. Nanking Massacre, Nanjing, Jiangsu Sheng, China,
1937–Historiography. 2. Nanjing (Jiangsu Sheng,
China)—History—20th century—Historiography.
3. Historiography—China. 4. Historiography—Japan.
I. Fogel, Joshua A., 1950– .

DS796.N2N346 2000
951'. 136—dc21 99-37864
CIP

Printed in the United States of America

08 07 06 05 04 03 02
10 9 8 7 6 5 4 3

The paper used in this publication is both acid-free and totally chlorine-free (TCF). It meets the minimum requirements of ANSI/NISO Z39.48-1992 (R 1997) (*Permanence of Paper*). ♾

Contents

Foreword

As a student of European history, I address with diffidence the contentious history of the Nanjing Massacre. Of course, I know why I was asked to contribute a preface to these essays: I have written about German controversies surrounding the historiography of the Holocaust. Within both Japan and China—the country of the perpetrators and the country of the victims—the Nanjing Massacre has assumed somewhat the same salience in public memory as the Holocaust in Europe and America. This is not to claim equivalence in any way; every mass killing is unique. In fact, the event that both Western and Japanese moral commentators often cite in the same sentence with Auschwitz as a paradigmatic site of slaughter is Hiroshima—sometimes (inappropriately, I believe) to claim equivalence and sometimes more rhetorically as a symbol of the brutalization of warfare in the twentieth century. Still, the Japanese army's killing spree at Nanjing at the close of 1937 has become the other emblematic massacre of the Pacific War, and it remains the epitome of the cruelty and aggression that the Japanese militarist regime unleashed. The Nanjing rampage seems all the more atrocious in that it involved not what has seemed so horrifying about the Holocaust—its bureaucratized planning and mechanized execution—but the often gleeful killing of perhaps hundreds of thousands of civilians by individual soldiers using sword and bayonet as well as bullet. The killings were all the more appalling in that they were unnecessary for the military objective, continued after the victory was secured, and apparently involved such joyful or at least indifferent murder. The accompanying rape and brutality short of murder—as in Bosnia more recently—served purposes of degradation and dehumanization as well as, possibly, sexual release.

The chapters in this volume confirm that important aspects of the atrocity remain uncertain, including precise figures and the chains of command and responsibility—but even those who most object to the story can no longer plausibly deny the overall record of wanton cruelty. Yet the purpose and achievement of these essays is not to confirm the record that conscientious investigators—Japanese as well as Chinese—have repeatedly established. It is to document the evolving historical evaluations and politicized debates about the massacre in both countries. As the authors emphasize, these passionate discussions have hardly been straightforward.

As a historian of German efforts to "master the past," I can most usefully signal some revealing comparisons and differences between the historical processing of German and Japanese responsibilities for atrocities committed in the name of their respective nations. (I will not speak to the Chinese story that Mark Eykholt tells here. What it demonstrates most intriguingly is that the Nanjing record has been a resource for popular mobilization often against a regime that would rather let sleeping dogs lie if economic or political advantage was to be gained from the Japanese. Chinese regimes have been most vulnerable perhaps when they seemed unable or unwilling to mobilize their resources of size and mass against foreign influences, as in 1900 or 1919, and the official manipulation of the Nanjing Massacre has revealed similar angry reactions.) One facile comparison, in fact, now represents the conventional wisdom for those of us who study the postwar self-scrutiny of the aggressor nations in World War II. This dominant script proclaims that whereas the Germans have largely faced up to their historical responsibility, the Japanese have done so far less completely, if at all. Postwar Germans have publicly acknowledged the aggressive designs of the Nazi state, the cruelty of their occupation policies, and the murder of the Jews. They have paid reparations, taught the shameful record to their children in schools, erected monuments to the victims, and in general have learned to shun the evils of the authoritarianism, military ambition, and anti-Semitism to which they seemed so prone. The postwar Japanese, according to the dominant script, find an equivalent disavowal of the past far more difficult and resort instead to avoidance and euphemism if not occasionally outright denial—at least until the outcry of their East Asian neighbors and the threat of adverse economic consequences compels some generic formulation of regret.[1] The public rhetoric of the successive presidents of the Federal Republic, Richard von Weizsäcker and Roman Herzog, and of chancellors from Konrad Adenauer and Willy Brandt to Helmut Kohl, also contrasts with the grudging statements of regret by Japanese statesmen. About the same time that the Yokohama Museum displayed a cautious 1995 anniversary exhibit, "Photography in the 1940s," a collection of German photographs documenting the Wehrmacht's mass executions of civilians in Eastern Europe was traveling from city to city—attracting sometimes indignant criticism but also long queues of viewers. The Germans were more prepared to look their behavior in the face—at a moment, too, it must be recalled, when the Smithsonian Institution was yielding to pressure that its partially critical description of the bombing of Hiroshima must be substantially revised.

Historians should remain distrustful of any easy generalization concerning nations as a whole. Modern nations represent communities of debate and dissent united by language or by shared tensions over language; by a sense of shared, though often contested, history; by a partial commitment, though again contested, to redistribute some material resources among citizens; and ultimately by some unitary representation in the world of states. When it comes to what nations think or believe, we generalize at our peril. We cannot even say how individuals master their past: Are aging soldiers defensive about their past behavior? Are they merely numbed? Are killings walled off as an aberration of a vanished life? Do they just fade in vividness as compared with the dangers confronted before or later, or the poignancy of lost comrades? Are they shrugged off because "war is like that"? Do soldiers actively suppress memories? Are they contrite or even tormented? Are wives and children compelled into strategies of denial or distortion? How do we read hearts and minds? How do we aggregate from undoubtedly diverse individual strategies of postatrocity coping to generalize about national behavior? Historians have fervently embraced the study of "collective memory" over the last two decades for reasons that themselves require historical analysis. But for all the attention paid to diaries, testimonies, graveyards, monuments, museums, and images, collective memory eludes our intellectual embrace just as Aeneas's father in Hades slips through his son's arms.

To content ourselves with a comparison between forthright Germans and prevaricating Japanese is to obscure much of the postwar history of both countries. The German path to "mastering" the past was less linear than often portrayed, and—as we learn from this volume—the Japanese debate has been more vigorous than commonly assumed. This does not mean that Germany and Japan have arrived at the same level of public acknowledgment or have reduced nationalistic, authoritarian, or merely nostalgic backlashes to an equally marginal level. Japanese public life does seem to impose a reticence (if we can generalize at all) that German public life has long since ceased to demand. Nonetheless, the evolution of collective memory in both countries has been uneven and turbulent.

If we must start with national generalizations we can say, in effect, that "the Germans" began with silence and then across a painful generational change moved toward self-scrutiny, whereas "the Japanese" began with a disavowal of their behavior and then moved toward self-righteousness, perhaps finally in the 1990s opening again to self-criticism under continued outside prodding. Pressures within German society compelled the more thoroughgoing self-interrogation, whereas pressures within

Japanese society tended to inhibit the criticism that the defeat of 1945 had initiated. Germans moved toward debate and the Japanese back toward conformity.[2] Japanese intellectuals and historians who were critical of their militarist regime accepted responsibility for the Nanjing Massacre within a year after the surrender. It was after 1960, to draw out of the chapters in this volume, that the "revisionist" reaction, doubtless present from the outset, became potent enough to claim that the critical historical accounts were distorted and to demand a rewriting of school texts that would eliminate harsh descriptions of Japanese aggression in East Asia. From the 1970s on, the public Japanese discussion has seemed dominated by such provocative actions: Prime Minister Nakasone's visits to the Yasukuni military shrine, the threatening of critics of Hirohito's wartime role, the repeated statements by LDP nationalists that Japan behaved no worse than any other nation-state in its international politics, the inhibitions about recognizing claims by victims such as Korean "comfort women," and the like. The spectacle has been apparently that of a nation tongue-tied by the dominance of a nationalist Right, or one silently in agreement with those seeking to renounce the early postwar disavowals of militarism.

This sequence is almost the opposite of what occurred in postwar Germany, where until the "Auschwitz" trials of 1964 the society remained rather quiet, not contesting the facts but apparently unwilling to discuss them publicly or present them in any detail in school curricula. Since the late sixties, however, the German silence has been shattered. The massive student demonstrations at the end of that decade represented in large part a harsh generational revolt against the silent complicity of the parents' generation from 1933 to 1945. Willy Brandt's famous gesture of kneeling in Warsaw, the 1978 televising of the American series *Holocaust,* and Richard von Weizsäcker's speech of May 7, 1985, are only the most conspicuous episodes in the German confrontation with its past. Only a small neo-Nazi fringe has openly challenged the history of war crimes and genocide as "the Auschwitz lie," to cite the title of the 1963 book that summarized the revisionist view. More consequential than any sympathizer's effort to deny the facts was the tendency to "normalize" the Holocaust that aroused such a vigorous debate in 1986–87. In this *Historikerstreit* reputable historians and journalists argued that although the murder of the Jews had certainly taken place, the crime was no worse than the wholesale terror in Stalinist Russia and, indeed, may have been an imitative response to Communist terror. In effect, the historians and writers who opened the debate were claiming that it was time for Germans to seek a healthy national pride without constantly picking at the scabs of events long past.[3]

To be sure, the Right did not prevail in the *Historikerstreit;* most scholarly opinion felt that the Right's spokesmen were seeking historical exculpation. The thesis that Hitler had borrowed the idea of extermination from the Communists (even if posed by Ernst Nolte only as a legitimate question historians should explore) was rejected by most public intellectuals. Why? As the contributions in this volume make clear, the historical confrontation with the past cannot be divorced from current politics. Political divisions and interests may not ultimately explain the gripping imperative to reassess the past, but they are important for rendering some historical views more or less acceptable.

One key political difference was the differing timing and impact of postwar Marxist critiques of Japan's militarist legacy and Germany's Nazi past (each generally characterized as "fascist" by the Left). For many reasons, the Marxist Left provided an important base for those intellectuals trying to confront their countries' authoritarian histories—at least in states Communists did not rule. In the German Democratic Republic the ruling Marxist-Leninist party felt no need for extensive historical self-examination. Instead it attributed the National Socialist regime to the capitalist order that it charged still persisted in the West but had been abolished in the East. But the spectacle of Communist repression in the East undermined any popular basis for the party in the West, and even as an intellectual tradition Marxism remained feeble until the mid 1960s. I do not mean to suggest that Marxism was the only impulse behind repudiating the past. The German Resistance had drawn on many ideological currents, and Konrad Adenauer understood that for West Germany to emerge as a sovereign nation it must, above all, make reparations to Jewish survivors and Israel and seek political reconciliation with France. Germans, moreover, began their own trials of concentration camp personnel in 1964. Nonetheless, there were limits to self-scrutiny: it was easier to try camp guards than to ask civil servants, judges, bankers, industrialists, and professors whether their enthusiasm or acquiescence had helped the murderous enterprise. Until the long transition from the Christian Democratic governments to the Social-Liberal coalition and the emergence of a vigorous and critical Left, Germans shied away from any radical confrontation over their history.

In Japan, however, it was Marxist historians and intellectuals who initially advanced the critique of wartime policies after 1945, and as conservatives recovered power they moved against the Left's version of the past as well as its political influence. There was no passage of power and alternation of parties in Japan. The Japanese Left expended its major political effort in contesting the international security structure within whose framework the Americans supported the LDP regime, offering, in effect, an alternative leftist nationalism. Although the German student Left of the late 1960s was also anti-American, it combined demonstrations against the American war in Vietnam with an attack on its elders' collaboration with National Socialism.

The identity of the victims has also made a difference. Nanjing was a massacre of enemy nationals. Germans committed many of these: the deportations and shootings of Polish intellectuals and local leaders, the savage reprisals against unarmed civilians at Lidice or Oradour-sur-Glane or Civitella in Tuscany. But the German atrocity that dwarfed all the others was the murder of European Jews without regard to nationality. And the murder of the Jews followed from the anti-Semitic worldview that was so central to the Nazi leadership (and whose grip on the German population as a whole remains so subject to intense debate). German self-interrogation about the murder of the Jews specifically came far more reluctantly than apologies for generic victims (among whom many Germans liked to include themselves). German Communists never liked to sort out Jewish victims from the heroic antifascists who had gone to concentration camps before Jews were deported as a collective group. Germans and Austrians who erected monuments dedicated them to the unspecified "victims" of Nazism, including their own air-raid losses. The identification of Jews as preeminent Nazi targets largely had to await the 1960s. The reparation agreements with Israel and former German Jews negotiated in the previous decade were intended as a move to close the moral books, not reopen them. The Holocaust remained a relatively subdued theme for the Jewish communities outside Germany, but as it became more and more salient after the Six-Day War of 1967, Germans too were led to examine this most appalling aspect of their past. Unlike Japanese apologists, most Germans could not invoke wartime conditions as even a spurious justification of the behavior. Nor could they easily say it happened far away without thinking about the Jews who had disappeared from their midst.

Numbers have also played a different role in the German and Japanese debates. As this book explains, the number of victims has been a highly charged issue, at least until recent efforts to agree on a plausible range by Chinese and Japanese historians. Japanese nationalists could argue that if the toll were only, say, 40,000 instead of 300,000, Nanjing was "no big deal." German right-wing nationalists might claim a lower toll—indeed, even Raoul Hilberg, the first authoritative historian of the murder of the Jews, aroused anger by cautiously tallying about five million rather than the canonic six million. But whatever numbers might or might not be agreed on (and the latest scholarly sums suggest that six million might be a cautious estimate), the magnitude was so great and appalling that only the ultra-Right or neo-Nazi revisionists continued to raise the issue.

Observers outside Japan for whom issues of historical responsibility are important obviously become angry with recurrent Japanese "stonewalling" on issues of war guilt. The first reaction is to ask what moral flaws are involved: insensitivity to foreigners, the lack of a religious tradition that stresses repentance, a "shame" versus a "guilt" culture, a pathological worry about internally divisive issues? But critics of Japan should recall how complex a path to historical openness was involved in the German case. They should also remember that the Austrian attitude—although it, too, in the last decade has moved toward far greater openness—was also one of collective denial and hostility toward those who questioned the comfortable postwar narrative of victimization. We might well ask whether Serbians will ever move beyond their own self-perception as victims rather than perpetrators during the Bosnian and Kosovar struggles.

Finally, we should remember that accepting historical responsibility may be less a question of unchanging cultural dispositions than of political alignments and disputes. Historical self-reflection cannot escape politics and will always be deeply affected by it because different versions of the past are so important for legitimating claims on power in the present. But, as the concluding chapter in this book points out, historical reflection can help us narrow the contests over the past: We can converge on the numerical claims, clarify the chains of command and the levels of responsibility, agree on the meaning of terms, establish the context of violence. This is hard work and historians undertaking it will have to overcome much resistance. The resistance, however, usually springs not from unchanging national psychology but from the balance of political forces and arguments over political values. If countries agree on democratic procedures they can usually keep the arguments from degenerating into violence. That is a message of hope and persistence, not despair.

Charles S. Maier
January 1999

Notes

1. Ian Buruma's remarkable book *The Wages of Guilt: Memories of War in Germany and Japan* tends to confirm this contrast between Japan and Germany even if the material on Japan documents some brave ef-

forts to contest the issue. For a subtle discussion of Japanese reticence (within the context of an essay on photography as a historical resource) see Julia A. Thomas, "Photography, National Identity and the 'Cataract of Times': Wartime Images and the Case of Japan."

2 See the contrast of East and West German attitudes in Herf, *Divided Memory: The Nazi Past in the Two Germanies.* Following public and official discourse, Herf attributes a steadier confrontation with the Nazi past than I would. At a fiftieth anniversary conference of the Nazi takeover held in 1983 the philosopher Hermann Lübbe claimed that the very silence on Germany's past during the 1950s testified to profound collective self-scrutiny. See Lübbe, "Der Nationalsozialismus im politischen Bewußtsein der Gegenwart." Although silence may have indicated shame on the part of many, it also signaled avoidance. For a stinging critique of the Adenauer government's attempt to hush up the past see Frei, *Vergangenheitspolitik: Die Anfänge der Bundesrepublik und die NS-Vergangenheit.*

3. For discussions of the *Historikerstreit* see my own *The Unmasterable Past: History, Holocaust, and German National Identity,* and Evans, *In Hitler's Shadow: West German Historians and the Attempt to Escape from the Nazi Past.* A German-language documentation was published as *Historikerstreit: Die Dokumentation der Kontroverse um die Einzigartigkeit der nationalsozialistischen Judenvernichtung.*

1

Introduction

The Nanjing Massacre in History

JOSHUA A. FOGEL

More than sixty years have passed since the series of historical events now called the Nanjing Massacre (also known as the Nanjing Atrocity and the Rape of Nanjing). Although historians have analyzed from every conceivable angle other aspects of World War II ranging from the Manchurian Incident of September 18, 1931—now considered the beginning of the war in the Asian theater—to the bombings of Hiroshima and Nagasaki in August 1945, this literature pales in comparison with that focused recently on what happened in Nanjing in 1937–38. There are journals and now a host of Worldwide Web sites devoted solely to the Nanjing Massacre and associated Japanese atrocities committed in East Asia during World War II, and Iris Chang's recently published book, *The Rape of Nanking,* has enjoyed astounding sales. At no time during the six decades since the event have tempers been more inflamed or research on this subject more intense than now. The Massacre and related events must be lifted beyond the popular level, however, to be studied with greater nuance and in consultation with a wider range of sources.

How could such a horrific event lie quietly for so long and only in the past few years explode with such force? How did the

Nanjing Massacre become a metonym for Japanese behavior in China over the entire half century before the end of the war? Indeed, how has the Nanjing Massacre become so profoundly entwined with—even emblematic of—contemporary Chinese identity, as Ian Buruma has suggested it has?[1]

Until recently the atrocities that took place in Nanjing in 1937–38 have not been accorded the importance or status they warrant in modern history, except by scholars. Certainly, this has increasingly become the perception of many Chinese, especially in the diaspora. This lack of attention to the Massacre has been partly attributable to the pride and determined self-reliance of the government in Beijing. The post–World War II world witnessed an extraordinary efflorescence of nationalism throughout East and Southeast Asia, and a concomitant unwillingness to play the victim any longer. After the collapse of the Sino-Soviet alliance the Chinese Communist regime assiduously rejected foreign aid or assistance of any kind, even in the face of a starving population and natural disasters (such as the Tangshan earthquake) of historically unprecedented proportions. Postwar East Asia's newly developed self-esteem has militated against countries' blaming others for their own failings. Thus, although the Chinese regime made the Japanese jump through any number of political hoops to reestablish diplomatic and trade relations, it did not demand reparations for the devastation that the Japanese had wrought during the war.

The denial by certain Japanese of the Nanjing Massacre over roughly the past two decades has contributed to a recrudescence of Chinese anger primarily at Japan but also at the Chinese regimes for not encouraging research on the subject earlier and exposing it to the world. The Japanese deniers of the atrocities are themselves part of a recent Japanese revival of nationalism that has cleaved to right-wing politics and rejected any foreign role in the articulation of Japanese identity. What actually happened in Nanjing is almost irrelevant in and of itself to these people—all that matters is that Japan's image not be stained, and therefore the atrocities must be denied.

With the rift between Taiwan and the People's Republic after

1949 and with increasing numbers of Chinese living in other Asian countries, the United States, and Canada, the complex issue of Chinese identity has been thrown into question. Unlike other peoples who have been exiled from their homelands and have had to forge an identity within a diaspora, the Chinese have had relatively little experience in this realm until recently. In roughly the past decade the Chinese diaspora has begun to speak in an altogether new voice. Where once it was split between those supporting Taiwan and those supporting the People's Republic, it now embraces a multiplicity of voices—embracing, for example, Tu Wei-ming's idea of cultural China, meaning all of those Chinese (living anywhere) who contribute to the growth of Chinese culture. The Communists and the Guomindang no longer control the discourse. As the diaspora searches for a distinct voice with which to articulate its distinct identity, it is finding that many issues have been swept under the carpet by both regimes. The Nanjing Massacre has become the most prominent of these.

The role that the Chinese diaspora has played in attempting to return the Nanjing Massacre to center stage may be attributable to yet another factor. One by-product of the modern era has been a kind of cultural deracination. Despite its obvious merits, the melting pot has led to the unfortunate result that few of us living in diaspora are well grounded in the sources, languages, and histories of the cultures putatively our own. Many are now returning to a search for an identity without the tools necessary to acquire it, often latching onto negative events in their history as elemental to their identity. Many Jews, no longer knowledgeable of their own traditions, languages, and texts as were their grandparents or great-grandparents, who learned them as a matter of course, cling to the state of Israel and the sanctity of the Holocaust as basic to their identity. Similarly, many Chinese in the diaspora with considerably less knowledge of their own traditions and history than their forebears have seized on the Nanjing Massacre as their own. Why choose a negative instance? Sadly, there are enough great massacres and atrocities to go around, and such an event committed against a people simply because of who they are endows them with an identity perceived as unassailable and irreproachable; it immediately links all members of an ethnic group in victimhood and ties them to their culture, albeit in a superficial way.

These and other factors have conspired to turn attention, especially among diaspora Chinese, back to the events of the war, and the atrocities committed by the Japanese in that war have often been wrenched out of context and elevated to untold heights. Of course, the Chinese are not the only people who have done this. Many Jews have done the same with the Nazi Judaicide of the war, as have Armenians with the Turkish massacres of 1915 and African Americans with the long history of slavery and discrimination in the New World. Although magnanimous citizens everywhere have been sympathetic to the pain and suffering of all peoples, only the attempted genocide of the Jews has thus far achieved virtually sacrosanct status. One can deny or downplay the Turkish massacres, as the Turkish government regularly does, and go on with one's life. No one denies slavery, but one can deny that the experience was thoroughly nightmarish from beginning to end, as Dinesh D'Souza has recently attempted to do, without derailing one's career.[2] By contrast, deniers of Auschwitz and the other Nazi death camps are immediately and justifiably relegated to pariah status, consigned at best to fringe groups, by all thinking human beings.

Of all these massive, man-made atrocities, only in the case of the Nanjing Massacre has a whole school—actually, several—developed that completely denies or significantly downplays it. How can this be? How can established Japanese intellectuals in many fields—though, importantly, few if any in Chinese or Japanese history—buy into the idea that the Nanjing Massacre is a phantom, an illusion, even a ruse concocted by the Chinese and their allies to ruin Japan's reputation? How can such people still defend Japanese mass murders of fifty and sixty years ago as the acts of "Asia's liberator"?

Frankly, it boggles the mind. More important, it also demonstrates that each of these mass atrocities of modern times is historically and morally distinctive. Lumping them together may serve some emotional end but it ultimately confuses rather than illuminates history, for this is one case in which comparative history may not serve us well. Asserting uniqueness does not mean that we cannot suggest a typology of such mass atrocities; it just means that we should not collapse them. Underscoring specific contexts in which such massacres occur contributes much more to the furtherance of our knowledge of the events themselves than does a cataloguing of superficial similarities or a use of borrowed and sensational appellations.

The three chapters that comprise this volume, each based on years of individual research, serve this end of contextualizing the Nanjing Massacre. The authors and editor presented a panel at the annual meeting of the Association for Asian Studies in March 1997 and then decided to compile the present volume. Each chapter considers a different aspect of the history and historiography of the Nanjing Massacre in China and Japan. Although the following three chapters examine some contemporaneous reports documenting the atrocities themselves, the bulk of the material they analyze dates from the end of World War II and the war crimes trials that ensued. They examine, in the kind of detail we have hitherto not seen in English, the voluminous Chinese and Japanese literature on this momentous event of 1937–38. Each attempts to answer the kinds of questions raised here.

It is a telling state of affairs historiographically that I must say in this introduction that none of us doubts that a great massacre occurred in and around Nanjing from December 1937 through February 1938. These essays are by no means devoted to disproving the claims of the deniers, however. We take for granted that those claims have been made for an assortment of unsavory political reasons or misguided emotional or nationalistic ones. To grant the existence of such an atrocity, though, only begs the question. Far more important to our purpose here is a consideration of how the Nanjing Massacre has been used both by those who aver and by those who deny it—that is, how it has been appropriated as an ideological tool or for nationalist mobilization. In particular, the chapters by Mark Eykholt and Takashi Yoshida confront the Nanjing Massacre in contemporary historiography in order to see the uses to which it has been put.

We have also refrained from engaging in what I call the "numbers game"—the practice of estimating and seriously debating the numbers of those killed and those raped in the Nanjing Massacre, in which certain Chinese push the figures higher and higher while certain Japanese do everything within their power to push the figures lower and lower. There are two different logics behind this game. The first is to render the Nanjing Massacre as gruesome an event as ever witnessed in world history and thus garner international attention and sympathy. In her recent book, for example, Iris Chang explicitly claims that the Nanjing Massacre was even more deadly than the European Holocaust.[3] The second logic is to normalize the events and portray them as understandable actions given the bloody circumstances of the war then underway, as some Japanese critics have attempted to do, purposefully taming the horrors surrounding the mass murders and offering them no special place in history. While those Chinese following the first logic now argue that more than 300,000 were killed and 80,000 raped, Japanese following the second argue that fewer than 100 were killed and very few raped. The contributors to this volume are all of a mind that a great massacre occurred, and whether 200,000 people were killed or 240,000 does not alter the dimensions of the horror.

No amount of discussion between the contending parties is likely to bridge this gap. Indeed, on a number of occasions in Japan advocates of these two views have confronted one another, made their respective cases, and uniformly failed to convince their opponents of a single item. In part, this inability to reach consensus results from the different concerns motivating these groups. Scholars of modern Chinese and Japanese history—irrespective of their political views—virtually all admit that a massacre occurred in the Nanjing area, though they may differ on numbers. Others involved in the debate—be they scholars from other fields or other professionals—seem all but oblivious to what constitutes historical fact. This is not a methodological or philosophical difference but an ideological one. Deniers of the Nanjing Massacre have acquired the strength of numbers to ignore the facts, the photos, and the personal memoirs. Their concern is with Japanese national pride and self-confidence, not with redressing a historical wrong.

In the final chapter in this volume Daqing Yang offers a more contemplative look at our subject in an effort to identify how we all might come to, if not agreement on what occurred in Nanjing sixty years ago, then at least some sort of consensus on the parameters of the event. I am less sanguine than he, but his reflections (those, incidentally, of a Chinese from Nanjing) make for deeply compelling reading. He confronts the difficult issues that only such a controversial and contested event can raise: history and memory, atrocity and amnesia, and the capacities of human beings to transcend nationality in the writing of history.

The aims of this book are several. We hope to place Chinese and Japanese historiography on the events that transpired in Nanjing into their contemporary settings in China (and Taiwan) and Japan, and to offer a more nuanced view of contemporary agendas. We examine what makes the Nanjing Massacre unique in modern Sino-Japanese (and world) history and why it has spawned such debate and emotions. Offering the English-reading public access to the voluminous material that has been published in East Asian languages over the past sixty years on this event, this book will serve to elucidate the complexity of details in the events surrounding the Nanjing Massacre as they are becoming better known in the English-speaking world.

The most important contribution this volume will make, however, will be to lay before its readers the highly complex debates in China and Japan since the war, and to attempt to explain why various schools of thought have come to the fore and why the debate has recently become so ferocious. This requires unpacking "Japan" (and "China"), identifying interest groups, ideological points of view, schools of thought, scholarly rifts, personal antagonisms, and political intrusions into scholarship, and dropping facile characterizations based solely on nationality. Far too often, for example, Japanese reluctance fully to admit the role of the Japanese military in the horrific events on the Mainland during the war has led uninformed critics to blame "the Japanese" for historical amnesia, yet much of the most advanced scholarship in the world on virtually every aspect of the war, atrocities included, comes from Japanese scholars.

Although there are many different Japanese constituencies, there remain certain compelling reasons to examine these issues from a national perspective as well. It was the Japanese army that invaded China and perpetrated the Nanjing Massacre, and it was Chinese soldiers and civilians, abandoned by their own army and government, who fell victim to the Japanese military. As a result, to this day Chinese write from the point of view of victims and their descendants; the events are being reclaimed by those distant from them often for reasons of changing identity. Japanese tend either to deny the events in an attempt to preserve a positive legacy for contemporary Japanese, or they write out of a deeply felt sense that Japanese wartime actions, although impossible to exonerate, may somehow be atoned for by detailed scholarship exposing all manner of atrocities including vivisection, use of poison gas, and chemical warfare. At the international level, the issues here have become the stuff of political and diplomatic controversy over the past two decades, exacerbating Sino-Japanese tensions.

The Chinese and Japanese sides of these issues form the basis, respectively, for the analyses of Mark Eykholt's and Takashi Yoshida's chapters in this volume. As they demonstrate, the political and intellectual environments in China and Japan are altogether different, to say nothing of the increasingly vocal role played by members of the Chinese diaspora.

In attempting to set these issues in a larger historiographical and philosophical context, Daqing Yang raises a number of questions about how a scholar (or a general reader) is to come to terms with an event so horrifying that it defies ratiocination. How do we make sense of an event rooted, at least at some level, in insanity?

A number of the questions raised in this book are also the concern of Holocaust scholars. Although their writings may offer historiographical guidance or correctives, the Nanjing Massacre is best studied on its own ground in China and Japan in the context of World War II in East Asia. When the atrocities associated with the toponym of Nanjing are situated within the context of the war and the debates about them situated in the historiography of the postwar period, then we will have gone a long way toward placing this massacre in history and historiography.

Notes

1. Buruma, "The Afterlife of Anne Frank," p. 7.
2. D'Souza, *The End of Racism: Principles for a Multiracial Society.*
3. Chang, *The Rape of Nanking: The Forgotten Holocaust of World War II.*

2

Aggression, Victimization, and Chinese Historiography of the Nanjing Massacre

MARK EYKHOLT

On August 15, 1937, Japanese planes bombed Nanjing, the capital of China. These raids continued until December 13, when Japanese troops entered the conquered city. For the next month Japanese soldiers killed, raped, looted, and burned. Hundreds of thousands of Chinese died. Six months later random atrocities were still occurring. This is the event known to history as the Nanjing Massacre.

For Chinese, the Nanjing Massacre is an immediate symbol of outrages committed by Japanese troops during the war and of China's victimization by imperialist aggression. As such, the Massacre is a highly sensitive event to Chinese people, causing anger when doubted and contempt when misconstrued. Thousands of books and articles have normalized the event in the minds of the Chinese people. Every year in August on the anniversary of Japan's surrender and again in December on the anniversary of Nanjing's fall, newspaper articles and public gatherings ritualize the Massacre and rekindle hatred for Japan's wartime deeds. Today, Chinese continue to view Japan's action as an unprovoked and unconscionable attempt to exterminate the Chinese spirit.

In the last decade, information about the Massacre has been spreading beyond East Asia. The stakes for China are high as the Massacre has become a defining event in how the world perceives Japan and China, and Chinese abroad actively take part in continuing the anti-Japan rhetoric about the Massacre. The audience has expanded but the goal continues to be to document the Massacre and prove to the world Japan's horrific wrongs against China. As a result, Chinese documentation is overwhelming but Chinese historiography remains captive to a cultural and national need to present China as a victim. Within this need, however, there are differences. The Chinese government does not aggressively pursue Japanese war guilt and does not demand reparations, whereas many Chinese both inside and outside China want the Chinese government to adopt a more aggressive stance toward Japan's wartime imperialism.

Trying to Believe the Massacre

The Massacre was only vaguely known until after the war. At the time of its occurrence, the only recorded evidence of atrocities was the writings of a few Chinese and Westerners who had stayed in Nanjing, writings that were then smuggled to the outside world.[1] Newspapers and journals in unoccupied China occasionally printed eyewitness accounts, but the narratives were just part of many war stories that filled the news in order to stir people to greater patriotism. In fact, a scholar who lived in the rural areas of Sichuan admitted that he had never heard of the Nanjing Massacre until he went to Nanjing in 1946, and even then people cared more about the deteriorating situation in Nanjing and China resulting from the Civil War.[2] The Nanjing Massacre was hardly the unifying event that it has become today for Chinese.

The Massacre also stretched the limits of believability. Diaries and personal accounts spoke of nightmarish and specific brutalities committed by the occupying Japanese forces, but no one could fathom the overall extent of the terror. Initially, Western witnesses spoke of hundreds and thousands of deaths and assumed a body count of about 10,000 in and around Nanjing. This count was quickly revised to 40,000 after an inspection of the city.[3] Yet these estimates pale in comparison to later burial figures that pushed the numbers closer to 200,000.[4] Though such complete numbers did not appear until after the war, burial teams began taking care of corpses at the start of 1938, and rumors of mass killings spread. Confronted by the spreading rumors and increasing body counts, some Westerners in Nanjing assumed that Chinese exaggerated family losses to get more relief supplies.[5] By spring, burial stories presented death numbers far beyond initial estimates. Again Westerners reacted with mistrust despite all they had witnessed. Minnie Vautrin, a Western missionary and teacher in Nanjing, listened to one Chinese report of thousands of bodies still unburied along the Yangzi River. She then asked the man if he did not mean tens or, at most, hundreds.[6]

This disbelief was rooted in the feeling that a modern people such as the Japanese could not act in such uncivilized ways. Actually, Westerners in Nanjing expected the Japanese to bring normalcy back to war-torn China. H. L. Sone wrote from Nanjing, "With the coming of the Japanese Soldiers we thought order would soon be restored and peace would come, and people would be able to return to their homes and get back to normal life again."[7] To George Fitch, another member of the Western community in Nanjing, the Massacre was like a terrible dream from which he expected to wake up. Minnie Vautrin voiced her belief that the Japanese must not have known what they were doing.[8] This same disbelief met news of the Massacre as it traveled abroad. Western missionaries in Japan accused their colleagues in Nanjing of lying. One missionary wrote, "The stories of Japanese military forces deliberately destroying hospitals and schools in China, and deliberately slaughtering innocent Chinese people are slanderous lies."[9] In the United States, people wrote angry letters to magazines that printed accounts of the Massacre.[10] One subscriber to *Reader's Digest* opined, "It is unbelievable that credence could be given a thing which is so obviously rank propaganda and reminiscent of the stuff fed the public during the late war."[11]

The stories were not rank propaganda. Yet even today overcoming disbelief requires attempting to understand how the Japanese military could commit the Nanjing Massacre. Chinese researchers on the Massacre often comment on this issue, and all reasoning, whether brief or elaborate, focuses on the brutal nature of Japanese militarism and, by extension, Japanese culture. On the brief end is one writer who simply wrote, "The reason such an atrocity occurred is, first, the savagery [*yeman*] and ruthlessness [*canku*] of the Japanese military, and two, the passive resistance of the Guomindang military and the incompetence of the Guomindang."[12] More elaborate comments add to the list of reasons the Japanese educational system, which emphasized Japan's military heritage, and the lack of any egalitarian or humanitarian spirit in Japan, cultural characteristics that resulted in a people mindlessly devoted to the Japanese nation.[13] Without a doubt the Japanese military acted ruthlessly in Nanjing, and this is partially due to the reasons just summarized. But analysis needs to look beyond the Japanese and their military tactics in order to realize a web of factors that resulted in the Nanjing Massacre.

The first factor is that inhuman behavior and advanced civilization are not exclusive categories. Scholars such as Zygmunt Bauman use this approach in researching the mass killings of the Nazi Holocaust. Bauman argues that the Holocaust uncovered aspects of advanced civilization that people often overlook: bureaucratic efficiency and control can be used for destruction; there is a dark side to modern life that includes violence, war, and exploitation.[14] The general trend in scholarship on the Nanjing Massacre is to present the Massacre as chaos—military discipline collapsed and Japanese troops went wild in Nanjing.[15] Yet there are no reports of soldiers abandoning their units, atrocities usually followed organized patterns, and random robberies and rapes accounted for a small fraction of the total. The truth is that discipline and order continued amid the murder and mayhem. They had to continue in order to maintain the efficiency necessary to carry out so much killing and destruction.

Japanese fighting forces had proven their discipline and superior capability throughout the twentieth century, beginning with the Russo-Japanese War of 1904–5 and continuing with Japan's various intrusions into Chinese territory. This same discipline and capability also made the Nanjing Massacre possible. For example, in order to kill thousands of captured Chinese troops, the Japanese army gathered the prisoners together, marched them under guard to specific locations, and then dispatched them in groups of fifty by mounted machine guns. Japanese officers oversaw at least some of these mass killings, corroborating evidence that the killings were orderly.[16] For the burning of Nanjing, soldiers received prepared-chemical strips to light their fires, and government buildings were spared because the military wanted to use them.[17] In the Xiaguan area of northwestern Nanjing, almost every building was razed except for the train station, an essential link for Japanese troop movements.[18] Prior to the burning, soldiers emptied stores of their goods and piled them onto military trucks. Soldiers were also organized into teams to collect rare antiques and documents. They raided libraries and private collections for ancient and valuable books, and military personnel removed religious icons and utensils from the many temples in Nanjing. Anything that Japanese or foreign collectors might want, the Japanese took.[19] Military trucks also carted away Chinese women to service Japanese soldiers. The women washed clothes during the day and were raped repeatedly at night. Complaints filed with Japanese diplomatic representatives show that officers directly involved themselves in these actions.[20] Finally, the fact that no Westerners were seriously injured means that Japanese troops had not gone berserk and military discipline had not collapsed. Rather, Japanese soldiers directed their actions at the Chinese population.

As for the Japanese individuals who committed murder, rape, and arson, experiments have shown that a need to obey superiors can overcome moral barriers, thereby leading individuals to commit acts they would normally avoid.[21] In Nanjing, officers not only ordered atrocities but took part in them as well, encouraging their men through words and actions to ignore their own misgivings and act in beastly ways. Many of these soldiers today look back at their actions and cannot understand why they acted in such terrible ways. Azuma Shirō, a Japanese soldier during the war, noted: "At home I was a good father, a good brother, and a good husband; however, after a month on the battlefield, I killed without remorse. I'm often at a loss as to why this happened."[22]

Theorizing that a modern bureaucratic system turned Japanese soldiers into brutes pushes sympathy in the wrong direction. Chinese in Nanjing were the victims. Furthermore, not all Japanese soldiers were reluctant pawns. Men sent pictures back to their families and friends in Japan, showing smiling soldiers standing next to naked women. Other pictures showed grim-faced soldiers raising swords over the necks of Chinese prisoners and proud soldiers carrying severed heads. The soldiers in these pictures were emboldened by their actions, and stories of Japanese war heroics in Nanjing border on the macabre.[23]

This leads us to a second factor, that of a Japanese military personality. Care must be taken because some have condemned Japan as uniquely capable of barbaric behavior. This was especially prevalent just after the Massacre occurred. A missionary writing in 1938 felt that a lack of Christian heritage made Japanese more prone to brutality, and a news report that same year called the Japanese sexual perverts obsessed with mutilation.[24] Such condemnations reflect two interlocking reactions to the Massacre. The first was the disbelief that met the reports coming out of Nanjing, a disbelief that connected brutality to primitive behavior. The second reaction was repugnance and moral condemnation, a condemnation that sought to single out Japan as different and demonic, thereby assuaging the souls of modernized observers who were not Japanese.

To condemn Japan as uniquely evil ignores many of the factors already mentioned, but that does not mean that there were no aspects of Japanese military training that made Japan's forces more prone to violence in their invasion of China. The bulk of Japan's frontline troops were poor farmers, industrial workers, and criminals, people who had lived rough lives of hard work with minimal reward. Once in the Japanese military system, they were treated harshly. Soldiers were routinely slapped and beaten by their superiors. Whole units were penalized with forced marches or punitive exercises for the actions of just one member. Complaints brought even worse retribution.[25] Ideologically, Japanese were taught that their imperial hierarchy lay at the center of world morality and that the Japanese were superior to all other peoples.[26] As part of this philosophy, China was made a focus of derision. Initially, some Japanese intellectuals used China as a foil in order to develop a more confident Japanese identity.[27] While Japanese wealth and power increased in the twentieth century, China continued to falter. Anti-Chinese attitudes spread in Japan as the popular voices of journalists and politicians condemned China as backward and encouraged Japanese expansion into Chinese territory.[28] By the 1930s Japanese school textbooks taught students to believe in Japan's superior position in Asia, to view China as a civilization in decline, and to consider Chinese people morally deficient.[29] This view permeated the Japanese military, leading to racial slurs and contempt.[30] Soldiers were told that expansion into China was Japan's destiny and that heroic behavior sought victory and death. The overall atmosphere of Japanese military life created soldiers who followed orders, ignored personal feelings, and treated anyone beneath them with the same contempt that they experienced themselves.

A mixture of harsh discipline and indoctrinated disdain created the potential for an event like the Nanjing Massacre, but to release that potential required the third and most important factor: the circumstances leading up to the assault on Nanjing. The Japanese attacked Shanghai and began bombing Nanjing in August 1937 with the expectation that all of China would fall in a matter of months. Instead, the siege of Shanghai required four months of bloody fighting. This angered the high command and the frontline soldiers who had watched their comrades die at the hands of the despised Chinese. When Shanghai finally fell in November, military planners and leaders turned their eyes to Nanjing, the capital of China, with the goal of retribution. Commanders pushed their units toward Nanjing, quickly outpacing supply lines and telling their men to survive on what they could scavenge. Soldiers robbed villages they passed through and Chinese they came across. Peasants were forced to carry equipment and goods for the Japanese troops, and villages were razed in order to efficiently end any threat of resistance. Brutalities were excused in the name of war and capturing Nanjing, and conquering the capital grew in importance with each new atrocity. These troops knew their job was to kill the enemy, and the barely acceptable conditions of frontline warfare grew worse, thereby amplifying the animal natures of these soldiers as they marched toward Nanjing. To further encourage their men, officers promised women and plunder. When the soldiers reached Nanjing, their expectations of revenge, sex, and goods combined with the heightened desire to make an example of Nanjing and prove Japan's dominance. The results were atrocities against both civilians and prisoners of war. During the first days of occupation too many Japanese troops entered the city walls and the situation quickly turned into a nightmare for the Chinese. Their government had fled, no Chinese authorities remained to protect them or mediate their cause, and Japanese troops poured into the city bent on violent retribution. Only when the frontline troops moved on in January and February 1938, as they were replaced by garrison troops, did the Massacre come to an end.

Military Trials Set the Stage

The Guomindang government in Chongqing, the capital of unoccupied China, was active throughout the war preparing to demand justice for Japanese aggression. As early as 1941, the government began collecting data on physical losses due to Japanese aggression.[31] The Chinese signed the Allied Declaration of St. James concerning the future disposition of war criminals in 1942, helped establish the United Nations War Crimes Commission in October 1943, and guided the establishment in Chongqing of the Far Eastern Subcommittee to the United Nations War Crimes Commission in May 1944.[32] Meanwhile, the government set up a fact-finding commission, called the War

Damage Investigation Committee *(Kangzhan sunshi diaocha weiyuanhui),* to facilitate the gathering of evidence. By the time the war ended and the war crimes trials in Tokyo and China began, the Chinese had fattened prosecutors' casebooks with burial records, interviews, diaries, and damage statistics.

Even with all this preparation, the Tokyo Trial failed to satisfy Chinese hopes for retribution. From the beginning, the United States used the office of General Douglas MacArthur, the Supreme Commander for the Allied Powers (SCAP), to dominate all phases of the trial. MacArthur chose the eleven judges who sat on the War Tribunal, and only three judges came from Asian countries—China, India, and the Philippines. The International Prosecution Section of SCAP chose to charge only 28 out of some 250 high Japanese officials in custody, and the Prosecution Section prepared the case against the war criminals.[33] Notable among those not tried were Emperor Hirohito and all economic officials connected with the business conglomerates *(zaibatsu).* The Charter for the Tribunal was written by Americans within the Prosecution Section, and President Truman personally appointed Joseph Keenan as chief prosecutor. Americans were even appointed to help the Japanese lawyers on the defense team.[34]

Joseph Keenan and the prosecution team decided to prove that from 1928 to 1941 the twenty-eight defendants had spearheaded a conspiracy to gain control of the Japanese government, and after 1941 had waged a war of aggression in the Pacific. In such a scenario, the war in China became either a means to highlight Japan's intended aggression in the Pacific prior to 1941 or a backdrop for Japan's assault on American interests after 1941. In other words, China was never a focus of the Trial. Disgruntlement over this state of affairs still simmers in China as evidenced by the comments of Professor Yu Xinchu of Nankai University. At a 1983 Tokyo conference on the Trial, Professor Yu recognized that the Trial did deal with the China-Japan War; however, he complained that the proceedings emphasized the Pacific War at the expense of all else, even though fighting against the United States lasted only four years, compared to a half century of Japanese aggression toward China.[35]

One reason for indicting only twenty-eight men was to wrap up the Trial quickly. Despite such hopes, the Trial turned into a lengthy affair and people lost interest. The prosecution took 192 days to present its case. Then the defense countered with several more months of witnesses and evidence. By the time it was over, 4,836 documents had been submitted and 419 witnesses had been questioned.[36] The trial transcript was fifty thousand pages, accounting for ten million words.[37] From beginning to end, the trial lasted more than a year and a half.[38] By comparison, the Nuremberg Trial ended eleven months after it began.[39] Other complaints concerned taboo topics such as the culpability of Emperor Hirohito, misdeeds by the United States and other Allied powers during the war, and the role that Chinese Communists played throughout the conflict and afterward. The defense team was not allowed equal access to evidence, and the judges strictly monitored the defense's use of evidence. The judges were more lax with the prosecution team because so much condemning evidence had been destroyed, evidence that would have built a much stronger case against the Japanese defendants.[40] B. V. A. Roling, the Dutch judge chosen to serve on the Tribunal, later admitted that the trial seemed to him a showcase to avenge Pearl Harbor and exonerate the U.S. government and the U.S. military for their own questionable aggressions.[41] Yet Roling still felt that the Tokyo Trial, like the Nuremberg Trial, served a good purpose: "It is true that both trials had sinister origins; that they were misused for political purposes; and that they were somewhat unfair. But they also made a very constructive contribution to the outlawing of war and the world is badly in need of a fundamental change in the political and legal position of war in international relations."[42]

In the end the Tribunal sentenced seven of the defendants to death. Of these, the judges connected only two defendants to the Nanjing Massacre: General Matsui Iwane, who had been the commander of Central China forces at the time of the Nanjing invasion, and Hirota Kōki, who had been foreign minister. The judges sentenced the remaining eighteen defendants to prison terms of seven years to life.[43] No country received war reparations. The Chinese judge chosen to serve on the Tribunal, Mei Ruao, was considered one of the bench's strictest hard-liners, and he declared the sentences far too lenient.[44] But the Tribunal's Charter stated that a mere majority of votes decided the final outcomes. Also, by the time the trial ended in 1948, the Cold War had begun and U.S. occupation objectives had changed from punishing Japan to rebuilding Japan as a bulwark against Communism in Asia. On December 24, 1948, MacArthur released the remaining seventeen men awaiting trial and announced an end to all international trials.[45] In 1950 China supported a Soviet Union proposal to reopen the Tribunal and try other war criminals, specifically Emperor Hirohito, but U.S. policy with respect to war crimes trials of Japanese had been made clear and nothing came of the proposal.[46]

China under the leadership of Jiang Jieshi (Chiang Kai-shek) had its own set of military trials for lesser war criminals that began in April 1946.[47] There is no doubt that China suffered more war crimes than any other Asian nation during the war and public thirst for vengeance was high. Chongqing established thirteen military tribunals, and these Chinese tribunals adopted the definitions of war crimes used at the Tokyo Trial. Lawmakers then added crimes of dealing in narcotics, promoting psychological warfare, and allowing aggression, thereby giving the Chinese trials the broadest definition of war crimes of any trials in Asia.[48] Chinese sentences were severe and any case could be retried if the Ministry of Defense so desired.

The Chinese trials had serious distractions, however, particularly the Civil War in China. When Guomindang leaders returned from Chongqing to retake control of China, they were less concerned with Japanese war criminals and more focused on preventing the Communists from reclaiming previously occupied territory.[49] This is one reason the trials did not begin until spring 1946, even though the Japanese had surrendered in August of the previous year. As the Civil War turned against the Guomindang in 1947, Jiang Jieshi hurried the trials, perhaps pushing for an early end because he realized that U.S. policy in East Asia was changing. The Chinese trials ended early in 1949, and Jiang Jieshi dropped all of China's reparation claims.[50] In 1952 Jiang and the government of the Republic of China on Taiwan signed a peace treaty with Japan and released eighty-eight war criminals.

The trials of Chinese collaborators also drew attention away from trials of Japanese war criminals, because those Chinese who had served Japan were the real focus of Chinese anger. From September 1945 until June 1946, a lead story about Chinese collaborators appeared almost every day in the Chinese press, and only the most notorious Japanese war criminals could elicit equal interest.[51] Chinese courts passed sentence on more than ten thousand Chinese for collaborating with the Japanese enemy by the end of 1947; 342 collaborators were executed and 847 received sentences of life imprisonment.[52] These numbers overwhelm those from Chinese trials against Japanese war criminals: Guomindang courts tried 883 men, convicted 504, handed out 149 death penalties, and sentenced 83 to life imprisonment. Even trials by other countries took a more serious stand against Japanese aggression. For example, the British had a higher conviction rate, the United States tried more Japanese, and the harshest courts were those of the Dutch.[53] In the absence of trials against collaborators, the Civil War, and the Cold War, the Chinese doubtless would have continued their momentum of the early 1940s, pushed harder, and convicted more Japanese war criminals. With those distractions, the Chinese court in Nanjing sentenced only four Japanese to death in connection with atrocities in the Nanjing Massacre.[54]

The war trials both helped and hurt representations of the Nanjing Massacre. The trials in China and Tokyo accepted uncritically the documents, diaries, and eyewitness accounts supporting the Massacre. The Tokyo Trial concluded that more than 200,000 Chinese had died, and the Nanjing court pushed the number to more than 300,000.[55] Therefore, national and international law courts had verified the Nanjing Massacre, validated the many types of corroborating evidence, and set precedents for death totals in the hundreds of thousands. On the other hand, attempts to cover up and deny the Nanjing Massacre were part of each defense case. For example, Matsui and one of his military assistants, General Mutō Akira, were questioned at length about the Nanjing Massacre. Matsui admitted that many soldiers had behaved badly but absolutely denied that anything on the scale of a massacre had taken place. Mutō had been in Nanjing during the first two weeks of the Massacre, but stated that he had seen no soldiers acting up. He did acknowledge that he had seen reports of looting and rape, but these reports only amounted to ten or twenty incidents.[56] Mutō and Matsui were just two of many leaders who tried to protect themselves and, more important, the reputation of their nation by downplaying and hiding the extent of Japan's war crimes. In the end only six Japanese were executed for the hundreds of thousands of Chinese who died, and of these, only four had actually participated in the killings, since Matsui and Hirota were military and civilian administrators, respectively. To execute only four men as retribution for the hundreds of thousands of people in Nanjing murdered by tens of thousands of Japanese soldiers was not justice in the eyes of the Chinese people.

Another shortcoming was that all of the trials focused blame on individuals and their actions, giving a sense that once the individual criminals were punished, everything would improve. More complicated factors of state, philosophy, and social ordering were ignored, factors that definitely played a role in Japanese aggression but might also have confronted victor nations with uncomfortable questions. For example, Taiwanese and Koreans were colonial subjects of Japan, and many participated in Japan's war effort. When the war ended, war tribunals treated them as Japanese subjects, and of the Japanese convicted of war crimes, 178 were actually Taiwanese and 148 were Korean.[57] By ignoring the colonized status of these individuals, nations such as the United States, Britain, and the Netherlands ignored their own colonial policies and pretended that they could continue with their foreign interests as they had prior to the war.

The rest of this chapter outlines the postwar growth of the Nanjing Massacre as a symbolic event in Chinese consciousness. Beneath this growth lies a deep dissatisfaction with the trials and a feeling that not enough has been done to recognize Japan's responsibility, punish Japanese for the war crimes committed, and root out the real causes of Japanese aggression against China.

Politicizing the Massacre in the Postwar Era

Postwar development and the Cold War consumed China as they consumed other countries in the world, and no Chinese groups pursued Japanese war guilt outside of the military tribunals. Japan was rebuilding itself as a pacifist nation, symbolized by Article 9 of the Japanese Constitution, which not only renounced war as a national right but also forbade the maintenance of any military potential. Indeed, the dropping of the atomic bombs and the terrible casualties that Japan suffered in the war caused Japanese to view themselves as victims of aggression. August 6, the day the United States dropped the atomic bomb on Hiroshima, became a national day to commemorate the death and destruction of that incident as well as the war in general.

Meanwhile, the Nanjing Massacre became one more political tool used by the Chinese government to keep public attention focused on development and unity. For example, during the Korean War, the Chinese government used the Massacre to stir up patriotism against the United States. An article in *Xinhua yuebao* (The New China Monthly) in 1952 condemned those Americans who had stayed in Nanjing to establish a Safety Zone. This Zone, called the Nanjing International Safety Zone, had been established in the center of Nanjing as a safe area for Chinese refugees. By the second week of Japan's occupation, the overwhelming majority of Chinese citizens remaining in Nanjing lived within its boundaries and received some protection from the rampaging Japanese troops. The *Xinhua yuebao* reported that American officials of the Zone had protected foreign property at the expense of Chinese lives, aided the invading Japanese troops, and sent Chinese to be executed by Japanese soldiers. The article included pictures of the Nanjing Massacre with the slogan, "Remember the Nanjing Massacre, Stop American Remilitarization of Japan!"[58]

By the 1960s popular and political voices interacted around the Massacre. Reflecting this interaction most notably was extensive research completed by historians at Nanjing University. They had gathered a great amount of data, including photographs, new statistics, and interviews with survivors, and in 1962 they collected it into an eight-chapter manuscript. This manuscript has since served as a basis for further work on the Massacre, even though it was hostage to the political ideology of the time. For example, the manuscript failed to assess the role of the Safety Zone and its foreign organizers objectively. The research correctly noted that Western leaders of the Safety Zone met the Japanese military as they entered the city, briefed them about the Safety Zone, and led some of the officers on a tour of the Zone. But then the manuscript condemned Zone leaders, saying that they excused Japanese atrocities such as the unprovoked killing of twenty Chinese that occurred after a meeting between the Westerners and Japanese. The Nanjing University researchers also misused documents to imply that Zone leaders cooperated in the killing of Chinese, refused to protest atrocities to the Japanese, and even wined and dined while Japanese carried out the Massacre.[59] No doubt these erroneous conclusions were part of the revolutionary and anti-imperialist atmosphere in China during this time, and research on modern history that did not praise revolutionary development and skewer the West in some way had little hope for recognition. The anti-Western bias was also only a small aspect of the overall research, the true value of which lay in the new and extensive documentation brought to light for others to see.

The Chinese government exercised direct political control over this research and classified the manuscript instead of allowing it to be published.[60] China had only recently rid itself of its last foreign influence, the Soviet Union, and the government wanted all Chinese to feel pride that their nation truly stood on its own. Publishing research on the Massacre would have focused attention back on a time of weakness and invasion, thereby drawing away from China's revolutionary progress. Though the manuscript was kept out of the public eye, in 1965 data from the manuscript was given to the Nanjing city government, which in turn showed the materials to interested Japanese visitors, encouraging them to remind their compatriots of Japan's crimes in China.

Published accounts of Guomindang generals provided the Chinese government with another political means to keep the memory of the Nanjing Massacre alive. These were generals who had participated in the battle against Japanese forces for Nanjing, and who had remained in China after 1949. Their battle memoirs appeared in the 1960s and lamented that the Guomindang had not done enough to protect the nation's capital, in turn denouncing Jiang Jieshi for a faulty defense plan.[61] In this way the Chinese government used the Nanjing Massacre to attack the Guomindang government in Taiwan, in effect implying that just as they did not defend China's capital against invading Japanese troops, Guomindang forces did not defend China, either.

As China moved into the 1970s, revolutionary fervor settled and China sought better relations with the West and Japan. The Nanjing Massacre continued to be more a political tool manipulated by the Chinese government than a large event in China's public history. Cultural and diplomatic contacts between China and Japan increased yearly, and negative encounters such as the Nanjing Massacre remained in the background of Chinese identity with respect to Japan. For example, for Chinese there are two symbolic dates in the war against Japan: September 18, 1931, when Japan invaded northeast China (Manchuria), and July 7, 1937, when Japan invaded north China. August is also an important month because the Japanese surrendered on August 15, 1945. Consequently, July, August, and September contain an important continuum of dates for the Chinese to commemorate their war against Japan. A cursory glance through Chinese newspapers of the 1970s during these months, however, show that friendship, not war, defined Sino-Japanese relations.

During the 1970s these critical months were filled with official visits between the two countries on an almost weekly basis, and these delegations were always referred to as friendship delegations, no matter whether their purpose was cultural, economic, or diplomatic. Chinese speeches and official commentaries on Sino-Japanese relations emphasized that the large majority of Chinese and Japanese wanted friendly relations, and in 1974 an entire month was set aside from September to October to celebrate "Japan-China Friendship Month." The symbolically important war dates of July 7 and September 18 always passed without comment, and August was never spoken of as the month that Japan surrendered. In fact, after China and Japan signed a formal treaty of peace and friendship in August 1978, August became a month to celebrate this treaty.[62] Although Japanese militarism was not swept completely under the rug, comments by Chinese leaders made it appear inconsequential to present-day relations. For example, a speech by Deng Xiaoping in August 1975 on Sino-Japanese relations depicted militarists as a minor factor in Japanese development.[63] In nationwide memorial services for Mao Zedong in 1976, Japanese militarism and the war were hardly mentioned, even though Mao's leadership against the Japanese during the war fueled his rise to power. Most telling is that memorial services fell on September 18, and government leaders in northeast China had the perfect opportunity to use Mao's death to commemorate their own experience of invasion by the Japanese. But they did not. In a 170-line speech by a northeast Party official memorializing Mao, only two lines spoke of fighting the Japanese.[64] This does not mean that China had sworn off celebrations and commemorations of its past history, but they occurred around other events, such as Army Day at the beginning of August and Communist Liberation in October.

Economics were the real linchpin of developing Sino-Japanese relations. Japanese business and political leaders saw China's potentially huge markets, vast natural resources, and cheap but skilled labor pool. At the same time, Japan's geographical and cultural proximity to China facilitated improved relations. In China, leaders wanted the advanced technology and capital resources of Japan for development, and the historical closeness between the two countries proved an additional aid to increasing contacts. Soon after normalizing relations with Japan in 1972, China began importing entire industrial plants from Japan.[65] Three years later Sino-Japanese trade approached U.S. $4 billion, and by 1979 almost fifty thousand people were traveling between the two countries each year.[66] Trade imbalances upset Chinese economic plans, so in 1979 Japan made available U.S. $1.5 billion in loans. As the 1970s ended, Japanese exports to China had ballooned to U.S. $5 billion per annum and consisted of industrial plants and high-technology products, and Chinese exports to Japan had surpassed U.S. $1 billion and were growing at almost 50 percent per year.[67] Sino-Japanese friendship became an integral part of China's development plans, and the Chinese government avoided criticism of Japan's wartime aggression such as the Nanjing Massacre in order to avoid disrupting relations between the two countries.

Textbook Revisions and the Turbulent 1980s

Sino-Japanese relations became more complicated in the 1980s due to, among other things, the growing attempts of groups within Japan to purge war atrocities from school textbooks and to whitewash Japan's invasion of China. Specifically, in 1982 news reporters both inside and outside of Japan accused Japan's Ministry of Education of toning down Japan's war imperialism in public school textbooks by changing terms such as *aggressive war* into *offensive war,* blaming atrocities such as the Nanjing Massacre on the resistance of enemy peoples, and claiming that Japanese invasions were actually Japanese advances into other countries.[68] These accusations set off a storm of protest and created opportunities to bring out many of the submerged aspects of Sino-Japanese relations, such as a desire by some Japanese to assert a more benign view of Japan's role in the war and a desire of many Chinese to remember publicly the negative aspects of past Sino-Japanese interactions. By the end of the 1980s friendship still dominated the public rhetoric between the two countries, but dialogue also included references to militarism, atrocities, and war commemorations, thereby clouding what had been a purified discussion of Sino-Japanese relations.

The Chinese government's response to the textbook issue was muted at first in comparison to the almost immediate responses from Hong Kong, Korea, and groups within Japan. Emphasis on friendship had characterized the Chinese government's approach to Japan in the 1970s, and China generally avoided public criticism of Japan. For example, Zhao Ziyang was visiting Japan in late June as the storm of protest was just beginning, and Zhao only emphasized the close friendship and economic ties between the two countries. Though never openly declared as a strategy, the Chinese government preferred to use diplomatic channels to voice its disagreement and save public announcements for pushing to improve Sino-Japanese ties. When private pressure did not bring satisfactory results, however, the Chinese government could turn to its powerful public voice in an attempt to force an accommodation. The textbook debates of 1982 followed this pattern.

Chinese news reports on Japan at the end of June and into July focused on friendly exchanges and the upcoming tenth anniversary of amicable Sino-Japanese interactions.[69] There were scattered reports on the textbook debate, but nothing on a par with the outspoken denunciations coming from other areas of East Asia. Influenced by the forceful stance of its neighbors, China's rhetoric heated up. Almost a month after the textbook issue began, an editorial in the *People's Daily,* the mouthpiece of the Chinese government, condemned Japan's textbooks and wondered whether they reflected a renewed militarism among some Japanese leaders.[70] Yet it was not until Japanese officials rejected such criticism and condemned other nations for interfering in Japan's internal affairs that China published a spate of articles attacking the Japanese Ministry of Education. These articles spoke of a conspiracy of Japanese militarists who wanted to make people forget the past in order to encourage future aggression, warned that this threatened Sino-Japanese friendship, and traced all such evil intentions to the Ministry of Education.

Meanwhile, the Chinese foreign ministry summoned Japan's ambassador in Beijing and lodged a formal protest.[71] By the end of July the textbook issue dominated all reporting on Sino-Japanese relations, and many of the articles carried threats of varying degrees. Most implied a disruption in friendly interactions and were couched in vague wording, such as, "We will never tolerate any distortion of historical facts."[72] The militant nature of the discussion, however, sometimes spilled over into more definite threats; one article against the Japanese militarists, for example, boldly stated: "They are no match for the Chinese people. Under the historical conditions of the 1930s and 1940s, the Japanese militarists survived for only eight years. If they step into their old shoes today, they will inevitably come to a more disgraceful end."[73]

Some Japanese officials continued to defend the textbooks, and pressure increased into August as Chinese scholars and writers publicized their efforts to keep memories of Japanese aggression against China alive. The first monograph on the Japanese puppet government in Manzhouguo (Manchukuo) was published, and a seminar in Heilongjiang a few weeks later recounted the Japanese invasion of Manchuria on September 18, 1931.[74] These were not sudden activities, as war commemorations and research continued each year, but the circumstances surrounding these activities were different because they suddenly received widespread attention through press releases. The same was true of the Nanjing Massacre. People throughout China and abroad read an account of a Massacre survivor that the *People's Daily* printed, and various Chinese newspapers reported a meeting in Nanjing aimed at exposing Japanese war atrocities.[75]

The textbook debate also became a means to play up the similarities between Taiwan and China, thereby encouraging a rapprochement between the Guomindang (GMD) government on Taiwan and the Communist (CCP) government in China. The *Wen Wei Po,* a CCP organ in Hong Kong, emphasized that compatriots in Taiwan and Mainland China equally experienced the miserable years of Japanese aggression. Only the second cooperation between the GMD and CCP allowed Chinese people to unite and defeat the Japanese invader.[76] The article repeatedly used the vocabulary of cooperation and unity when referring to the Chinese side while labeling the Japanese as aliens and oppressors, thereby playing up the mutual interests of people in Taiwan and China. In an openly nationalistic plea, the article used news reports surrounding the textbook issue to suggest reunification: "Since the newspapers of the CCP and KMT [GMD] could take the same side within 48 hours concerning an event, is there any reason why the CCP and KMT cannot carry out their third cooperation on the problem of the unification of the motherland?"[77]

The textbook controversy for China peaked in August. China canceled the scheduled visit of Ogawa Heiji, Japan's minister of education, and threatened to cancel the visit of Prime Minister Suzuki Zenkō that was planned to coincide with celebrations of the tenth anniversary of Sino-Japanese friendship.[78] Chinese and Japanese officials were holding talks about how to resolve the textbook issue while Chinese newspapers continued to publish critical reports. On August 10, Chinese historians held a forum honoring victory over Japan in the war, and the following week there were exhibitions, forums, and published reminiscences in China to commemorate the end of the war. On the Japanese side, Prime Minister Suzuki visited the Yasukuni Shrine on August 15 to commemorate Japan's war dead, thereby following through on a plan set the previous April.[79] This opened another issue that plagued Sino-Japanese relations: visits by government officials to pay homage to the war dead at the Yasukuni Shrine. Because the Shrine held the remains of executed war criminals such as Tōjō Hideki, the Chinese government and governments of other Asian nations complained that Shrine commemorations glorified Japan's militarists.

The textbook controversy took an abrupt turn on August 18 when the Japanese news service reported that China had once again welcomed a visit by Prime Minister Suzuki.[80] A week later the prime minister publicly pledged to resolve the textbook controversy, and on August 25 China celebrated the tenth anniversary of normalized relations with Japan.[81] The sudden turn-around was not announced by any public declarations that a breakthrough had occurred, but Chinese and Japanese negotiators must have come to a settlement that allowed for an end to the criticism and a recreation of amicable exchanges between the two nations. Since business and cultural exchanges had never ceased despite the angry rhetoric, the resumption of diplomatic visits and an end to negative press reporting quickly restored the friendly public atmosphere that had characterized Sino-Japanese relations prior to July and the textbook controversy. Prime Minister Suzuki visited China at the end of September, and Chinese newspapers printed articles warmly celebrating ten years of renewed Chinese and Japanese friendship. The textbook controversy had ended and cooperation was once more the public stance of the Chinese government.

The 1982 controversy proved how volatile Sino-Japanese relations could be. Although nothing more than diplomatic protests and newspaper criticism resulted, the heated nature of these protests and criticisms as well as the inability of either side to fully accept the other's position showed that many issues remained unresolved beneath the bilateral economic and political interactions that were taking place on the surface. Furthermore, the textbook issue soon escalated into a Chinese discussion of not just the war, but specific symbols of Japanese aggression such as the Nanjing Massacre. A flood of suppressed Chinese feelings poured forth in meetings, publications, and reminiscences, and Chinese people proved all too willing to dig up the negative past that their government's rhetoric professed to want to move beyond. Finally, the textbook debate also showed the willingness of some to use these controversies to further political agendas, in this case the hope for eventual reunification of Taiwan with the Chinese motherland.

Throughout the rest of 1982, 1983, and 1984, there were no alterations to the managed script of Sino-Japanese amity on the scale of the 1982 textbook controversy. Exchanges continued on a weekly basis, and instead of commemorating war anniversaries such as the beginning of war on July 7 or the invasion of Manchuria on September 18, there were celebrations of the

Sino-Japanese Peace and Friendship Treaty in August and the normalization of Chinese and Japanese relations in September. The controversy of 1982 did open the way for two new aspects to the relationship, aspects that in the past had been ignored as detrimental to continued interaction. First, Japanese conservatives could openly speak of Japan's war in Asia as a war to liberate Asian countries from Western colonialism, a view that directly contradicted China's stance that the war had been one of aggression and colonization. Monuments, films, and exhibitions that praised the war effort, as well as Yasukuni Shrine visits, all became media events as the Japanese public debated their nation's role in the war. Second, Chinese celebrated war anniversaries and talked of atrocities in the public media as China, too, engaged in a more open discussion of the war and its effects on China. Meanwhile, friendship continued.

The year 1985 marked the fortieth anniversary of China's victory over Japan, and protests again threatened the façade of amity between Japan and China. At the beginning of July Chinese newspapers reported on Japanese textbook revisions in what had become an annual affair. The reports were short-lived and moderate in tone, merely reporting what had and had not been changed. In a symbolically much larger event, on August 15 Prime Minister Nakasone Yasuhiro became the first postwar head of government to worship at the Yasukuni Shrine in an official capacity.[82] China's first response was low-key: Chinese representatives merely noted, "The Japanese people have different opinions on this matter."[83] A week later the Chinese stance hardened. Government spokespeople condemned the visit as pandering to militarism, and CCP representatives made it clear that they opposed officially sponsored visits.[84] These complaints were at the forefront of multifaceted reporting about Japan as the Chinese government tried to recognize the war anniversary while also promoting good Sino-Japanese relations. The activities of Wang Zhen, a high government official, highlighted the difficult balancing act. In his capacity as honorary president of the China-Japan Friendship Association, Wang met with the president of Tokyo Electric and Chemical Equipment Company on August 12 to celebrate the opening of the company's Beijing office.[85] The next day, Wang, this time in his capacity as a Politburo member and war veteran, attended the opening of a war exhibit in Beijing.[86] At the war exhibit ceremony, Wang used the war to emphasize a familiar theme of GMD and CCP cooperation, and speeches emphasized the important part that GMD forces had played in defeating the Japanese invaders. Throughout the rest of August the Chinese media were filled with a mixture of reports on Japanese atrocities and Japanese friendship delegations.

Another element that entered the complicated propaganda milieu was a connection between war, patriotism, and development. For example, in an article for the *Jingji ribao* (Economic News) titled "Patriotism Is a Great Spiritual Inspiration for Modernization," a strong connection was made between patriotic fervor, economic development, and national improvement, thereby allowing the Chinese government to play both ends of the Sino-Japanese relationship. On the one hand, the government used anti-Japanese war sentiment to bolster public momentum for economic reform. On the other hand, the government emphasized friendly relations with Japan as a means to gain the capital and technology necessary to push forward economic reform.

The issue of the anti-Japanese war and patriotism surrounded the opening of the Memorial for Compatriot Victims of the Japanese Military's Nanjing Massacre *(Qin-Hua Rijun Nanjing datusha yunan tongbao jinianguan)* in Nanjing on August 15, 1985. The Memorial stands well back from the street in an area far from Nanjing's downtown, chosen because a Massacre burial site had been unearthed there. Upon first entering, the visitor faces a stone wall with "VICTIMS 300,000" inscribed on it, showing the central importance of this death total to Chinese representations. A stairway leads to an open sand field scattered with thousand of tiny stones and a few dead trees, and a huge statue of a woman stands strong and tall, towering above this barren field. The stones and trees abstractly make one think of desolation, but the statue is overpowering, cut with strong angles and shaped with an energy often seen in government sculptures that commemorate revolutionary heroes and victory. A walkway takes the visitor around the stone field and along a wailing wall on which are etched figures of people being bound and taken away, bits and pieces of bodies, fire, and a nude woman. The human figures link the viewer with the atrocities committed at Nanjing, thereby enhancing the Memorial's effect and bringing home images of how brutal imperialism has been to the Chinese people. Halfway along the walkway, the visitor enters a small building with yellowed human bones inside, bones from Massacre grave pits unearthed during excavation of the Memorial. The names of tens of thousands of victims are written on the wall spaces between the displays of bones, invoking feelings of loss, destruction, and humiliation. Exiting, the visitor once again walks along the stone field. The revolutionary statue is central to all of this, adding a heroic overtone to the loss, tying everything to China's revolutionary victory and, by extension, the Communist Party. There is no individuality or obvious political division. Instead the feeling is communal and collective. These are displays for all people, commemorating a time when the motherland suffered before uniting under Communist leadership to stand up to its enemies.

From here the visitor enters the main building. Maps, eyewitness accounts, pictures, numerical data, surrender papers, and information about the postwar trials provide documentation of Japanese atrocities and guilt. Many of the displays are in Chinese, Japanese, and English in order to explain the Massacre to all peoples. Gone is the abstraction of the sand garden outside. The objects are real, their authenticity guaranteed, in part, by the explanations and their placement within the Memorial. Near the end is a mock setup of the Tokyo Trial as the Massacre blends into the war, thereby heightening the Massacre's symbolic power. The blending of one into the other is also seen in the opening of the Memorial on August 15, the day of victory over Japan, instead of in December when the Massacre began. The Massacre is part of the war. Talk of the war also reflects talk of the Massacre and vice versa. Furthermore, since the Memorial did not open until 1985, it is also part of the complicated situation surrounding war and Sino-Japanese relations in the present day rather than in the past.

The Memorial asserts the government's view of the Massacre. For example, the displays close with a homily on brotherly love and international cooperation, specifically between China and Japan. It seems oddly out of place amid the reconstruction of so much violence until we realize that the government's approach is to move beyond the Massacre and hold out a hand of friendship to Japan in the name of China's development. At the exit, there is another treatise about a new China built up through revolutionary reform. Ending the Memorial in this way, the government successfully valorizes the Massacre by placing it within China's revolutionary development. In other words, the Memorial is a journey through the imperialism, anger, retribution, and reconstruction of the war, but the focus is on connecting this journey to the leadership of the Communist Party in today's China. Any doubts about this were dispelled in 1996 when the Communist Party, fearful that Chinese people were ignoring this monument to the glory of Communist strength and wisdom, made visits to the Memorial mandatory for schoolchildren. This was part of a larger program to reenergize loyalty to the Party among Chinese citizens.[87] The Memorial is one more way that the Chinese government asserts its control over how people commemorate the war with Japan.

After the Memorial's opening, events in September 1985 showed that feelings within China were more intense than those presented by the government's balanced approach to Sino-Japanese relations. The two months of articles and events highlighting the anti-Japanese war as well as government encouragement of people to show their patriotic spirit resulted in student demonstrations in Beijing against Japan. They began on September 18 as students at Beijing and Qinghua Universities commemorated the fifty-fourth anniversary of Japan's invasion of Manchuria. The demonstration by about five thousand students on the campus of Beijing University received official approval, and student speakers made sure to follow the government line that commemoration was meant to promote Sino-

Japanese friendship.[88] After the ceremony about one thousand students marched through the streets to Tian'anmen in an unapproved action, shouting, "Down with Japanese militarism," "Down with Nakasone," and "Strongly oppose the second invasion." The term *second invasion* referred to Japan's economic penetration of China through Chinese government invitations for more investment and technical assistance. University officials initially reacted by denying that demonstrations had occurred, then claiming that all demonstrations had been spontaneous, and finally admitting that the campus gathering had been approved.[89] This confusion did not last long, and by the end of the month government spokespeople used the student protests to once again warn Japan that friendship and not militarism was the correct path to follow in relations with China.[90]

Protests spread to other cities in China and continued through October. They showed that students directly linked Nakasone's Yasukuni Shrine visit to Japan's current invasion of China; in other words, militarism still lay behind Japan's interests in China. For example, a big-character poster at the Beijing University protests showed a Japanese saying, "I used to be a Japanese imperialist, decapitating 50 people in Shenyang (during the war), but now I'm selling you colour televisions."[91] Evident in such criticisms but never clearly stated was a sentiment among the students that their government was partially responsible for this second invasion, and criticism of government concessions to Japan had appeared clandestinely two years earlier. The circumstances surrounding this criticism were mysterious, but a radio report in Mandarin denounced the government for granting too many concessions to Japan, for ceasing to demand war reparations, and for generally betraying China's best interests.[92]

Spokespeople for the Chinese government continued to put a different spin on these and other protests, insisting that all were helping renew revolutionary patriotism and promoting a new spirit that would push forward the government's Four Modernizations. Central to this government spin was the role of the Communist Party in having defended the nation against Japan and in building up China after the war. The Guomindang came in for a share of the credit in having protected China as the government continued to search out means for compromise with its former political enemy. To those within China, the difference between the government and the students was obvious. Said one unnamed official of the Beijing protests: "This anti-Japanese demonstration, if it was indeed spontaneous, reflects a deep mistrust of Japan among the Chinese people, which continues several decades after the war. The mistrust contrasts sharply with the official relations between Beijing and Tokyo, which are very good."[93]

The student protests continued sporadically. Government officials were compared to Li Hongzhang, a famous Chinese leader at the turn of the century who, in this context, was infamous for selling China out to the Japanese in the Treaty of Shimonoseki that ended the Sino-Japanese War of 1894–95. Japanese cars were burned and Japanese citizens in China attacked. So violent were some of these anti-Japanese demonstrations that Vice President George Bush had to alter his travel plans when he got to Sichuan province.[94] Under the direction of Li Peng, students and others were arrested throughout October and November in an attempt to stifle the protests.[95] This angered the students. They planned further demonstrations to commemorate December 9, the day in 1935 when Chinese students protested Japanese actions in north China, a day considered the beginning of the popular anti-Japanese movement that led to war with Japan. The government organized its own celebrations surrounding December 9, and official speeches emphasized the power of youth when it followed the leadership of the Communist Party. This would be the main thrust of government propaganda, and students were encouraged to make constructive criticism within boundaries set by the CCP.[96]

The students had no such intentions. What had begun in September as anti-Japanese feeling had now expanded into widespread criticism of the Chinese government. Fraud, embezzlement, and corruption within the Party were specific complaints, and students wanted a greater public voice in the affairs of the nation. A general complaint was that after thirty-five years of

Communist rule, China was still a backward country.[97] Just as the government used anti-Japanese feelings to promote an agenda of unity and development, the students used anti-Japanese feeling as a pretext to voice their anger against the Communist Party, which they felt was unresponsive to the sentiments and needs of the Chinese people. In a further twist on the complicated atmosphere of protests and conflicting goals, Xinjiang students used the protests to stage their own demonstrations against nuclear testing and discrimination in Xinjiang.[98]

Protests disappeared from press reports in January. A mixture of suppression and government intervention ended demonstrations. The rest of 1986, at least until December, passed with no serious upheavals. The customary complaints about textbook revisions appeared in July, and Yasukuni Shrine visits caught the media's attention in August. Prime Minister Nakasone canceled an official visit to the Shrine in a gesture of goodwill, meaning that he ignored pressure from within his own party to put aside international opinion, visit the Shrine, and uphold Japan's sovereignty.[99] When his minister of education, Fujio Masayuki, insisted on publicly denying Japanese aggression in the war, Prime Minister Nakasone not only dismissed Fujio from his post but also admitted Japan's wartime aggression in front of the Japanese Diet.[100]

December brought forth the continuing tension between Chinese students and the government, exploding once again around December 9 commemorations. Along with the anti-Japanese feelings that surrounded this anniversary, students complained of poor living conditions and expressed a desire to have a say in who would be their student representatives. As the protests grew, anti-Japanese and antiforeign feeling remained an undercurrent, as seen in one Beijing wall poster that chastised the excessively passive nature of the Chinese people, a passivity that was responsible for again inviting foreign invasion similar to past invasions that had destroyed China.[101] Protesters, however, moved far beyond lamenting the "second invasion." Not only did they repeat the criticisms against Party corruption and oppressive control that had been part of the previous year's demonstrations, they also demanded freedom of speech, open elections, and other democratic concessions. Marches of up to seventy thousand people occurred in Shanghai and other cities as workers joined the students with their own complaints against high living costs and inadequate living conditions.[102] These were the largest demonstrations in China since the Cultural Revolution, and the government had to step in and forcefully repress them. In the aftermath, Hu Yaobang, the general secretary of the Communist Party and a leading spokesman for liberalization of the political system, was blamed for the upheaval and lost his position in the government.

The year 1987 brought more of the same as textbook revisions, Shrine visits, and symbolic war dates all became sources of tension within China and between China and Japan. That year Japan returned a Chinese-owned student dormitory to Taiwan, creating a diplomatic storm as China accused Japan of supporting a two-China policy and undermining the treaties between China and Japan. Japan also helped mediate the transfer of a Chinese pilot who defected to Taiwan. On both issues, the Chinese government put intense pressure on Japan's leaders and Deng Xiaoping threatened to cut back on economic and technical cooperation.[103] Furthermore, the Chinese government made a connection between those who supported a two-China policy in the Japanese government, those who had militaristic tendencies, and past war aggression.[104] As political leaders on both sides tried to manage these disagreements, citizens created further problems. Vandals in Japan reacted to Chinese demands by defacing several monuments to peace and friendship within Japan, and on December 9 Chinese students again rose up in protest.[105]

Chinese officials also became more outspoken during 1987 about their expectations of Japanese aid, a result of Japan's tightening trade regulations after the "Toshiba Machine Incident" when Toshiba was found to have given sensitive technical information to China. Senior Chinese officials urged Japan to offer more assistance, and even Deng Xiaoping said that Japan should contribute more to China's development because China had renounced war reparations in the 1972 Japan-China

Joint Communiqué.[106] Complaints continued into the next year, 1988, and in July Sun Pinghua, president of the China-Japan Friendship Association, threatened to take China's business elsewhere when he voiced a none-too-subtle Chinese saying, "If you cannot light up the lantern in the east, then you should light up the lantern in the west."[107] The very next month Japan offered a generous loan program to China. The Chinese response was immediate; as one official noted, "Sino-Japanese economic relations are in better shape than ever."[108]

The 1980s was in many ways a rocky decade for Sino-Japanese relations. Open protests exploded in 1982, 1985, 1987, and 1988, and from 1985 on students and other citizens within China made clear their disagreement with the government's soft policy toward Japan. The government was not insensitive to the feelings of its people, as seen in 1982 when it also accused Japan of having developed its economic base on the backs of colonized Chinese, but the government only resorted to aggressive language when the Japanese government refused to make concessions. The government's more aggressive stance, in turn, triggered greater anti-Japanese feelings among the Chinese people. Once concessions came, the government reverted to its policy of forgiveness and expected protests to end as well. If they did not, the government pressured protesters off the streets. The back-and-forth nature coincided with growing public dissatisfaction over corruption, lack of freedom, and rising cost of living, resulting in anti-Japanese protests that grew into antigovernment protests. The government's response was to keep reform and development going on government terms, and generally this meant keeping a lid on protests that might upset Sino-Japanese relations and public order.

On the positive side, Sino-Japanese relations had matured through the ups and downs of the 1980s. The war became a topic for debate and discussion, and this led to negative actions such as Japanese vandalism of peace statues in Japan or Chinese attacks on Japanese citizens in China. Both governments solved these problems and others at the diplomatic level, and the variety of opinions witnessed in protests and ceremonies, though expressed more openly than ever before, did not derail the improvement of relations. In fact, cooperation increased as loans and exchanges reached new highs. The Chinese government expressed the maturation of its own attitude toward Japan in July 1988: "In the past, in our propaganda work, we often put stress on . . . Sino-Japanese friendship and did not put stress on the troubles in . . . Sino-Japanese relations because we thought it improper to simultaneously stress both Sino-Japanese friendship and the troubles in the Sino-Japanese friendship. Moreover, for a period in the past, we overestimated the positive side of . . . Sino-Japanese relations and made some improperly optimistic remarks on . . . Sino-Japanese relations."[109] The rest of 1988 was marked with what had become the usual articles on textbook revisions and war atrocities, and after the loan agreements nothing occurred to create open protests.

Student protests in Beijing and other cities made 1989 an altogether extraordinary year. They grew directly out of the memory of Hu Yaobang, who had recently passed away, and commemoration of the May Fourth Incident, a series of first student and then public demonstrations in 1919 to oppose foreign interference and reform Chinese society. The students in 1989 also wanted to reform China, and they used Hu Yaobang as a symbol of political liberalization to demand a larger public voice in Chinese affairs. However, Hu Yaobang had also promoted better ties with Japan and the outside world. Consequently, there was no direct connection between imperialism, anti-Japanese feeling, and the 1989 demonstrations. For students to have highlighted such feelings would have undermined the basis of their activism, namely the memory of Hu Yaobang and his internationalist ideas.

Even though anti-Japanese feeling was never a focus in the protests leading up to the government's assault on student strongholds near Tian'anmen on June 4, the tension between public and government views of Japan existed within the strong emotions expressed. *Maiguo* or "selling out the nation" had become a term heard often as protests grew in the 1980s against the government's soft policy toward Japan, and this resentment joined the myriad others that fed student dissatisfaction with the rulers they viewed as corrupt and inattentive to the real desires of the people. For example, one Chinese student was asked why he disliked Li Peng. The student replied that Li Peng brought humiliation to China through visits abroad and only knew nuclear power and economics.[110] Just a month earlier, Li Peng had been in Japan negotiating new economic deals for China. Hu Yaobang's death, the spark that began the student demonstrations, had occurred during Li Peng's visit.

Growing protests throughout the 1980s culminated in 1989, and when the government silenced the students in June, they also silenced all public demonstrations against Japan and the war. Further adding to this repression was the fact that Japan more quickly than any other world leader reopened contacts with China. Within a little more than a year, Japan had renewed its loan agreements with China, and Japan's foreign minister condemned Western efforts to isolate China.[111] China responded by suppressing any anti-Japanese reports or actions. When the Japanese government decided to formally recognize a Japanese lighthouse constructed on the Diaoyu (Senkaku) Islands, protests erupted in Taiwan and Hong Kong. In China, however, information about these protests was suppressed. Furthermore, when students applied for a protest permit, not only was the permit denied but the students were investigated because of the government's continued fear that any activism might again grow out of hand. The government also did not want to sour Sino-Japanese relations at a time when international support for China had fallen so far.[112]

This state of affairs continued into the 1990s as students and citizens learned to ignore politics and focus on more open sectors of society, such as economics. On the sixtieth anniversary of the invasion of Manchuria, a series of publications and commemorations took place while at the same time China prepared for the visit by Prime Minister Kaifu Toshiki.[113] The year 1992 saw the usual reports on Yasukuni Shrine visits and war memories, but the real news was the visit to China by Emperor Akihito at the end of October. In 1993 Japan began a massive investment plan in China, part of a trend that saw trade volume between the two countries increase by at least 20 percent each year from 1991 to 1994.[114] By the end of 1994 this trade would top U.S. $43 billion, as Japan was China's primary trading partner and one-fifth of all China's trade went to Japan.[115]

The comments of several Japanese officials, calling the Nanjing Massacre a story made up by the Chinese and denying Japan's war atrocities, could not overshadow the positive nature of Sino-Japanese ties.[116] Japanese cabinet ministers who denied specific atrocities publicly apologized for their insensitive comments and resigned their positions. The sincerity of their apologies was irrelevant because merely the apology itself paid homage to and reaffirmed a story that China and Japan were friends separated by a narrow strip of water, that their friendship dated back two thousand years, and that the war was a mistake carried out by a few militarists whose modern-day influence must be controlled.[117] Once the apology was uttered and compliance to the public script was made apparent, these officials continued their careers in another setting, and their private denials of the Massacre and other war atrocities could continue, just as millions of Chinese citizens privately expressed their anti-Japanese feelings while their government carried on a public story of enduring friendship and cooperation between Japan and China. Official denials followed by public apologies and resignations became one more trend, adding to the convolution of understanding the Nanjing Massacre and the war.

The year 1995 marked the fiftieth anniversary of the Japanese surrender, and commemorations marked the brutalities and outrages the Japanese troops had committed in China. Chinese commentators warned of an ever-present militarist trend in Japan and exhibits displayed pictures, documents, and artifacts to stir up the patriotism of the Chinese people against foreign aggression. News releases promoted the role of the Communist Party in defeating Japan and building a strong new China. Japan diplomatically reacted with humility to these ceremonies, and Prime Minister Murayama Tomiichi officially apologized for Japan's war of aggression.[118]

Current issues interacted with old memories and both became woven into the fabric of deepening Sino-Japanese relations. China undertook a series of nuclear tests that continued through 1995 and brought criticism from Japan and other nations. When China ignored these complaints, Japan in August decided to suspend its economic aid for 1995. China protested, thereby beginning another round of diplomatic debates that, invariably, elicited references to Japan's past militarism and its war debt. One Chinese official complained that Tokyo should reflect on its own wartime atrocities instead of criticizing others.[119] Another official stated, "The linking of financial cooperation with political issues has hurt the feelings of the Chinese people," a truly tongue-in-cheek comment considering China's or most other nations' approach to foreign policy.[120]

Incomplete Scholarship and Unresolved Issues

The Chinese scholar Tang Meiru argues that the 1970s and 1980s were a time of increasing confidence among Chinese, a confidence that made people willing to face past war humiliations and added to the fervor of war protests.[121] As Chinese power and influence continued to grow, the government actively released stories and information that upheld a narrative history of imperial domination and suffering while promoting China's status in the world. The increasing respect that other nations accorded China justified this status, allowing Chinese to safely contrast past weakness and victimization with present strength. A government editorial in 1995 declared: "The China of today is not China of 50 years ago. Through a protracted hard struggle, particularly since the 17 years of reform and opening up to the outside world, China's economic and comprehensive national strength have grown greatly."[122] China's past suffering and present confidence created both sympathy and fear. Nations such as Japan were made to recognize an obligation to China for past wrongs, and China was ever ready to bring up the past as part of present-day politics.

That the victimization card should work at all has a lot to do with developments in the twentieth century, especially since World War II, concerning victims and humanitarian relief. Formation of the United Nations, international antiwar protests of the 1960s, and U.S. president Jimmy Carter's insistence that human rights were a serious political issue all pushed forward a hope for international covenants to protect victims of war and violence.[123] The Third-World Movement, which began after World War II with nations declaring themselves sovereign and independent of foreign domination, also created momentum to create international bodies where less technologically developed areas could raise their voices against more advanced ones, all in the hope of preventing aggression. This movement received a boost in the 1970s and 1980s when conflicts in Vietnam, Afghanistan, and numerous other areas focused attention on peoples that rarely received consideration in world affairs. These were the same decades during which China began to open up to the world, and the Nanjing Massacre was one of many symbols that served to unify the face China presented to nations abroad.

Confidence has its flip side as well, and as China opened to the world in the 1970s Chinese began to see just how far behind China's economy, science, and quality of life were compared with those of the United States, Europe, and, most important, Japan. Japan had become a dominant economic power, and some saw this as Japan's unjustified reward for a half century of militarism in the Pacific. For many Chinese the 1980s brought a new era of Japanese economic imperialism that was once again raiding China of its wealth for the benefit of Japan.

One outlet for the confusion that renewed Sino-Japanese contacts brought was increased scholarship on war atrocities, specifically the Nanjing Massacre. In response to Japanese denials of the Nanjing Massacre, Nanjing University in cooperation with the Number Two Historical Archives in Nanjing formed the Committee to Compile Materials on the Japanese Military's Nanjing Massacre *(Qin-Hua Rijun Nanjing datusha shiliao bianji weiyuanhui)* to research the Nanjing Massacre. In 1984 the Committee interviewed more than seventeen hundred survivors of the Massacre and placed their testimonies in the 1985 Massacre Memorial.[124] They also undertook research into death totals and concluded that 190,000 people had been massacred in groups and 150,000 had died in random atrocities, bringing the total number of dead to 340,000.

Artists and writers involved themselves in commemorations as well. In conjunction with the opening of the Nanjing Massacre Memorial in 1985, smaller monuments were constructed throughout Nanjing to commemorate Japanese atrocities at other sites in the city. Well-known calligraphers wrote inscriptions such as: "The invading Japanese troops massacred our 300,000 compatriots in Nanjing in December 1937. As many as 2,000 were killed in the vicinity. . . . This monument is erected in order that future generations will never forget and will be determined to strengthen China and make her prosper forever."[125]

The year 1985, the fortieth anniversary of victory over Japan, witnessed a series of published works on the Nanjing Massacre. The novelist Zhou Erfu published a historical novel titled *Nanjing de xianluo* (The Fall of Nanjing), finishing a project that had been inspired by the textbook controversy of 1982.[126] Xu Zhigeng, who in 1987 would publish his study of the Massacre, titled *Nanjing datusha* (The Nanjing Massacre), released information he had collected in a commemorative series of articles published in Beijing.[127] Gao Xingzu, a professor of history at Nanjing University who had coauthored the 1962 study of the Massacre and a leading expert on the subject, published *Rijun qin-Hua baoxing: Nanjing datusha* (Japanese War Atrocities: The Nanjing Massacre). Carefully footnoted and providing detailed information on atrocities and people involved, this book provided the best research yet on the Massacre and continues to be a standard work on the Japanese invasion and occupation of Nanjing. From here public attention to the Massacre mushroomed, and Chinese translations of Japanese works also began to appear in Chinese bookstores.[128] Before the decade was out, news writers and novelists involved themselves in projects that depicted Nanjing under invasion and occupation, and in 1988 the Nanjing Film Studio released a coproduced film on the

Massacre. Titled *Tucheng xuelei* (The Blood and Tears of a Massacre), the movie told the story of a young Chinese doctor in Nanjing who was killed after filming the endless atrocities committed by invading Japanese troops.

Chinese archive collections also committed some of their materials to publication. In 1987 the Number Two Historical Archives cooperated with other archives and published hundreds of documents concerning the Massacre.[129] The next year they began publishing a fifteen-volume work on the entire war period in another cooperative effort to make public a small portion of the extensive documentation on the Massacre and the war.[130]

Fictional and nonfictional accounts, reminiscences, news reports, and films have continued to appear in the 1990s, and the search for new information never ends. Throughout this burgeoning interest the government continues to control access to primary documents. The Number Two Historical Archives and the Nanjing City Archives contain unknown quantities of documents concerning the Massacre, but researchers who wish to view them are carefully screened because most information is reserved for government-approved scholars and projects.[131] As the Massacre increases in importance, the Chinese government intends to monitor it as much as possible, just as it tries to monitor China's relationship with Japan.

Scholars in Taiwan and Hong Kong are also active in Massacre scholarship, though not to the extent of researchers in China. As is the case in Mainland China, this scholarship focuses on a few crucial issues. Foremost is the number of deaths in the Massacre. Scholars continue to unearth data on sites where groups of soldiers and civilians died, on how many people were buried, and on how people died, all in an attempt to build on death totals first established in the war crimes trials. As stated before, the official estimate of 300,000 was inscribed on the Nanjing Massacre Memorial entrance in 1985, and Chinese scholars have pushed that number well beyond 300,000. Such death totals are aggressively defended in print, especially against Japanese research that denies the Massacre or tries to belittle any death estimates in the hundreds of thousands.[132]

This focus on numbers and actual atrocities keeps the Massacre within the bounds of human understanding, thereby maintaining specific identity with human suffering and death. However, by focusing on data and first-hand accounts, Chinese research also opens an avenue for dissenters to question and poke holes in the specific information, hoping by extension to cast doubt on the overall story of the Massacre.[133] Further muddying the calculations of death totals is a lack of concreteness. Burial documents are a mixture of actual numbers and estimates, and no differentiation is made between Chinese or Japanese, soldiers or civilians. An unknown number of bodies were cast into the Yangzi River and disappeared, so Chinese calculations make up for this by adding many tens of thousands of bodies to the burial estimates. Finally, the highest estimates include killings that occurred well outside the boundaries of Nanjing City. What results is a range of estimates from a few tens of thousands by the most serious doubters to several hundreds of thousands by the most avid supporters.

The figure of three hundred thousand or more deaths is also a numeric symbol of Chinese suffering, a concrete measure of imperialist aggression in China. The immediate aggression was from the Japanese invasion and initial occupation of Nanjing. As the capital of China, Nanjing's suffering during the Massacre reflects China's suffering throughout its war with Japan. Yet Japan was only the last in a line of aggressors that waged war on Chinese soil. Consequently, the Massacre joins a string of events, such as the Opium War and the burning of the Summer Palace, that represent the violence of imperialism, and death figures are a central part of the Massacre as a larger symbol of the destruction that foreign encroachment wrought on Chinese soil. Three hundred thousand deaths is more than just a number over which scholars argue. It is a multilayered symbol that for Chinese signifies the unjustified pain inflicted on China by Western and Japanese power, and those who try to lessen or deny this number are, by extension, attempting to deny imperialist aggression.

A second concern of Chinese scholarship on the Massacre is

blame. Scholars search through archives and diaries, looking for key words that might prove that the Japanese command ordered the Massacre. Every year more Japanese come forward and admit that atrocities occurred and that their commanders ordered them to carry out mass killings. In Japanese diaries, another source of evidence, wording is often vague, which stirs debate on exactly what officers did and did not order. For example, brigade commander Yamada, who was in charge of the 103rd Brigade at the time of the Massacre, was put in charge of Chinese prisoners. His diary records that on December 15 he received the order to "take care of" *(shimatsu seyo)* the prisoners. In diary entries a few days later, Yamada writes that he took care of the prisoners, and he never mentions prisoners again. For most researchers, "take care of" is a euphemism for "execute," and this has led to further research into the language that surrounded and covered up Japanese war atrocities.[134] However, this has also led to exaggerated interpretations of the vague comments uttered or written by soldiers and officials in an attempt to prove that the Massacre was not a sudden event but had been premeditated at the highest levels of the Japanese command.[135] Just as with concrete death totals, pinning responsibility on the Japanese high command pushes the limits of good scholarship and gives way to emotionalism and political agendas.

A third aspect of research concerns war reparations from Japan. When Japan surrendered, war reparations were an ongoing issue between China and Japan. As U.S. policy toward Japan changed after 1945, the Guomindang government followed the U.S. lead and stopped pushing for reparations. In the 1952 peace treaty between the Republic of China and Japan, the GMD government renounced Chinese claims to war compensation. When Japan and China normalized relations in 1972, China also renounced reparations, seemingly making moot any need for Japan to compensate China for destruction caused by the war. However, many private citizens want Japan to pay reparations, take responsibility for the destruction caused in the war, and thereby pave the way for true international reconciliation. Continued Japanese refusal to answer such demands creates an atmosphere of distrust between the Chinese people and the Japanese government that, in turn, makes other Sino-Japanese issues difficult to solve. In 1987 the comments of Chinese leaders, tying reparations to Japanese aid, brought the problem into the open and clearly showed that China's leaders are also aware of this potentially explosive issue. The prying open of the "comfort women" issue has brought the debate over compensation further into the open. In the 1990s both reparations and "comfort women" became part of the Chinese government's political dialogue with Japan. In July 1992, just prior to Emperor Akihito's visit, Chinese officials for the first time publicly asked the Japanese government to compensate "comfort women."[136] In an even stronger stand, Li Peng, while talking with a group of visiting Japanese business executives, told them that economic aid and war reparations were connected: "During the 1930s and 1940s, China suffered enormously from the invasion by Japan. The sum of aid given by the Japanese government cannot compare with the amounts of damage that China suffered."[137] Stated by one of China's most senior leaders during ongoing commemorations of the fiftieth anniversary of the Japanese surrender, Li's comments made clear that China expected increased aid from Japan because China did not demand war reparations.

Private Chinese citizens also demand compensation as well as a public apology, but Japanese worry that compensation on one issue will lead to demands for reparations on many others, leaving the Japanese government with a potentially mammoth monetary burden. Furthermore, giving public money and a public apology will anger conservatives who still feel that no guilt should be connected to Japan's war effort. Chinese look at the war in Europe and see that Germany has apologized profusely while also paying out billions of dollars in compensation. This is the standard, fair or unfair, to which they hold Japan.[138]

As in any contested scholarship, there is both hearsay and strong empirical work surrounding these and other issues of the Massacre. The volatile atmosphere surrounding the Massacre means that often exceptional scholarly ability and extensive documentation are limited by a Chinese focus on attacking Japanese denials and emphasizing worst-case scenarios. The massacre at Mufu Hill *(Mufushan)* can provide an example of how a need to condemn Japan negatively affects Chinese researchers who are trying to document the Massacre. At the Tokyo Trial, the prosecution told of an incredible massacre in the Mufu Hill area outside of Nanjing. A witness, Lu Su, came across two wounded Chinese, one a soldier and the other a policeman. They told Lu that the Japanese had interned and been starving 57,418 Chinese of all ages. On December 18 the Japanese killed everyone still alive. Lu Su's account was transcribed and submitted directly as prosecution evidence in Tokyo, and the Tribunal accepted the transcription without question. When a defense lawyer tried to object or question the veracity of such a report, the Tribunal ignored his concerns.[139] This massacre at Mufu Hill and Lu Su's number of 57,418 continue to appear in Chinese scholarship. Chinese researchers do not compare the Mufu Hill massacre to other reports of similar massacres in the area, do not ask how and why Japanese soldiers corralled so many people into one place, and do not wonder how Lu Su's informants came up with such a specific number. The report appeared in the 1962 research done by Nanjing University, in the 1985 work by Gao Xingzu, and in an extensive look at the Massacre completed in 1994.[140] In every book the authors repeat the story and go on to emphasize that the prisoners were first shot, then bayoneted, and finally burned as a way to further play up the barbarity of the whole situation. The information has also made its way into English accounts of Japanese atrocities, again being used without question or comment as if the Mufu Hill atrocity was based on sound documentation.[141]

Contrast this to Japanese work on the same incident. Scholars who deny the Massacre such as Suzuki Akira question why so many people were holed up in such a militarily strategic location, implying that possibly they were Chinese soldiers preparing to fight or that the story was fabricated.[142] A scholar with a more moderate stance toward the Massacre, Hata Ikuhiko, compares the many different accounts that depict a series of killings in the Mufu Hill area and concludes that Chinese are wrong to see these as a string of separate incidents. Hata feels that all are stories about just one set of killings.[143] Finally, Japanese scholars in full agreement with Chinese accounts of mass killings and atrocities examine the many conflicting accounts about murders in the Mufu Hill area in order to better understand which numbers and sites are the most believable.[144]

The strong emotions that affect Chinese scholarship also continue to create tension between a public and a government view of war and Japan. Contradicting government pronouncements of improving relations, a 1995 survey of residents in Beijing found that 85 percent of the respondents believed Japan was not to be trusted. In Shanghai 79 percent felt this way. As for Japanese cooperation, 57 percent of Beijing respondents said that Japan had failed to provide cooperation with China, and more than 70 percent felt that Japan had not compensated people for the atrocities committed in the last war.[145] Despite the claim of the Chinese government to "two thousand years of friendship" with Japan, Chinese people still carry strong anti-Japanese feelings.

This strong feeling appears as well in the war research atmospheres of Hong Kong and Taiwan. There is little tolerance for Nanjing Massacre research that does not focus on Japanese responsibility, and the intimidating environment scares away especially younger scholars who question some aspects of Massacre scholarship or who are interested in broader issues of the Massacre.[146] There is an extensive and varied literature on the Holocaust that could act as a reference for ideas and approaches to the Nanjing Massacre. For example, many Chinese scholars have investigated reasons why the Japanese military acted with such cruelty, but their explanations consider little more than an inherent weakness in either Japanese character or Japanese society. Left out or de-emphasized are situational explanations and broader approaches that point to the inhuman aspects of all modern societies. The nature of memorials, memory, the psychological effects of the Massacre, and representations are further topics that have been left out of Chinese research on the Massacre. The focus of research is instead on documenting the extent of Japanese atrocities and making Japan admit its responsibility, nothing more and nothing less.

Chinese in the United States have also become more active in the 1990s with respect to the Nanjing Massacre and other Japanese war atrocities. After the death of Emperor Hirohito in January 1989 and just prior to his funeral in February, a group calling itself the Ad Hoc Committee on the Case against Hirohito purchased a full-page advertisement in the *New York Times* in which it accused the late Japanese emperor of war atrocities and criticized U.S. president George Bush's decision to attend the funeral.[147] Hirohito's lifelong escape from legal prosecution and the events at Tian'anmen Square four months later stimulated Chinese scholars and Chinese students abroad to get more involved in Chinese issues. This, in turn, promoted a sense of increased activism among these groups, and the explosion in information technology fed this activism as groups created Nanjing Massacre websites on the Internet.[148] One group of Chinese scholars in the United States began publishing *Riben qin-Hua yanjiu* (Studies of Japanese Aggression against China).[149] This journal publishes scholarly work centered on different themes concerning Japanese aggression against China and draws submissions from well-known scholars in China, Taiwan, Japan, and elsewhere. The editors hope to keep memory of atrocities such as the Massacre alive and wish that China would do more to make Japan face its war responsibility. The Alliance for Preserving the Truth of the Sino-Japanese War is another group in the United States that puts on exhibitions and collects materials. Recently it has become active on the Internet, spreading news and information, contributing to several list-servs, and establishing its own website.[150] The Alliance teamed up with several other World War II victims' groups in 1997 to support a U.S. House of Representatives Resolution (HR 160) that called on the Japanese government to offer an official apology and recognize its wartime atrocities.[151] Drafted by Congressman William O. Lipinski (Democrat, Illinois) and cosponsored by ten legislators from both the Democratic and Republican parties, the resolution demanded that Japan compensate military and civilian prisoners of war and establish a humanitarian fund to compensate survivors of Japanese brutality.[152]

The expanded scope of Massacre scholarship is also reflected in international conferences. In December 1995 an international symposium on "Reassessing the Sino-Japanese War (1937–45): New Sources and Interpretations" was held in Vancouver, Canada, with researchers from Europe, North America, China, Taiwan, and Japan. By bringing together different nationalities and research approaches, this conference and others like it move beyond the mutual agreement of a Chinese-only conference and expand both the issues under examination and the possible approaches. In Vancouver some of the participants questioned the use of labels such as "collaboration," "resistance," and "puppet," thereby looking at the narratives of patriotism that limit study of the war and events like the Nanjing Massacre. Others closely examined the maneuverings and rationale of Chinese governments under Japanese occupation. In other words, these scholars pointed the lens at China rather than exclusively at Japan or other foreign powers. General conclusions did not differ from those that preceded, namely that the Japanese had brutally invaded an innocent China, but these researchers did examine life during the war and under occupation with a broader lens.[153]

Children of Chinese immigrants are also helping to spread information and ideas about the Nanjing Massacre. Growing up with a Chinese past in a non-Chinese environment gives them cultural and linguistic skills necessary to bring Chinese information to a non-Chinese audience. In the United States, Christine Choy and Nancy Tong have used their documentary film, *In the Name of the Emperor,* to discuss the Nanjing Massacre. Through interviews, film footage of the invasion, and a larger discussion of the war, these two filmmakers also express their dissatisfaction with the late Japanese emperor Hirohito and Japanese ignorance of the war. Author Iris Chang heard about the Massacre from her grandparents. She used these stories as a basis for her own research and has written an account in English, titled *The Rape of Nanking: The Forgotten Holocaust of World War II.* As part of her quest, she helped uncover the diary materials of John Rabe, the German head of the Safety Zone Committee in Nanjing during the invasion. This diary is an important primary document. Even though it offers little new with respect to what is known about the Nanjing Massacre, it does add further eyewitness corroboration of the horrific atrocities committed by invading Japanese troops. In her book, Chang presents some of the documents and stories that inform the emotion-filled Chinese views of the war and Japan, mixing good research and biased speculation to portray an evil and secretive Japan. Written in English, Chang's work targets an American audience with no personal investment in the Nanjing Massacre and probably little knowledge of it. Hence, she does a service by spreading information about the Nanjing Massacre while unfortunately spreading hearsay as well. As more exhibitions, conferences, movies, and books come to the English-speaking world and enter international information networks such as the Internet, the Nanjing Massacre and its debates expand beyond China.

Conclusions

The Massacre began as a specific incident experienced by many hundreds of thousands of Chinese. Those who survived had no concept of the overall event, but knew that family members, neighbors, and numbers of people outside of their personal circles had suffered. Even people who had access to broader information, such as Western missionaries in Nanjing, had no idea of the extent of the atrocities.[154] People in Nanjing could not do more because to see the whole Massacre at the time it occurred required an awareness and comprehension beyond human ability. After 1945 the dimensions of the Massacre emerged more clearly, as did its consequences, and the Massacre has become part of both official and popular histories in China, meaning, among other things, that the half-tints and complexities have been ignored in order to reduce this event to the level of us and them, winners and losers, the good guys and the bad guys. Historiography supports this view while ceremonies ritualize the

Massacre. In short, the Massacre has been transformed from a war atrocity experienced by Chinese in Nanjing on a local scale to an international symbol of suffering that, in one sense, brings together all who identify with China and/or oppose Japan. At this level the Massacre is a strong unifying event for all Chinese people.

At another level the Massacre has become a tool for political struggle, even inter-Chinese struggles. The Chinese government uses the Massacre for political ends, and a national fervor has developed around the Massacre and other war atrocities. This gives the government a potent weapon with which to try to intimidate Japan, and the Chinese government has shown that it will use the media, protests, and diplomatic threats to see that Japan accords it the respect it feels it deserves. In the past China was one of many victims of Japanese nationalism. Now China's own nationalism has become a weapon to use against Japan. On the other hand, China also uses the Massacre to play up China's victimization. China is a powerful nation whose influence is on the rise, and it can safely contrast its past weakness and victimization with its present strength and refusal to allow itself to be dominated again. In short, China uses the Massacre to play both sides of a power coin, that of intimidator and victim, and the balance can be uncertain, as witnessed by the differences between popular and official feelings within China.

The Chinese government has had trouble managing these differences, and Chinese students have proven willing to use anti-Japanese protests as a base for their own antigovernment protests. In the 1980s this led to street violence, arrests, deaths, and hard-nosed political repression. By the end of the decade, the government had silenced dissent within China and dissenting voices moved abroad, stirring others to spread information about events such as the Nanjing Massacre in the West.

The growth of information surrounding the Nanjing Massacre comes from this event's ability to encompass a great deal of China's modern past, especially as it coincides with Japan. There are other symbolic events as well, such as the "comfort women" issue, the biological experiments of Unit 731 outside the northern city of Harbin, the "three alls" campaign, and massacres in other cities. However, the Nanjing Massacre overshadows these events for several reasons. First, information has existed about the Massacre from the day it began, and more information appears yearly to hold people's attention and keep research going. Because this information includes Chinese records, Japanese reminiscences, and Western accounts, there is a legitimacy that spans national borders. Adding further legitimacy are the trials held in Tokyo and China after the war. These trials dealt at some length with the Nanjing Massacre, while other events such as the biological experiments of Unit 731 or the forced prostitution of "comfort women" were ignored. The Massacre occurred in the national capital and at the beginning of the war, thereby making it symbolic not only because of the atrocity itself, but also because of geographical and chronological location. The focused and brutal nature of the Massacre also sets it apart from other symbolic events. For example, biological experiments and the abusive treatment of "comfort women" occurred over a long period of time, as did the "three alls" campaign. Only massacres in other cities carried the immediate impact of Nanjing, but the Nanjing Massacre exceeded them in scale. For all these reasons, the Nanjing Massacre has proven to be an enduring symbol for Chinese grievances and a source of Chinese unity. The Massacre also resonates with feelings abroad because it calls up anti-Japanese emotions that remain strong in other nations that fought Japan in the war. As China becomes more involved in various international arenas, its opinions become more easily transported abroad. With more Chinese living overseas than ever before, these opinions acquire human transmitters throughout the world. Thus, the Nanjing Massacre may continue to grow in international importance.

Intimidation, victimization, politics, social turmoil, and war memories are all linked to the Nanjing Massacre. Though the atrocity occurred decades ago, it has moved through time to connect, tentacle-like, with other issues, such as those of "comfort women," the Bataan Death March, and militarism in today's Japan. The result is a colonial story of an innocent China and an evil Japan. This discourse can be extrapolated to other periods of foreign aggression and connected to other symbols of Japanese aggression. The site no longer needs to be located in China, and the colonial power can be other than Japan. There is also a timeless quality to the Massacre because most Chinese who protest against Japan were born after the war. Their knowledge of the Massacre comes from family stories, school lessons, and newspaper accounts. Their information usually comes without much of the wartime context or the world situation at the time, and the feelings are patriotic and emotional, which in turn inspire hatred of Japan and tend to ignore the complicated situation surrounding the Massacre and its postwar metamorphosis.

There is a need to reiterate numbers and stories in order to keep the Massacre alive and maintain pressure on Japan to acknowledge its aggression in the Pacific War. The Tokyo Trial established trends for numbers, for stories, and for varied evidence, and the Chinese have continued these trends. Conversely, the Japanese government's insincerity about Japan's war responsibility keeps Chinese minds focused on the data and documents of the Massacre. Perhaps some day soon Chinese scholars will be able to use the plethora of evidence at their disposal and high standards of critical inquiry to venture beyond a description of the horrors and toward a direct effort to understand the meaning and implications of the Massacre. There is more to the Massacre than now exists in Chinese historiography.

Notes

1. H. J. Timperley compiled some of these accounts in *What War Means: The Japanese Terror in China, A Documentary Record,* as did Hsu Shu-hsi in *The War Conduct of the Japanese, Documents of the Nanking Safety Zone,* and *A Digest of Japanese War Conduct.*
2. Tang and Zhang, *Nanjing: 1937 nian 11 yue zhi 1938 nian 5 yue,* p. 16.
3. Fitch Papers, box 52, Nanking, "Notes on the Present Situation,"

March 21, 1938, p. 2; Bates Papers, Record Group 11, box 157, file 2993, Ginling College, letter from Minnie Vautrin, March 21, 1938, Yale Divinity School Library; Timperley, *What War Means,* pp. 59–60.

4. Kasahara, *Nankin nanminku no hyakunichi: gyakusatsu o mita gaikokujin,* p. 316; Song, "Shenpan Nanjing datusha an zhufan Gu Shoufu de huiyi," p. 18.

5. Smythe, *War Damage in the Nanking Area, December 1937 to March 1938: Urban and Rural Surveys,* p. 8n. 1.

6. Vautrin Diary, April 11, 1938.

7. Fitch Papers, box 52, "Letters from Nanking," copy of a letter from Professor H. L. Sone of Nanking Seminary to Dr. F. P. Price in Shanghai, January 16, 1938. Minnie Vautrin made a similar comment in her diary. See Vautrin Diary, February 2, 1938.

8. Fitch Papers, box 52, letter to family, January 15, 1938; Vautrin Diary, January 2 and June 8, 1938.

9. Varg, *Missionaries, Chinese, and Diplomats: The American Protestant Missionary Movement in China, 1890–1952,* p. 263.

10. Fitch Papers, box 52, letter to John Magee, April 23, 1938.

11. "We Were in Nanjing," p. 41.

12. Luo, "Shenpan Riben zhanfan: junshi fating de zujian jingguo," p. 30.

13. See, for example, Xu, *Xueji: qin-Hua Rijun Nanjing datusha shilu,* pp. 268–69, and Tang and Zhang, *Nanjing,* p. 19.

14. Bauman, *Modernity and the Holocaust.*

15. This is reflected not only in the missionary diaries and letters of the time but also in continuing scholarship up to today that widely refers to the poor training of Japan's frontline troops and the lack of leadership from military superiors.

16. Brackman, *The Other Nuremberg: The Untold Story of the Tokyo War Crimes Trials,* p. 191.

17. Smythe, "What Happened in Nanking," p. 383.

18. Bai, *Jinri zhi Nanjing,* p. A7.

19. Han, "Qin-Hua Rijun zai Nanjing de wenhua dajielüe."

20. Timperley, *What War Means,* pp. 182, 193, 195. Because atrocities were organized and officers took part, I infer official complicity in the Massacre. I trace this complicity no farther than those officers who were in Nanjing, however, because we do not yet have any evidence of Massacre orders coming from higher levels of the Japanese military outside of Nanjing.

21. See, for example, Milgram, *Obedience to Authority: An Experimental View.* See also the experiment of Philip Zimbardo referred to in Bauman, *Modernity and the Holocaust,* pp. 166–67.

22. Tang and Zhang, *Nanjing,* p. 160.

23. A well-known story is of a sword-killing competition between two Japanese heroes. The competition had to be extended twice and finally ended after each man had decapitated more than one hundred people. This story is widely commented on in Japanese and Chinese research. Osaka's *Mainichi shinbun* carried a report on February 9, 1938. Tokyo's *Nichinichi shinbun* and the *Japan Advertiser* (English edition) also carried reports. In the appendix to Timperley's *What War Means* there are comments on the *Japan Advertiser* report.

24. *China Weekly Review* 84:8 (April 23, 1938), pp. 207–8; Fitch Papers, box 52, letter to George Fitch from K. S. Lee, July 3, 1938.

25. Rummel, *China's Bloody Century: Genocide and Mass Murder since 1900,* p. 154; Brackman, *The Other Nuremberg,* pp. 275–76; Tang and Zhang, *Nanjing,* pp. 162–63.

26. A good discussion of the emperor system and its effect on military discipline is in Yuki Tanaka, *Hidden Horrors: Japanese War Crimes in World War II,* pp. 198–208.

27. For example, Motoori Norinaga, Hirata Atsutane, Yoshida Shōin, and Fukuzawa Yukichi all derided China in their writings. In the twentieth century even Ishibashi Tanzan, while claiming to support Chinese sovereignty, encouraged Japanese occupation of northeast China.

28. Fogel, *The Literature of Travel in the Japanese Rediscovery of China, 1862–1945,* pp. 210–30.

29. Wray, "China in Japanese Textbooks," pp. 119–23.

30. Dower, *War without Mercy: Race and Power in the Pacific War,* p. 286.

31. Chi, "Zhanhou Zhongguo xiang Riben suoqu peichang yanjiu."

32. Piccigallo, *The Japanese on Trial: Allied War Crimes Operations in the East, 1945–1951,* p. 158.

33. Minear, *Victor's Justice: The Tokyo War Crimes Trial,* p. 102.

34. Piccigallo, *The Japanese on Trial,* pp. 10–14.

35. Yu, "Comments," p. 98.

36. Roling, *The Tokyo Trial and Beyond: Reflections of a Peacemonger,* p. 52.

37. Brackman, *The Other Nuremberg,* p. 22.

38. The Military Tribunal was established in January 1946, the prosecution's opening statement was delivered in May 1946, the defense ended its case in June 1947, and the Tribunal's verdicts were announced in November 1947. See Piccigallo, *The Japanese on Trial,* pp. 10, 18–23.

39. Brackman, *The Other Nuremberg,* p. 223.

40. Roling, *The Tokyo Trial and Beyond,* pp. 54, 59–60; Minear, *Victor's Justice,* pp. 120–22.

41. Roling, *The Tokyo Trial and Beyond,* pp. 79–81.
42. Ibid., p. 89.
43. Two defendants died during the trial and one was declared incompetent to stand trial. By comparison, at the Nuremberg Trial twelve men were sentenced to death, seven received prison terms of ten years to life, and three were acquitted. See Brackman, *The Other Nuremberg,* p. 223.
44. Ibid., p. 388. Kojima Noboru, who has written extensively about the Tokyo Trial, speculated that Mei voted for eleven death sentences. See Minear, *Victor's Justice,* p. 91n. 44.
45. Awaya, "In the Shadows of the Tokyo Tribunal," p. 83.
46. Minear, *Victor's Justice,* p. 117n. 88. Chinese continue to lament the change in U.S. policy toward Japan that meant that only twenty-five war criminals were tried at Tokyo. See, for example, Gao, *Rijun qin-Hua baoxing: Nanjing datusha,* p. 101.
47. The sometimes unclear distinctions are between A-class criminals who committed crimes against peace and humanity, and B-class or C-class criminals who committed conventional war crimes such as murder and rape.
48. Piccigallo, *The Japanese on Trial,* pp. 159–62.
49. Pepper, *Civil War in China: The Political Struggle, 1945–1949,* pp. 9–16; Luo, "Shenpan Riben zhanfan," p. 30.
50. The Communists did not drop claims to reparations, but this was a moot point because the Communists did not represent China in international bodies. As for trials of Chinese traitors, some never faced prosecution because of the need to evacuate from central China. As the Guomindang fled, they released those Chinese sentenced to less than life imprisonment. See Meng and Cheng, "Chengzhi hanjian gongzuo gaishu," pp. 111.
51. Piccigallo, *The Japanese on Trial,* p. 170n. 67.
52. Hong, *Jindai Zhongguo waidie yu neijian shiliao huibian,* pp. 759–800; Meng and Cheng, "Chengzhi hanjian," pp. 110–11.
53. Piccigallo, *The Japanese on Trial,* pp. 95 (U.S.), 120 (Britain), 173 (China), 183–84 (Netherlands).
54. Yang, "A Sino-Japanese Controversy: The Nanjing Atrocity as History," p. 16.
55. International Military Tribunal for the Far East, *The Tokyo War Crimes Trial,* pp. 40147–48. Later in the trial summary of charges against Matsui Iwane, the Tribunal quoted a figure of 278,586, which came from the prosecutor of the Nanjing Trial. See p. 41221. The Tribunal said that settling on an exact figure was impossible, but from the figures quoted we can conclude that the judges approved of a number greater than 200,000. See p. 40147.
56. Brackman, *The Other Nuremberg,* pp. 182–85.

57. "The Tokyo Trial in Historic Perspective: Question and Answer Period," p. 112.

58. Yang, "A Sino-Japanese Controversy," p. 16. Accounts by H. J. Timperley and Hsu Shu-hsi presented the Safety Zone officials as heroically doing their best to save Chinese in a nightmarish situation. Over time accounts in Chinese, Japanese, and English have come to support this view of the Westerners who worked in the Zone.

59. Gao et al., "Riben diguozhuyi zai Nanjing datusha," part 2, "Brutal Killings Committed by the Japanese Invasion Force in the Safety Zone," March 23, 1996.

60. In 1979 a classified publication of the book was issued in China for internal circulation only, generally meaning for government officials and others with inner-circle connections. Over time this publication became available to most Chinese interested in the Massacre. In 1995 a Chinese scholar obtained a copy and carried it to America where sections were translated and posted on the Internet at http://www.cnd.org/njmassacre/njm-tran.

61. Yang, "A Sino-Japanese Controversy," p. 16.

62. Foreign Broadcast Information Service, "Sino-Japanese Treaty Anniversary Marked by Press, Arts," *Daily Report: China,* August 13, 1979, pp. D1–D3.

63. Foreign Broadcast Information Service, "Teng Hsiao-ping Comments on War, Japan Peace Accord," *Daily Report: China,* August 18, 1975, p. A3.

64. Foreign Broadcast Information Service, "Heilongjiang Holds Memorial Rally, 18 Sep.," *Daily Report: China,* September 20, 1976, pp. L1–L6.

65. Kojima Reiitsu, "Accumulation, Technology, and China's Economic Development," pp. 248–49.

66. Foreign Broadcast Information Service, "Ta Kung Pao Views Sino-Japanese Trade" and "Sino-Japanese Treaty Anniversary Marked by Press, Arts," *Daily Report: China,* December 19, 1975, and August 13, 1979, pp. A5 and D1–D3.

67. Beasley, *The Rise of Modern Japan,* p. 267; Foreign Broadcast Information Service, "Japanese Media Cited on China Treaty Anniversary," *Daily Report: China,* August 17, 1979, p. D1.

68. Foreign Broadcast Information Service, "Distortion of Japanese History Textbooks Cited" and "Renmin Ribao Criticizes Japan's Revised Textbooks," *Daily Report: China,* July 7 and 21, 1982, pp. D2 and D3–D4. These changes are discussed at length in Takashi Yoshida's chapter in this volume.

69. See, for example, Foreign Broadcast Information Service, "Wan Li Meets Japan Amity Group Officials" and "Wan Li Meets Japanese Newspaper, TV Official," *Daily Report: China,* July 6, 1982, p. D1.

70. Foreign Broadcast Information Service, "Renmin Ribao Criticizes Japan's Revised Textbooks," *Daily Report: China,* July 21, 1982, pp. D3–D4.

71. Foreign Broadcast Information Service, "Kyodo: PRC Protests Japanese History Rewrite," *Daily Report: China,* July 27, 1982, p. D1.

72. Foreign Broadcast Information Service, "Zhongguo Qingnian Bao Article," *Daily Report: China,* July 28, 1982, p. D4.

73. Foreign Broadcast Information Service, "Japanese Officials Defend Textbook Changes," *Daily Report: China,* July 28, 1982, p. D3.

74. Foreign Broadcast Information Service, "Renmin Ribao on 'History of Puppet Manzhouguo'" and "Heilongjiang Seminar," *Daily Report: China,* July 28 and August 10, 1982, pp. D6–D7 and D3.

75. Foreign Broadcast Information Service, "Nanjing Survivor's Account" and "Nanjing Meeting," *Daily Report: China,* August 5 and 8, 1982, pp. D5 and D2.

76. For most of Chinese history, the GMD and CCP have been enemies. However, they cooperated for the first time in 1923–27 to unify the Chinese nation, and for the second time in 1936–45 to fight the Japanese, though even these periods of cooperation were often fraught with animosity and distrust.

77. Foreign Broadcast Information Service, "Press Views Japanese Textbook Controversy," *Daily Report: China,* July 29, 1982, p. W3.

78. Foreign Broadcast Information Service, "Japanese Minister's Visit Deemed Inappropriate" and "AFP Report on Suzuki Visit," *Daily Report: China,* August 2 and 3, 1982, pp. D1 and D1.

79. Foreign Broadcast Information Service, "Historians Mark Anniversary of Victory over Japan" and "Japan, China Commemorate War Anniversary," *Daily Report: China,* August 12 and 17, 1982, pp. D2–D3 and D8–D10.

80. Foreign Broadcast Information Service, "Kyodo: Wan Li Says Suzuki Visit Still Welcome," *Daily Report: China,* August 18, 1982, pp. D3–D4.

81. Foreign Broadcast Information Service, "Suzuki Pledges Solution" and "Japanese, Chinese Groups Celebrate Normalization," *Daily Report: China,* August 25 and 26, 1982, pp. D1 and D1–D2.

82. Foreign Broadcast Information Service, "Nakasone Visit to Yasukuni Draws Criticism," *Daily Report: China,* August 19, 1985, pp. D1–D2. Past visits had always been in a private capacity, even though some prime ministers signed the logbook with their official titles. See, for example, Foreign Broadcast Information Service, "Japan, China Commemorate War Anniversary," *Daily Report: China,* August 17, 1982, pp. D8–D10.

83. Foreign Broadcast Information Service, "CPC Officials Com-

ment on Sino-Japanese Relations," *Daily Report: China,* August 14, 1985, pp. D1–D3.

84. Foreign Broadcast Information Service, "Xinhua Commentary Condemns Yasukuni Shrine Visit" and "Yao Yilin Answers Reporters Questions," *Daily Report: China,* August 22 and 27, 1985, pp. D1–D2 and D1.

85. Foreign Broadcast Information Service, "Wang Zhen Meets Japanese Corporation Delegation," *Daily Report: China,* August 14, 1985, p. D3.

86. Foreign Broadcast Information Service, "Wang Zhen Attends Anti-Japanese War Exhibition," *Daily Report: China,* August 13, 1985, pp. D1–D2.

87. "Nanjing Students Forced to Visit Massacre Memorial Hall."

88. Foreign Broadcast Information Service, "Students Mark '18 Sep. Incident' in Beijing," *Daily Report: China,* September 19, 1985, p. D1.

89. Foreign Broadcast Information Service, "AFP Reports Demonstration," *Daily Report: China,* September 19, 1985, p. D1.

90. See, for example, Ibid.

91. Ibid., p. D2.

92. Foreign Broadcast Information Service, "Ba Yi Scores PRC Leaders' Concessions," *Daily Report: China,* August 15, 1983, pp. D1–D2.

93. Foreign Broadcast Information Service, "AFP Reports Demonstration," *Daily Report: China,* September 19, 1985, p. D2.

94. Foreign Broadcast Information Service, "Cheng Ming on Background of Student Unrest," *Daily Report: China,* December 13, 1985, pp. W1–W2.

95. Foreign Broadcast Information Service, "Anti-Japanese Student Demonstrators Arrested" and "Cheng Ming on Background of Student Unrest," *Daily Report: China,* November 25 and December 13, 1985, pp. D1 and W1–W2.

96. See, for example, "Speeches, Ceremonies Mark 'December 9th Movement,'" *Daily Report: China,* December 9, 1985, pp. K1–K12.

97. Foreign Broadcast Information Service, "Commentary Notes Causes of PRC Student Unrest," *Daily Report: China,* December 6, 1985, p. V1.

98. Foreign Broadcast Information Service, "Xinjiang Students Hold Beijing Nuclear Protest," *Daily Report: China,* December 23, 1985, pp. K2–K4.

99. Foreign Broadcast Information Service, "Nakasone Cancels Visit to Yasukuni Shrine" and "Wan Wei Po Opposes Homage to Yasukuni Shrine," *Daily Report: China,* August 15 and 18, 1986, pp. D1 and D3–D4.

100. Foreign Broadcast Information Service, "Nakasone Admits Japan Aggression against China," *Daily Report: China,* September 18, 1986, p. D1.

101. Foreign Broadcast Information Service, "Qinghua University Students Put up Posters," *Daily Report: China,* December 23, 1986, p. R2.

102. Foreign Broadcast Information Service, "10,000 Students Stage Protest March in Shanghai," *Daily Report: China,* December 22, 1986, pp. O1–O14.

103. Foreign Broadcast Information Service, "Deng Said Considering Reprisals Against Japan," *Daily Report: China,* July 2, 1987, p. D1.

104. Foreign Broadcast Information Service, "Wen Wei Po Criticizes 'Japanese Rightists,'" *Daily Report: China,* September 11, 1986, pp. D2–D3.

105. Foreign Broadcast Information Service, "Students, Authorities Clash" and "Chinese Peace Statue in Nagasaki Defaced," *Daily Report: China,* December 8 and 14, 1987, pp. 9–10 and 7.

106. Foreign Broadcast Information Service, "Lecture Views Sino-Japanese Ties," *Daily Report: China,* September 3, 1987, p. 4.

107. Foreign Broadcast Information Service, "Journal Interviews Official on Sino-Japanese Ties," *Daily Report: China,* July 11, 1988, p. 7.

108. Foreign Broadcast Information Service, "Official Praises Japanese Loan Program," *Daily Report: China,* August 17, 1988, p. 15.

109. Foreign Broadcast Information Service, "Journal Interviews Official on Sino-Japanese Ties," *Daily Report: China,* July 11, 1988, p. 7.

110. Foreign Broadcast Information Service, "NHK Feature on Movement," *Daily Report: China,* May 9, 1989, p. 33.

111. Foreign Broadcast Information Service, "Japan Urges West Not to 'Isolate China'" and "Japan to Resume Loan Package to PRC," *Daily Report: China,* July 6 and 11, 1990, pp. 6 and 5.

112. Foreign Broadcast Information Service, "Request for Anti-Japanese Rally Probed," *Daily Report: China,* December 19, 1990, p. 7.

113. Foreign Broadcast Information Service, "Commentary Notes Prospects for Sino-Japanese Ties" and "Anniversary of '18 September' Incident Marked," *Daily Report: China,* August 23 and September 20, 1991, pp. 9–11 and 22–25.

114. Foreign Broadcast Information Service, "Japan Plans 'Massive Investment Plan' for China" and "Japanese Loans Cause 'Staggering' Currency Losses," *Daily Report: China,* July 12, 1993, and December 12, 1994, pp. 19–20 and 12–13.

115. Foreign Broadcast Information Service, "Official Sees Sino-Japanese Trade 'Blossoming,'" *Daily Report: China,* December 12, 1994, pp. 13–14.

116. Foreign Broadcast Information Service, "Spokesman Views Japanese Environment Minster's Remark," *Daily Report: China,* August 15, 1994, pp. 5–6.

117. "Two thousand years of friendship" and "separated by a narrow strip of water" are clichés that often appear in official Chinese proclamations concerning Sino-Japanese relations.

118. Foreign Broadcast Information Service, "Japan's Murayama Apologizes for World War II," *Daily Report: China,* August 17, 1995, p. 6.

119. Foreign Broadcast Information Service, "'Deep Regret' Expressed over Japanese Aid Cut," *Daily Report: China,* August 21, 1995, p. 5.

120. Foreign Broadcast Information Service, "Nuclear Test 'Excuse' for Japan to Suspend Grants," *Daily Report: China,* September 19, 1995, pp. 19–20.

121. Tang and Zhang, *Nanjing,* p. 16.

122. Foreign Broadcast Information Service, "Editorial Marks 7 July Incident Anniversary," *Daily Report: China,* July 13, 1995, pp. 13–15.

123. Elias, *The Politics of Victimization: Victims, Victimology, and Human Rights,* pp. 10–19, 196, discusses this development at some length. Though Elias focuses on human beings as victims, many of his ideas are also applicable to nations that claim victimization.

124. Wu, "Nanjing datusha shijian zhi zaiyanjiu," p. 64.

125. Yang, "A Sino-Japanese Controversy," p. 26.

126. Ibid. Unless otherwise noted, information in this paragraph comes from this work.

127. Xu, *Xueji,* pp. 480–81.

128. For example, Tanaka Masaaki's work on the Nanjing Massacre was translated into Chinese as *"Nanjing datusha" zhi xugou* (The Illusion of the "Nanjing Massacre").

129. Zhongguo dier lishi dang'anguan et al., *Qin-Hua Rijun Nanjing datusha dang'an.*

130. Foreign Broadcast Information Service, "New Books View Japanese Aggression," *Daily Report: China,* August 18, 1988, pp. 7–9.

131. This comes from personal experience in these archives as well as the stories of colleagues, both Chinese and non-Chinese.

132. For example, see Duan, "Bo Rijun Nanjing datusha 'xugou' lun."

133. This is exactly the approach of Suzuki Akira in *"Nankin daigyakusatsu" no maboroshi,* and Tanaka Masaaki in *"Nanjing datusha" zhi xugou.*

134. This diary and interpretation of the term *take care of* appear often in scholarship on the Nanjing Massacre. See, for example, Hora,

"Nankin jiken to shiryō hihan," p. 113, and Gao, *Rijun qin-Hua baoxing,* pp. 31–32.

135. For example, Li Enhan, one of Taiwan's foremost authorities on the Nanjing Massacre, wrote an article that emphasized a few vague comments by General Matsui while downplaying clearer commands to argue that the Massacre was ordered by Matsui. See Li, "Nanjing datusha de tusha mingling wenti."

136. Foreign Broadcast Information Service, "Japan Urged to Compensate 'Comfort Women,'" *Daily Report: China,* July 7, 1992, p. 8.

137. Foreign Broadcast Information Service, "Li Peng Links Japanese Aid with Repayments for Invasion," *Daily Report: China,* September 19, 1995, p. 18.

138. Germany was not a lone aggressor in the European war. Also, Germany was a central force in Western civilization. For these reasons, Germany has been able to distance its war heritage from its history as a member of modern civilization. Japan had neither of these advantages, and its war history ties directly into its modernizing history. These factors make the case of Japan different than that of Germany. Finally, in historical terms, the German apology and paying of compensation are more an exception than the rule.

139. International Military Tribunal for the Far East, *The Tokyo War Crimes Trial,* pp. 4538–51.

140. Xu, *Xueji,* p. 131.

141. Rummel, *China's Bloody Century,* p. 137.

142. Hora, "Nankin jiken to shiryō hihan," p. 117.

143. Hata, *Nanjing datusha zhenxiang: Riben jiaoshou de lunshu,* pp. 138–39.

144. For example, Hora, Fujiwara, and Honda, *Nanking daigyakusatsu no kenkyū,* pp. 128–49.

145. Foreign Broadcast Information Service, "Poll Reveals PRC, ROK Distrust of Nation," *Daily Report: East Asia,* August 17, 1995, pp. 9–10.

146. On a trip to Taiwan in 1996 I had extended discussions with two different Chinese graduate students concerning the Nanjing Massacre and how it has been researched. I asked them why they did not pursue their ideas as a dissertation topic. They both simply said that they would not be allowed to do so, which I took to mean that their advisors either disagreed with their ideas or realized such research would be academic suicide.

147. *New York Times,* February 16, 1989, p. B15.

148. Nanjing Massacre websites can be located by typing the words "Nanjing" or "Nanjing Massacre" in a web search.

149. The publisher is Society for Studies of Japanese Aggression

against China *(Riben qin-Hua yanjiu xuehui)*, and the address and phone number are 110 Mark Court, Carbondale, IL 62901, (618) 549-4993.

150. Alliance for Preserving the Truth of the Sino-Japanese War Worldwide Web URL: http://www.sjwar.org, e-mail: sjwar_board@sii.stanford.edu. The group's address and phone are P.O. Box 2066, Cupertino, CA 95015-2066, (415) 398-7758. Ignatius Ding, the Alliance's secretary, often posts information to several list-servs. His e-mail address is ding@capella.cup.hp.com.

151. Some of the other groups are American Defenders of Bataan and Corregidor, Center for Internees Rights, Inc., and Washington Coalition for "Comfort Women" Issues.

152. "News Reported in Japan," on h-asia@h-net.msu.edu, May 6, 1997. Information on Resolution 160 (HR 160) can be found at the Alliance website listed above as well as the congressional website: http://Thomas.loc.gov.

153. Zhang Li, "'1937 nian zhi 1945 nian Zhong-Ri zhanzheng zhi zai jiantao: xin ziliao yu xin jieshi' guoji yantaohui."

154. This is borne out by estimates of deaths in the tens of thousands by Westerners in Nanjing, such as those in the writings of George Fitch at the Harvard-Yenching Library and at the Hoover Institution of War, Revolution, and Peace Archives at Stanford University; in the diary of Minnie Vautrin at the Yale Divinity School Library; and in the letters of Miner Searle Bates, also at the Yale Divinity School Library. These initial estimates proved wholly inadequate as war crimes trials and burial records documented death totals that exceed 100,000 and possibly exceed 300,000.

3

A Battle over History

The Nanjing Massacre in Japan

TAKASHI YOSHIDA

On December 13, 1937, the Japanese army captured the city of Nanjing. The judgment of the International Military Tribunal for the Far East (May 1946–November 1948) described what happened in Nanjing as follows:

> The Japanese soldiers swarmed over the city and committed various atrocities. According to one of the eyewitnesses they were let loose like a barbarian horde to desecrate the city. It was said by eyewitnesses that the city appeared to have fallen into the hands of the Japanese as captured prey, that it had not merely been taken in organized warfare, and that the members of the victorious Japanese Army had set upon the prize to commit unlimited violence. Individual soldiers and small groups of two or three roamed over the city murdering, raping, looting, and burning. There was no discipline whatever. Many soldiers were drunk. Soldiers went through the streets indiscriminately killing Chinese men, women, and children without apparent provocation or excuse until in places the streets and alleys were littered with the bodies of their victims. According to another witness, Chinese were hunted like rabbits, everyone seen to move was shot. At least 12,000 non-combatant Chinese men, women and children met their deaths in these indis-

criminate killings during the first two or three days of the Japanese occupation of the city.[1]

The Tribunal estimated that more than 20,000 Chinese men of military age were killed, and approximately 20,000 cases of rape occurred in Nanjing during the six weeks after the city fell.[2] The total number of people killed in and around the city during the first six weeks of the Japanese occupation was, according to the Tribunal, more than 200,000, a figure based on the fact that funeral societies and other organizations buried more than 155,000 bodies.[3]

Such was the judgment of the Trial, and since then this view has become standard in Japanese school textbooks and among progressive historians who have opposed any incursions of the imperial past into postwar education.[4] These progressives, active and influential in the postwar Japanese public arena (in academic discussions, political debates, and the mass media), have long battled with conservatives and nationalists over postwar historiography regarding the Japanese imperium. Thus, the terms used to describe the warring groups of scholars and their allies outside the academy have different meanings in Japan than in the United States. In the United States, the term *progressive* is virtually synonymous with liberal revisionism. In Japan, however, the term *revisionist* is associated with conservatism and is at odds with the progressive view of history.

From the end of the war until the early 1970s, some Japanese revisionists, such as Tanaka Masaaki, a World War II veteran, tried to discredit the conclusions of the Tribunal as "victors' justice," but their efforts received little attention. From the 1970s on, the dominant view, that a massacre occurred in Nanjing in 1937–38, has increasingly been challenged by revisionists, including conservative politicians, World War II veterans, scholars in various disciplines, business executives, and popular commentators *(hyōronka)*. Outraged by these revisionist challenges, progressives responded quickly to refute revisionist claims that the Massacre did not occur. The struggle between the two camps over the Nanjing Massacre has raged for more than twenty-five years, and the contest over how to characterize the Nanjing Massacre along with other Japanese wartime atrocities is not likely to end in the near future.

Historiography of the Battle over the Nanjing Massacre

Before the 1970s: The Rise and Decline of Progressive Influence

Beginning on September 11, 1945, class A war crimes suspects were arrested, and by the end of December 1945 more than one hundred former Japanese leaders were in the Sugamo Prison. According to a poll conducted by the United States Strategic Bombing Survey after Japan's defeat, 44 percent of the Japanese people (excluding former military personnel) thought that Japan must become a more peaceful and democratic nation. Only 5 percent expressed a wish that Japan return to the prewar system. Although 22 percent of the respondents, according to the same survey, had little idea of how Japan should change, the physically and spiritually exhausted majority agreed that it was necessary to build a new Japan that would be different from the country in wartime.[5] For instance, another poll conducted among the Japanese residing in Beijing in 1945 showed that 80 percent of them were willing to sacrifice as much as they did during the war in order to rebuild Japan.[6]

Although many people were dissatisfied with the shortage of food supplies, 70 percent of interviewees at the end of 1945 said that they were satisfied with Allied occupational policies.[7] The half-starved populace attributed postwar miseries such as starvation to their own wartime leaders.[8] These people, as well as most Japanese newspapers, supported the activities of the War Crimes Tribunal.[9] For instance, on April 30, 1946, *Nihon keizai shinbun* considered it "the duty of the Japanese to carefully follow the trial of the 28 wartime leaders who initiated the military dictatorship."[10] On the same day, an editorial in *Mainichi shinbun* echoed this feeling: "We believe that this [the Trial] is earnestly desired not only by the Japanese people suffering from the extreme difficulties caused by the defeat, but by the whole human race."[11] On May 1, 1946, *Tōkyō shinbun* printed three letters to the editor supporting the Tribunal and calling for the punishment of the twenty-eight war criminals who had dragged Japan into the war.[12]

The Tribunal served as a stage for openly displaying Japanese wartime atrocities to the Japanese public. Japanese newspapers circulated the Trial's details throughout the country, and accounts of the Nanjing Massacre finally became headline news. On July 26, 1946, the testimony before the Tribunal of Robert Wilson, a doctor who witnessed Japanese brutalities in Nanjing, prompted *Asahi shinbun* to write that "the horrible acts of the Japanese Army have now been revealed to the people for the first time."[13] On July 27, 1946, the headline of a report on the Trial in *Asahi shinbun* read, "Insatiate Atrocities for Three Months." Three days later, *Mainichi shinbun* reported the testimony of Miner Searle Bates, a history professor at Nanking University at the time, who claimed that "more than 12,000 non-combatants were slaughtered" and that "8,000 cases of rape" took place within a month.[14] Moreover, on July 31, 1946, an editorial in *Yomiuri shinbun* condemned the irresponsibility of the journalists who witnessed the Massacre but stopped short of reprimanding the military.[15]

In addition to the punishments exacted by the Tribunal, 193,612 wartime political, economic, and social leaders were purged from national and local offices, the press, and private companies in conformity with guidelines established in January 1947.[16] Furthermore, 5,211 teachers and administrative staff members (0.9 percent of the total figure of 568,000) who supported wartime militarism and nationalism were purged from schools and boards of education.[17] On December 31, 1945, Japanese history as well as moral education *(shūshin)* and geography were prohibited from being taught in schools because the prewar content of these subjects was regarded as militaristic and nationalistic by the Supreme Commander for the Allied Powers. Tōyama Shigeki, a historian, has called this day the starting point of Japanese historical education in the postwar period.[18]

In November 1946, almost one year after the ban on the teaching of Japanese history, the Occupation authorities permitted the instruction of history to resume. School textbooks edited by the Ministry of Education did refer to the Massacre, although the description of the Massacre was not detailed. The elementary school textbook *Kuni no ayumi (ge)* (The Course of the Nation, vol. 2, 1946), for instance, stated: "Our army devastated *[arashi]* the capital of China, Nanjing." The junior high school and high school textbook *Nihon no rekishi (ge)* (Japanese History, vol. 2, 1946) read: "Atrocities *[zangyaku kōi]* committed by our army at the time of the capture of Nanjing resulted in an all-out anti-Japanese struggle by the Chinese."[19]

Historical writing and the critical examination of history extended beyond elementary and high school textbooks. In the halls of higher education, Rekishigaku Kenkyūkai (or Rekken, the Historical Science Society of Japan), established in 1932, held its first and second postwar meetings in November and December 1945. The participants reflected upon wartime national historical education that was used to lead the nation into the war, and they unanimously agreed that they had to take responsibility for historical education in order to keep the nation from engaging in war again. At the third postwar meeting of Rekken in January 1946, discussion centered on criticisms of *tennōsei* (the emperor system), and the proceedings were published in February 1946 as *Rekishika wa tennōsei o dō miru ka* (How Historians View the Emperor System). According to the book's foreword, "History will become science only if it serves the people, and the people must regard historical science [Marxism] as a guiding compass."[20] In other words, Rekken participants rejected the wartime history education that was used to teach "unscientific imperial myths and morals," as well as to justify national sacrifice for the emperor and Japanese expansion overseas.

These progressive historians, most of whom were Marxists or influenced by Marxism, could not have challenged imperial myths during the war without risking imprisonment. With the end of war, however, they published numerous books. For instance, Ishimoda Shō's *Chūseiteki sekai no keisei* (The Formation of the Medieval World), which was written during the war, was finally published in 1946. It received critical acclaim from Marxists and non-Marxists alike.[21] Other books challenging the wartime imperial-centered monopoly on the writing of history include: Takahashi Kazuo's *Yuibutsu shikan Nihon rekishi nyūmon* (Introduction to Japanese History from a Historical Materialist Perspective, 1946); Inoue Kiyoshi's *Kuni no ayumi hihan: tadashii Nihon no rekishi* (Critique of *The Course of the Nation:* The Correct History of Japan, 1947); Tamaki Hajime's *Nihon rekishi* (Japanese History, 1948); and Hani Gorō's *Nihon jinmin no rekishi* (History of the Japanese People, 1949). Progressive historians not only wrote actively, but also participated in democratic and peace movements, such as "The Struggle to Protect People's Rights" (Minshuteki shokenri o mamoru tatakai) and "The Petition Campaign for the Stockholm Appeal to Prohibit the Use of Atomic Weapons" (Genshi heiki shiyō kinshi no Sutokkuhorumu apiiru shomei undō) in 1949–50.[22]

However, from the early 1950s on, as the Cold War took shape, the progressives endured a rising challenge from what they called "reactionary forces" and they struggled to resist what they regarded as a revived imperialism and militarism.[23] In 1950 the so-called red purge was initiated by the American occupying force, and more than ten thousand members and sympathizers of the Japanese Communist Party were purged from the government, mass media, and the private sector.[24] Simultaneously, those who had been purged for supporting wartime militarism were permitted to return to public posts.

In the face of perceived Communist threats, a conservative Japan gained renewed support from the United States. Japanese envoy Ikeda Hayato's promise to the U.S. government in 1953—that "the Japanese government will be responsible for facilitating a spontaneous spirit of patriotism and self-defense among the Japanese"[25]—began to be inscribed in school textbooks in the mid 1950s. The Japanese Democratic Party (Minshutō) demanded that school textbooks be compiled by the state. It also published a booklet, *Ureubeki kyōkasho no mondai* (Deplorable Problems in Textbooks) in 1955, which insisted that Japanese textbooks were polluted by dangerous distortions and should be called "red textbooks" *(akai kyōkasho).*[26] The Ministry of Education subsequently increased its control over textbook authorization, and one-third of school textbooks were rejected by the government for not meeting new government standards.[27] The ministry demanded that textbooks avoid tough criticism of Japan's role in the Pacific War, and the government regarded as inappropriate any description of Japan as invading China.[28] From the mid 1950s until the 1970s, therefore, the description of the Massacre completely disappeared from school textbooks, mirroring this conservative shift of the Ministry of Education.

As noted earlier, progressive historians also allied themselves with more broadly based popular movements. In 1960, the Liberal Democratic Party (Jiyū minshutō), the successor to the Democratic Party, pushed a bill through the House of Representatives ratifying the U.S.-Japanese Security Treaty in spite of strong public opposition.[29] Throughout May and June 1960 there were almost daily demonstrations. On May 14 alone, one hundred thousand people joined the mass demonstration. Nearly six hundred historians signed petitions, and many of them actually participated in the protest movement.[30] After the bill was passed, the area around the Diet building was filled with demonstrators. On June 20, the treaty automatically became law without receiving the approval of the House of Councilors, and 330,000 protestors surrounded the building. Millions of people nationwide were involved in the antitreaty movement.[31]

In the reaction to the political and social upheaval of the 1960s, new works that reconsidered the meaning of the "Greater East Asian War" appeared and found widespread support among the public. For instance, Ueyama Shunpei, a philosopher, wrote "Dai tō-A sensō no shisōshi teki igi" (The Significance of the Greater East Asian War in Intellectual History) in *Chūō kōron* (September 1961). Ueyama challenged "the established [progressive] view of the war in the press," the view that had been advocated by the United States and that justified the Allies' conduct during the war. To Ueyama, Japan's war was simply one of many wars among sovereign states whose ultimate aim was to safeguard national interests. He argued that a sovereign state could not judge other sovereign states, and he raised serious doubts about the justice of the Tribunal in light of acts by the former Allied powers in the Korean, Algerian, and Suez Wars.[32]

Hayashi Fusao, a novelist, published a series of articles titled "Dai tō-A sensō kōteiron" (The Affirmative Thesis on the Greater East Asian War), which later became a two-volume book,[33] beginning in the September 1963 issue of *Chūō kōron.* The articles argued that the Tribunal was simply an act of vengeance by the victors and had nothing to do with "justice," "humanity," or "civilization"; that the war, which Hayashi regarded as inevitable, was a part of the Hundred-Year War against Western aggressors; and that the "hundred-year war" was never a war of aggression, as claimed by the Tribunal.[34] Hayashi's articles won some support from the media. One of the four leading newspapers, *Yomiuri shinbun,* praised Hayashi's article and urged Japan to free its history from the propaganda of Communism.[35] Another influential newspaper, *Asahi shinbun,* argued that Japan contributed to the emancipation of Asian peoples from the West and that the role of the Pacific War should be re-examined.[36]

The government fostered this spurt of nationalism as well. In 1966, the government revived the February 11th national holiday, calling it the "National Foundation Day" *(kenkoku kinenbi).* This holiday, earlier known as *kigensetsu,* was first established in 1873 and lasted until Japan's wartime defeat; it celebrated the enthronement day of the mythic first Japanese emperor, Jinmu. Business circles such as Nikkeiren welcomed the establishment of the holiday. In 1968, moreover, the government sponsored the one hundredth anniversary of the Meiji Restoration across the nation in order to nostalgically commemorate the Japan of the Meiji period (1868–1912), during which Japan became modernized. The government's objective in commemorating the anniversary was to teach young people the significance of the Meiji period and to instill national pride in them after their "patriotism had been weakened by postwar education."[37]

Within the climate of historical revision and growing conservative fervor, the history of the Nanjing Massacre did not escape reinterpretation. In 1966, Shimono Ikkaku, a former general of the Sixth Army who participated in the battle of Nanjing, together with Gotō Kōsaku, a former newswriter for *Mainichi shinbun* who marched toward Nanjing with the army, insisted that the Sixth Army never participated in the Massacre as claimed by the Guomindang government; that Tani Hisao, who was sentenced to death at the War Crimes Tribunal in Nanjing, was innocent; and that the Massacre was a "lie" of world history.[38] By contrast, in the following year historian Hora Tomio published *Kindai senshi no nazo* (Riddles of Modern War History) in order to commemorate the deaths caused by the Japanese invaders. These two works, partly because of their small publishers and partly because of the overshadowing publicity of the military conflict in Vietnam, did not find a large audience among the Japanese public.

From the mid 1960s to the early 1970s the conflict in Vietnam attracted attention among Japanese and caused many of them to rethink their understanding of World War II. In 1965 the United States began indiscriminate bombing of North Vietnam and sent land troops to South Vietnam. In the spring of 1965, 78 percent of Japanese respondents answered "yes" when asked whether they were concerned about the war. Between 1965 and 1972, this percentage never fell below 61 percent. In the spring of 1972, 71 percent were still concerned with this issue in Japan.[39] American activities in Vietnam, such as atrocities committed against civilians and chemical warfare, were reported in detail in the Japanese press and on the television networks. Japanese sympathies, as Edwin Reischauer observed, were with the Vietnamese.[40] The United States was regarded as being in the wrong, and America's popularity had plummeted by 1973.[41]

The American atrocities in Vietnam also fueled the progressives' interest in exposing Japanese atrocities in the Asia-Pacific War (1931–45). In 1968, Ienaga Saburō, a historian who had sued the government over its textbook authorization system three years earlier, stressed Japanese aggression in China from 1931 through 1945 in his *Taiheiyō Sensō* (The Pacific War).[42] Shirota Tsuyoshi, a high school history teacher who had been shocked to find that a number of his students supported the United States' war effort in Vietnam, was led to question postwar Japanese education about wartime history. This education, it seemed to him, had focused too much on what had happened to the people in Japan instead of what had happened to the people at the battlefront during the war. Shirota, therefore, used *Sankō* (Three Bolts of Lightning), a book containing memoirs of atrocities committed by Japanese soldiers, as supplementary material in order to teach his students about the victims of Japanese wartime aggression.[43]

The 1970s: A Battle over "Killing Competitions"

In July 1971, President Richard Nixon announced that he would visit Beijing by May 1972. This announcement fueled an increasing desire in Japan to normalize relations with China.[44] In August 1971, senior Liberal Democratic Party (LDP) politician Miki Takeo met with an envoy from China who had come to Japan for the funeral of Matsumura Kenzō, an LDP politician who ardently supported improved relations between China and Japan.[45] Japanese business circles welcomed the movement and sent representatives to China in the summer of 1972, assuring China that normalization was the general wish of the Japanese business world. Japanese trade with China increased from $1.1 billion (1972) to $2 billion (1973) to $3.3 billion (1974).[46]

From August to December 1971, Honda Katsuichi's serialized work *Chūgoku no tabi* (Travels in China) appeared in the evening edition of *Asahi shinbun* as well as in *Asahi jānaru* and in *Shūkan asahi*. Inspired by his experience in the Vietnam War, Honda sought to portray the behavior of the Japanese military during the Sino-Japanese war from the Chinese perspective. He visited villages and interviewed survivors of Japanese atrocities and their families in Pingdingshan, where three thousand civilians were massacred in 1932; in Dashizhuang, where human remains of tens of thousands of murdered Chinese mine workers were found; in Nanjing, the site of the Nanjing Massacre of 1937–38; and in a village in northern China where 1,230 people were massacred out of a population of 1,300. The stories of the survivors were vivid and graphic, and Honda published them together with photos of survivors in tears alongside skulls and human bones. These stories, after being revised and expanded, were published in book form under the same title in 1972.[47]

Honda explained that his objective in publishing "Chūgoku no tabi" was threefold. He stressed that neither the government nor journalists had made an effort to face up to Japanese atrocities in China and to investigate what really occurred there. He also argued that although there was a widespread domestic movement to preserve the history of Japan's own sufferings, such as the bombings of Hiroshima and Nagasaki, the Japanese public was unaware of Japan's own history of committing atrocities during the Fifteen-Year War (1931–45). In addition, he suggested that his documentation would, through fostering an understanding of China's wartime experience, explain why China remained nervous about a revival of militarism in Japan.[48]

The widely read "Chūgoku no tabi" series stimulated extensive debates among readers and popular critics. Although Honda received strong support and encouragement, he was also criticized and even threatened. Honda most intensely resented apologist responses such as: "War is like that. Other armies were also committing atrocities during the war." He thought that such opinions were "the viewpoint of those who perpetrate, but not of those who suffer from, aggression." He attributed such views to one hundred years of "reactionary" education since the Meiji period and noted that they proved how little he could do by himself. In the same year as the publication of *Chūgoku no tabi,* Honda published *Chūgoku no Nihongun* (The Japanese Army in China). The content was similar to, and often identical with, that of *Chūgoku no tabi.* The primary difference was that *Chūgoku no Nihongun* used many more and larger photos than his earlier work. Honda stated that his main objective in publishing the second book was to "study what the reactionary government does not want us to teach ourselves."[49]

Honda's most intense challenges came from "henchman-intellectuals" *(yōjinbōteki chishikijin)*—those who viewed Japanese wartime aggression from the viewpoint of aggressors, not from that of victims. Intense rebuttals were written by Yamamoto Shichihei, a World War II veteran and a popular commentator, and Suzuki Akira, a journalist who identified himself as a "nonfiction writer." These critiques primarily focused on Honda's account of the story of "the killing by sword competitions" on the way to Nanjing in 1937, a story that Honda heard from two Chinese survivors of the Massacre. The survivors told Honda that two second lieutenants, whom Honda later identified as Mukai Toshiaki and Noda Tsuyoshi, competed to see who could use his sword to kill one hundred Chinese first between two suburbs of Nanjing, 6.25 miles apart. Their superior offered a prize to the winner. Mukai killed eighty-nine and Noda killed seventy-eight. Since neither man reached his goal, their superior ordered them to compete again. In the second competition, although they both killed more than one hundred Chinese, it was not clear who had reached the goal of one hundred first; thus, there was yet another competition, and this time the goal was to kill 150 Chinese across five miles from a suburb to the city of Nanjing.[50]

Yamamoto Shichihei claimed that the competitions had no basis in fact, and he criticized Honda for reporting this myth as truth. According to a calculation based on his own military experience, Yamamoto pointed out that for Mukai to have killed eighty-nine people in 6.25 miles, he would have had to kill a person every 1 minute 36 seconds. This, Yamamoto asserted, was physically impossible.[51] The fact that Honda did not initially disclose the names of the two lieutenants also buttressed Yamamoto's belief that the story was concocted. Honda countered that the competitions were covered by the newspaper *Tōkyō nichinichi shinbun* on November 30 and December 13, 1937, and that anonymity was granted in order to protect the privacy of the two officers and their families.[52] In his column in *Shokun!*, which was later published as *Watashi no naka no Nihongun* (The Japanese Imperial Army through My Eyes) in 1975, Yamamoto continued to argue that the competitions were a piece of fiction.

According to Yamamoto, he wrote his book to relay his experience in the army because the postwar generations were ignorant of the Japanese military and its wartime actions. Furthermore, he argued, the image of the wartime military had been distorted by the mass media. To Yamamoto, the killing competitions were created by a *Tōkyō nichinichi shinbun* journalist in order to bolster popular support for the war, and Honda was merely accepting this propaganda as truth after the war. Recognizing that what he experienced in the army was only a portion of military life, Yamamoto recounted his story to contradict what he regarded as "stupidities," such as the killing competitions.[53]

In contrast with Yamamoto's simple denial, Suzuki Akira, born in 1929, focused on how such an "illusion" as the killing competitions had been created. He expressed his concerns in an article in *Shokun!* in April 1972, titled "'Nankin daigyakusatsu' no maboroshi" (The Illusion of the "Nanjing Massacre"). To Suzuki, Honda had distorted the event by fabricating the story as if "the game" happened outside of battle. Suzuki argued that the Nanjing Massacre had become a disputed myth and a symbol of the cruelty of the Japanese people throughout the period because people wanted to forget rather than to study the full truth revealed by the Tribunal. He cited the testimony to the Tribunal of Japanese survivors of Chinese atrocities in Tongzhou (July 1937) and insisted that such testimony, like that of Chinese survivors of the Massacre, must be exaggerated.[54]

Suzuki published these articles in *Shokun!* and eventually gathered them in a single collection, *"Nankin daigyakusatsu" no maboroshi* (1972). Contrary to Honda's *Chūgoku no tabi* and *Chūgoku no Nihongun,* which were written from the Chinese survivors' point of view, Suzuki wrote his works from the viewpoint of Japanese soldiers, based on interviews with Japanese, such as former soldiers, the bereaved family of the soldiers, and former war correspondents. He sympathized with the two second lieutenants who were sentenced to death because of the killing competitions reported in *Tōkyō nichinichi shinbun* and with other Japanese soldiers who had to kill against their will.[55] Suzuki's book received wide critical acclaim. He won the prestigious Ōya Sōichi Prize for nonfiction in 1973, and he was granted one thousand dollars and an around-the-world airplane ticket by the publisher Bungei shunjū.

Both Yamamoto's and Suzuki's characterizations of the Nanjing Massacre as illusory met ardent opposition from progressives such as Hora Tomio. Hora revised his earlier *Kindai senshi no nazo* and published *Nankin jiken* (The Nanking Incident) in 1972. In contrast with Honda's emphasis on oral interviews, Hora focused on the documentary record. He used a variety of Japanese, English, and Chinese primary and secondary sources, including the evidence submitted to the Tokyo War Crimes Trial and newspapers published in China and the United States during the Massacre.[56] In 1975 Hora's refutation of Yamamoto's and Suzuki's arguments was published as *Nankin daigyakusatsu: "maboroshi" ka kōsaku hihan* (The Nanjing Massacre: Criticism of the Making of an Illusion). In the preface to the book, Hora did not hide his rage over Yamamoto's and Suzuki's attempts to erase the entire history of the Massacre and their claims that the killing competitions were merely a myth. To Hora, "reactionaries" such as Yamamoto and Suzuki, who were driven by emotion to turn history upside down, were intolerable. Hora pointed out that it took eight days for the Japanese army to advance the distance cited in the first killing competition. Thus, Yamamoto's calculation based on the assumption that the army advanced 6.25 miles in 150 minutes was wrong. Regarding Suzuki's assertions, Hora countered that the two second lieutenants were proud of the articles that depicted them as war heroes. Hora also argued that Suzuki should have interviewed Chinese survivors rather than constructing his story based solely on what he was told by some ten former soldiers and officers.[57] Neither Yamamoto nor Suzuki responded to the issues Hora raised in his challenge.[58]

As journalists and academics brought the debates over the

Massacre into the public spotlight in the 1970s, the Nanjing Massacre appeared again in some school textbooks. The textbook publishers and authors were inspired by the judgments of the Tokyo District Court (1970) and the Tokyo High Court (1975) in favor of Ienaga Saburō, who had brought his case before the court and demanded that the Ministry of Education withdraw its disapproval of the high school history textbook, *Shin Nihon shi* (A New History of Japan), which he had edited.[59] Although the Nanjing Massacre was still absent from elementary school textbooks, junior high school textbooks such as those published by Nihon shoseki and Kyōiku shuppan in 1975,[60] for instance, mentioned that forty-two thousand Chinese residents, including women and children, were killed during the Massacre. Although two other publishers mentioned the Massacre, the other four did not mention it at all. High school Japanese history textbooks—Jiyū shobō's *Shin Nihon shi* (A New History of Japan) in 1974, Teikoku shoin's *Shin Nihon shi* (A New History of Japan) in 1977 and *Kōtō Nihon shi saishinban* (An Advanced History of Japan: A New Edition) in 1978, Jikkyō shuppan's *Nihon shi kaiteiban* (A History of Japan: Revised Edition) in 1977, and Sanseidō's *Shin Nihon shi kaiteiban* (A New History of Japan: Revised Edition) in 1978—all described the Massacre, but no numerical death toll was mentioned in them.[61]

For schoolteachers, however, Honda's *Chūgoku no tabi* and Ienaga's lawsuit raised questions of war responsibility and Japan's role as a victimizer *(kagai no mondai)*. Some schoolteachers began to voice concern that their students now had little idea about the war.[62] Until the 1970s, Japanese students had personally experienced the aftermath of the Asia-Pacific War: some had lost their fathers or other relatives; some grew up with memories of wartime suffering, recollections that included bombings, evacuations, and food shortages; others saw reminders of the war each day when they encountered handicapped veterans, widows, and orphans or when they walked past the debris of ruined buildings. After the textbook controversy in the 1980s, however, many more teachers began to stress Japan's role as aggressor instead of solely as victim.

The 1980s: The Proliferation of Histories of the Massacre

Agitated by the judgments in the lawsuit in favor of Ienaga Saburō and by the inclusion of Japan's wartime atrocities in school textbooks, conservatives revived their attacks on the textbooks in the 1980s. Okuno Seisuke, then the minister of justice, commented in July 1980 that the absence of patriotic language in the current textbooks was quite troublesome.[63] In November 1986, the Liberal Democratic Party (LDP) published *Shin ureubeki kyōkasho no mondai* (New Deplorable Problems in School Textbooks), once again expressing concern over the re-emerging "colored [red] textbooks" *(iro no tsuita kyōkasho).*[64] The Liberal Democratic Party Subcommittee on Textbook Issues (Jimintō kyokasho mondai shō iinkai) agreed to write a bill in order to tighten government control over textbooks in May 1981.[65]

The shift to conservatism was reflected in the government authorization *(kentei)* system for high school textbooks for 1982, as the government tried to tone down the words used to describe Japanese aggression during the Asia-Pacific War (1931–45). For instance, because of the government guidelines, "Japan's aggression *[shinryaku]* in China" was replaced with "Japan's occupation *[senryō]* of Manchuria" in Tōkyō shoseki's *Sekai shi* (World History); "Japan's aggression *[shinryaku]* in the three eastern provinces" became "the Manchurian Incident *[jihen]* and the Shanghai Incident *[jihen]*" in Sanseidō's *Sekai shi* (World History); "the Japanese actions were considered aggression *[shinryaku]*" was changed to "the Japanese actions were considered illegitimate *[seitō na mono de nai]*" in Yamakawa shuppan's *Yōsetsu sekai shi* (A Detailed World History); "the Meiji government's repeated wars and aggressions *[shinryaku]*" was toned down to "the Meiji government's continued expansion policy *[taigai bōchō]*" in Yamakawa shuppan's *Sekai no rekishi* (A History of World); and "this aggression in South East Asia" *(kono Tōnan Ajia shinryaku)* was changed to "this advance into South East Asia" *(kono Tōnan Ajia shinshutsu)* in Teikoku shoin's *Shinshō sekai shi* (A New and Detailed World History).[66]

The revision of high school textbooks was widely reported

in Japanese national newspapers on June 26, 1982. *Asahi shinbun* reported it in a front-page article; the long headlines stated: "Textbooks Return Further 'Toward Prewar' Position; the Ministry of Education Tightens the Standards of Textbook Authorization, Especially on High School History [Textbooks]; the Term 'Aggression' Toned Down; Honorific Language Added to Descriptions of the Emperors in the Ancient Period."[67] *Mainichi shinbun, Yomiuri shinbun,* and *Sankei shinbun,* too, emphasized the government's shift in their headlines on the same day, noting that *aggression* had been replaced with *advance.*[68]

The Japanese government's revision did not remain a domestic news item, but became an international issue. In July 1982, the Chinese government officially protested the attempt by the Japanese Ministry of Education to revise textbooks by replacing the term *aggression (shinryaku)* with *advance (shinshutsu)* and by altering descriptions of the Nanjing Massacre.[69] In August of the same year, the South Korean government also protested the Japanese government's attempt in textbooks to justify wartime Japanese colonialism in Korea. Also in August, labor unions in Hong Kong submitted a protest to the Japanese Council there. In September, the Vietnamese government asked the Japanese government to correct textbook wartime descriptions of the Japanese occupation of Vietnam. Between July and September 1982, according to Tokutake Toshio, at least 2,439 articles on Japanese textbook revision appeared in newspapers throughout Asia.[70]

In response to international pressure, on August 26, 1982, then-cabinet minister Miyazawa Kiichi promised that the government would correct *(zesei)* descriptions in the textbooks. In November the textbook standard began to require "necessary concern for international understanding and international cooperation."[71] This government movement toward capitulating to "foreign intervention" offended revisionists in Japan and sparked their challenge to wartime Japanese history. The revisionists once again focused on accounts of the Nanjing Massacre that, they claimed, were dominated by leftist academics and journalists.

Revisionist articles and books began to appear with ever greater frequency. In September 1982, Watanabe Shōichi, a professor of English at Sophia University, for instance, claimed that no textbook authors had been ordered to replace *aggression* with *advance* in 1982 and that Japanese newspapers pressured the Japanese government to undertake "a diplomacy of apology" *(dogeza gaikō)*. Watanabe argued that Japanese national newspapers all mistakenly believed that changing *aggression* to *advance* in the textbooks was the result of the government's textbook authorization policy, when in fact it was not.[72] He also contended that 200,000 or 300,000 could not possibly have been massacred in Nanjing and praised Suzuki Akira's *"Nankin daigyakusatsu" no maboroshi*.[73]

Among these revisionist articles in the 1980s, however, the most sensational challenge was made by Tanaka Masaaki. Tanaka had served as the secretary to General Matsui Iwane, the commander in chief during the atrocities in Nanjing, who was sentenced to death at the Tokyo Trial for his role in the Massacre. In his book *"Nankin gyakusatsu" no kyokō* (The Fabrication of the "Nanjing Massacre"), published in 1984, Tanaka argued that there had been no indiscriminate killing at all in Nanjing and that the so-called Nanjing Massacre was a fabrication, mere propaganda manufactured by the Tokyo Trial and the Chinese government. The book objected to those who believe in the Massacre, or "the great massacre faction" *(daigyakusatsuha)* in Tanaka's terminology, because they

> trust the documents and claims put forward by the Chinese government and prosecutors of the Tokyo Trial;
>
> do not distinguish between combatants and noncombatants, and killing combatants during a battle is not a massacre but rather a military achievement;
>
> ignore the situation on the battlefield and the great losses of Japanese soldiers during the war;
>
> disregard China's use of guerrilla tactics, illegal under international law;
>
> overlook atrocities committed by Chinese soldiers;

> ignore the fact that the Tribunal was victors' justice, and that its purpose was to prove artificially and unilaterally the inhumanity and cruelty of the Japanese army; and
>
> overlook the facts that perjury laws were not applied to the Trial and that the Trial overemphasized the incident in Nanjing.[74]

Tanaka's book encouraged conservatives and nationalists who had been previously frustrated by postwar accounts of imperial Japanese history—accounts that, in their view, emphasized Japanese atrocities and inhumanity as well as demonized imperial Japan. More than one hundred people, all of whom denied the existence of atrocities in Nanjing, offered Tanaka documents from private collections to support his conclusions.[75] Some scholars also rallied behind Tanaka. Watanabe Shōichi wrote a preface for Tanaka's book in which he praised Tanaka's efforts to eradicate the illusion of the Nanjing Massacre, which, in Watanabe's opinion, stained the honor of Japan and the Japanese. To Watanabe, Tanaka's book proved that the Massacre was physically and practically impossible.[76]

Revisionist views that the Massacre was a mere fabrication were largely supported by conservative publishers such as Sankei shuppan and Bungei shunjū. The newspaper *Sankei shinbun* asked its readers on October 24, 1983, to provide evidence and historical materials in order to help Tanaka's research on the alleged atrocities in Nanjing.[77] *Shokun!* and *Bungei shunjū,* monthly journals published by Bungei shunjū, as well as *Seiron,* a monthly journal published by Sankei shuppan, carried articles written by revisionists such as Watanabe Shōichi, Kobori Keiichirō (a professor of comparative literature at the University of Tokyo), Tanaka Masaaki (a World War II veteran), Itakura Yoshiaki (an independent researcher of the Massacre), and others.[78]

As progressives initiated lawsuits related to Massacre historiography, so did the conservatives. After Ienaga Saburō brought his third lawsuit in January 1984 against the Ministry of Education, accusing it of forcing him to revise textbook histories to place the wartime Japanese period in a better light, Tanaka and his allies also sued the Ministry of Education in March 1984. Contrary to Ienaga, Tanaka demanded the deletion of the terms *aggression (shinryaku)* and the *Nanjing Massacre (Nankin dai-gyakusatsu)* from junior high school and high school textbooks and seven million yen in compensation for the suffering that he and his supporters endured because of the 1982 textbook dispute. On May 28, 1987, the Tokyo District Court ruled against Tanaka without examining a single witness. The court declared that "psychological sufferings claimed by the plaintiffs are nothing but displeasure and irritation attributed to historical and political views that they disagree with, and the claim is not to be regarded as a damage that needs to be redeemed." Although Tanaka lodged a final appeal, the Supreme Court dismissed the case in December 1989.[79]

Progressives, infuriated by such revisionist challenges, set up the Study Group on the Nanjing Incident (Nankin jiken chōsa kenkyūkai) in March 1984. Throughout the 1980s and until the present, this group has had some twenty members, including historians, journalists, lawyers, company employees, and teachers, and it holds meetings monthly or bimonthly. Although the values of the founding members were different because of the diversity of their professions, the founders all agreed that they had to face the past wrongs committed by Japan and the Japanese, no matter how shameful the wrongs were. The Study Group emphasized that historical consciousness was necessary in order to build "a fortress for peace" *(heiwa no toride)* among the Japanese.[80] The members of the group have actively published their studies on the Massacre. From 1984 until today, more than fourteen books and dozens of articles discussing the Massacre have been published by the members of the Study Group.

Hora Tomio was an active member of the Study Group and repeatedly published new work on the Massacre. In 1985 he edited a two-volume, 750-page compilation of historical documents related to the Nanjing Massacre. The first volume included documents about the Nanjing Massacre presented at the Tokyo War Crimes Trial, including the indictment, transcripts of the proceedings, the judgment, and even evidence that was not read in the court. The second volume included translations of English documents such as Tillman Durdin's articles in the *New York Times,* H. J. Timperley's *Japanese Terror in China,* Lewis Smythe's *War Damage in the Nanking Area,* and Hsu Shu-hsi's *Documents of the Nanking Safety Zone.*[81] Based on his rich knowledge of the Massacre, in 1986 Hora published *Nankin daigyakusatsu no shōmei* (The Proof of the Nanjing Massacre), in which he refuted in great detail Tanaka Masaaki and some of the new adherents to the revisionist cause, such as Itakura Yoshiaki. Hora went over claims made by Tanaka in *"Nankin gyakusatsu" no kyokō* and pointed out Tanaka's mistakes, misinterpretations, and distortions of historical evidence. For instance, in his book Tanaka had claimed that Miner Searle Bates, a history professor at Nanking University who testified at the Tokyo Trial for the prosecution, gave false testimony about atrocities in Nanjing. Tanaka cited a *Tōkyō nichinichi shinbun* article dated December 15, 1937, in which Bates said that he was grateful for the orderly Japanese army in the city so that Nanjing was again peaceful.[82] To check the claims made by Tanaka, who had distorted more than nine hundred passages of General Matsui's diary in 1985, Hora examined *Tōkyō nichinichi shinbun* in order to make sure that Tanaka cited from it without any distortion. Although Hora did not find that Tanaka manipulated the text, he concluded that Tanaka's claim was an unsupported accusation because of a letter that Bates sent to a friend dated December 15, 1937. In this letter, Bates described his horror at the atrocities in Nanjing and his feeling of disgust whenever he heard Japanese officers claiming that they were fighting to "save" Chinese people.[83]

Meanwhile, Study Group members such as Honda Katsuichi (a journalist), Fujiwara Akira (professor emeritus of history at Hitotsubashi University), and Watanabe Harumi (a lawyer) helped Ienaga in his third lawsuit, filed in 1984 against the government. One of the textbook passages that the ministry had ordered Ienaga to rewrite in order to receive government approval was a description of the Nanjing Massacre. Honda and Fujiwara testified at the court hearing in support of Ienaga, and Watanabe was one of the lawyers helping Ienaga pursue his case.[84]

War veterans who experienced the battle in Nanjing added their stories to the literature on the history of the Massacre in the 1980s.[85] Both Sone Kazuo and Azuma Shirō, who wanted their personal experiences in China to be remembered by today's youth, did not hesitate to expose the cruelties and shame of their experiences.[86] Motivated by revisionist challenges, Sone wrote frankly of his own experience with executions, looting, and rape in his three books: *Shiki Nankin gyakusatsu* (A Private Narrative of the Nanjing Massacre); *Zoku shiki Nankin gyakusatsu* (A Private Narrative of the Nanjing Massacre, Part II); and *Nankin gyakusatsu to sensō* (The Nanjing Massacre and the War). Sone received considerable support, both spiritually and materially, from his fellow soldiers in writing his first work, *Shiki Nankin gyakusatsu.*[87] Sone responded to criticism by further exposing his experiences in *Zoku shiki Nankin gyakusatsu.* Azuma, too, felt compelled in the face of revisionist challenges to publish the diary accounts of the Massacre that he had recorded during the war.[88]

In addition, the Kaikōsha, an organization of war veterans and their bereaved families, asked their members (some eighteen thousand) to describe their experiences in Nanjing in its newsletter, *Kaikō* (October 1983). At first Kaikōsha expected to receive accounts from members that could prove the innocence of the Japanese military in Nanjing. A very different course of events ensued, however. The organization received accounts that acknowledged atrocities in Nanjing in 1937–38. The then vice-commander in chief, for instance, revealed the systematic killing of prisoners of war in Nanjing. Such accounts were published in *Kaikō* between 1984 and 1985 and later published as *Nankin senshi* in 1989. In the March 1985 issue of *Kaikō,* Katogawa Kōtarō, an editor of *Kaikō,* issued a personal and profound apology to the Chinese as a former member of the Japanese army.[89]

Still, the revisionists clung to their assertion that the Massacre had never taken place. Tanaka Masaaki continued to publish books such as *Matsui Iwane taishō no jinchū nisshi* (The Field

Diary of General Matsui Iwane) in 1985 and *Nankin jiken no sōkatsu* (A Summary of the Nanjing Incident) in 1987, in which he continued to argue that the Massacre was a mere fabrication. Itakura Yoshiaki, who identifies himself as a scholar of the Nanjing Incident *(Nankin jiken kenkyūka),* wrote articles attempting to discredit Sone Kazuo's work by stressing his distortion of his true rank and position in the army.[90]

Conservative senior LDP politicians continued to lend their support to the revisionist viewpoint. In September 1986, Fujio Masayuki, then minister of education, declared the Nanjing Massacre to be a fabrication and subsequently refused to withdraw his statement.[91] In May 1988, Okuno Seisuke, then the national land agency chief, also openly asserted that there had been no Nanjing Massacre.[92] Both comments not only offended Japanese progressives, but also sparked protests by neighboring countries such as China and Korea. Although both officials left office, they refused to admit that what they had said was incorrect. In fact, Fujio insisted that his challenge had succeeded in raising an important issue for his country about Japan's imperial past.[93] Similarly, Okuno quit his position simply because he did not want to jeopardize the Takeshita administration in the Diet because of the expected challenges by the opposition parties, not because he thought what he had said was false.[94]

The proliferation of historical accounts of the Massacre was not limited to Japan in the 1980s. To counteract such revisionist movements, detailed studies of the Massacre began to appear in Chinese history journals after the Japanese government's textbook revision. In 1985 the Memorial for Compatriot Victims of the Japanese Military's Nanjing Massacre (hereafter, the Memorial) was opened to the public in Nanjing. In the Memorial human skeletons, photographs, and written accounts of the Japanese atrocities were displayed. The official Chinese estimate of those killed by the Japanese invaders was set at three hundred thousand.[95] In the United States, Chinese Americans in the late 1980s formed organizations such as the Chinese Alliance for Memorial Justice (established in 1987 in New York).

As the events and number of victims became an international

topic in the 1980s, almost all Japanese textbooks came to include some mention of the Massacre. In 1986, six out of seven elementary school textbooks mentioned the Massacre, although the number of deaths was not reported.[96] In 1984, Tōkyō shoseki, the largest publisher of junior high school history textbooks, cited figures introduced by the Tokyo Trial and the Chinese government.[97] The text stated that those who were killed "are said to have been more than 200,000. In addition, in China, more than 300,000 were considered to have been killed, including soldiers killed in action." By the end of the 1980s, all junior high school textbooks included some mention of the Massacre. Japanese high school history textbooks, though usually not mentioning the number of deaths, discussed the Japanese atrocities in Nanjing. Jiyū shobō's *Yōsetsu Nihon no rekishi* (1984) and *Shin Nihon shi* (1985) were considered the most progressive among high school history textbooks. These two textbooks recounted that approximately 200,000 people, including women and children, were massacred in Nanjing within a month after the fall of the city, as well as mentioning the official Chinese death figure of more than 300,000.[98]

The textbook changes in this period corresponded to the rise among schoolteachers of "victimizer's consciousness" *(kagaisha ishiki)* and the question of war responsibility. Both of these issues were sparked in turn by the textbook controversy. Adachi Yoshihiko, a high school teacher, questioned whether wartime Japanese fascism as evidenced by the Nanjing Massacre was being fully taught in the classroom. He also stressed that fuller illustration of the Asia-Pacific War was impossible without studying the Japanese people as perpetrators.[99] Komatsu Yutaka, a junior high school teacher, argued that merely emphasizing Japanese victimhood would be self-indulgent and that excluding the sufferings of non-Japanese would evince an attitude no different than Japan's wartime racism.[100] In comparison to historical work in earlier periods, the increased number of articles on Japanese wartime atrocities and war responsibility was quite noticeable. This trend was especially clear in *Rekishi chiri kyōiku,* a monthly pedagogy magazine.[101] Kasahara Tokushi, a professor of Chinese history at Utsunomiya University and a member of the Study Group on the Nanjing Incident, actively contributed to *Rekishi chiri kyōiku* and provided historical analysis of the Massacre to history teachers.[102] In addition to its increased attention to the Massacre, *Rekishi chiri kyōiku* also pursued inquiries into a number of other controversial topics, including Hirohito's war responsibility, Japan's treatment of war prisoners, Japan's chemical and biological warfare, "comfort women," forced labor, and other matters relating to Japanese war crimes. Articles on these issues began to appear more frequently than ever in this period.[103]

With the progress of the study of the Nanjing Massacre among academics and the increasing number of war veterans admitting their atrocities in Nanjing, revisionists finally realized that it was impossible to completely deny the Nanjing Massacre. Therefore the revisionists altered their strategy by the late 1980s. For the first time, they admitted that some killing and perhaps even limited atrocities had occurred at Nanjing. However, they simultaneously claimed that the indiscriminate killing of 200,000 people insisted on by the Tokyo Trial or the 300,000 deaths insisted on by the Chinese government never took place. They argued that the Nanjing Massacre was a historical fabrication, claiming that relatively few people were killed and, of the deaths that did occur, only a small number were illegal under the laws of war. In addition, the revisionists stressed that the incident was no more horrifying than many other atrocities committed by various nations in the twentieth century. In their opinion, the event in Nanjing did not deserve the special attention it had received.[104]

The 1990s: Old Issues, New Strategies

The death of Emperor Hirohito on January 7, 1989, marked the passing of the Shōwa era (1926–89). Hirohito's death and the coronation of Emperor Akihito received massive media coverage. These events prompted a public debate on the history of the Shōwa era, particularly Japan's role in the Asia-Pacific War

(1931–45). As Hirohito lay dying, his responsibility for the war was widely debated around the world. Even an English tabloid, the *Sun,* was concerned with news of Hirohito's poor health and his responsibility for the war; the *Sun* expressed its regret on September 21, 1988, that Hirohito had never been charged with war crimes during his lifetime. The *Sun* article offended Watanabe Michio, a senior LDP politician, who responded on September 27 that the Tokyo Trial had judged that the emperor was not a war criminal and that the Allied countries agreed that he was not responsible for the war.[105] Similarly, Nomura Shūsuke, an extreme right-wing activist, further argued that the emperor was by no means responsible for the war and that he symbolized the heart of Japan. In opposition, the organization Wadatsumikai, which had published *Kike wadatsumi no koe* (letters written by mobilized college students who died in the war), held the emperor responsible for Japan's wartime aggression.[106] Meanwhile, members of the Ad Hoc Committee on the Case against Hirohito sponsored a memorial service for the victims of Japanese aggression in New York, characterizing Hirohito as the other Hitler.[107]

On the other side of the globe, the Berlin Wall was torn down in November 1989, and many celebrated "a new relationship" between the East and the West. *Japan's Diplomatic Bluebook,* a yearly public report by the Ministry of Foreign Affairs, read, "A[t] this time of historic change, Japan, which already bears considerable responsibility and plays an important role for the stability and prosperity of the international community, must make an even greater effort to fulfill its responsibilities and act more vigorously."[108] In 1991, fifty years after the attack on Pearl Harbor, Prime Minister Kaifu Toshiki gave a policy speech in Singapore asserting that understanding the past would be a key to Japan's playing a more active political role in the future.[109] In *Gekkan keidanren* in April 1992, Japanese business leaders such as the presidents of Fuji Xerox, Asahi kasei, and Daiē also stated that acknowledging responsibility for the Asia-Pacific War would be central to expanding their business presence in Asia.[110]

A significant change that few could have predicted occurred

in Japanese politics in the early 1990s. In August 1993 Hosokawa Morihiro became the first non-LDP prime minister in thirty-eight years. On August 10 he issued a public statement at a press conference that the Asia-Pacific War was an aggressive and unjust war.[111] On August 23, 1993, at the first keynote address he delivered to open a Diet session, Hosokawa apologized for past Japanese aggression and colonial rule. On November 6, when he met President Kim Young Sam (Kim Yŭng-sam), he again apologized for Japan's past colonial rule over Korea. Furthermore, one year later, Murayama Tomiichi, a member of the Japanese Socialist Party, became prime minister and led a coalition government that agreed to offer an apology for past aggression to other Asian countries.[112] Such a conciliatory domestic environment provoked intense challenges from revisionists among various occupations, many of whom were already successful in their own careers and had ready access to the media, and prompted them to make louder noises than ever. Again, the issue of the Nanjing Massacre became one of their battlefronts.

In reaction to Hosokawa's public stance of offering apologies to neighboring countries, 105 LDP members from different factions within the party formed a private study group called the Committee to Examine History (Rekishi kentō iinkai) during the same month that Hosokawa became prime minister, and the group invited nineteen revisionist speakers to teach them the version of wartime Japanese history that they wanted to support. The group's efforts included a lecture about "the fabrication" of the Massacre, delivered by Tanaka Masaaki on May 10, 1994.[113] Other speakers included Uesugi Chitoshi, who identifies himself as a scholar of history textbooks; Satō Kazuo, a professor of international law at Aoyama Gakuin University; Fuji Nobuo, a World War II veteran; and Kobori Keiichirō, a professor of comparative literature at the University of Tokyo, all of whom asserted that the Massacre was a fabrication.[114] These lectures were published as a single monograph titled *Dai tō-A sensō no sōkatsu* (An Outline of the Greater East Asia War) in 1995.

As in the 1980s, some senior politicians continued to publicly challenge the postwar history of imperial Japan with greater frequency. In the 1990s, senior LDP politician Ishihara Shintarō (1990), justice minister Nagano Shigeto (1994), environmental agency chief Sakurai Shin (1994), international trade and industry minister Hashimoto Ryūtarō (1994), education minister Shimamura Yoshinobu (1995), and management and coordination agency chief Etō Takami (1995) have all made statements de-emphasizing Japanese aggression during the war. Both Ishihara and Nagano have referred specifically to the Massacre, asserting that it was a fabrication.[115]

These frustrated conservatives and nationalists began to organize groups in 1994 and 1995 to protest government initiatives to offer an official apology to the Asian nations that had suffered from Japanese militarism. In 1994, for instance, Okuno Seisuke organized a group of 161 lawmakers who opposed the resolution.[116] In 1995 Kase Toshikazu, a former ambassador to the United Nations, became the president of a civic group called Shūsen 50 shūnen kokumin iinkai (People's Committee for the Fiftieth Anniversary of the End of the War), which was a combination of Okuno's group, some veterans' associations, and other conservative organizations. This conservative coalition promoted a nationwide campaign and collected 4.56 million signatures from people who opposed the "masochistic" apology resolution.[117]

Just as Yamamoto Shichihei, Suzuki Akira, and Tanaka Masaaki, among others, were the faces of the revisionists in the 1970s and 1980s, Fujioka Nobukatsu, a professor of education at the University of Tokyo, has probably been the most recognizable face of the revisionists in the 1990s. In January 1995 Fujioka established Jiyūshugi shikan kenkyūkai, or the Study Group on the Liberal Historical View, whose primary objective was to rewrite "the Tokyo War Crimes Trial's presentation of history," which, in its eyes, demonized Japan's imperial past.[118] Fujioka founded the monthly journal *"Kingendai shi" no jugyō kaikaku* in September 1995, and revisionists contributed articles such as "Was Japan 'Fascist' during the War?"; "International Law in History: 'Aggression' and 'Aggressive War'"; and "An Introduction to Books That Reconsider the 'War.'"[119]

In the midst of persistent revisionist writings, in June 1996 the Ministry of Education authorized new editions of seven junior high school textbooks. To Fujioka and his colleagues, the new descriptions of modern Japanese history in these textbooks were "unconscionably full of evil distortion, masochism, and anti-Japanese qualities."[120] Of the seven junior high school history textbooks that began to be used in April 1997, every single book mentions the Massacre. Even more disturbing to the revisionists were the textbooks' estimates of the number of Chinese massacred. Only Teikoku shoin's history textbook does not mention the number of the dead; Kyōiku shuppan's, Ōsaka shoseki's, Shimizu shoin's, and Nihon bunkyō shuppan's textbooks include the Chinese official figure of 300,000. The other textbooks, Tōkyō shoseki's and Nihon shoseki's, estimate the death toll in Nanjing to be about 200,000.[121]

According to Fujioka, the textbook numbers were "fabricated" *(detarame)*, and the Chinese official figure of 300,000 was simply a lie. He insisted that the Chinese military was responsible for the deaths of Chinese soldiers because they were killed not by the Japanese but as a result of the failure of the Chinese leaders to surrender. He argued that if the Chinese military had agreed to surrender, most of the Chinese soldiers would never have been killed. Although he acknowledged Japanese atrocities against civilians, there were, according to Fujioka, no more than forty-seven. He stressed that "200,000 civilians could not possibly have been massacred unless ghosts were killed."[122]

Deeply offended by these new history textbooks, Fujioka and his supporters founded a group with the goal of rewriting modern Japanese history textbooks (Atarashii kyōkasho o tsukuru kai) in December 1996. Seventy-eight people—including business people, academics, novelists, critics, and athletes, such as Agawa Hiroyuki (novelist), Hayashi Mariko (novelist), Itō Takashi (professor emeritus at the University of Tokyo), Kamiya Fuji (professor at Tōyō Eiwa Jogakuin University), Kobayashi Yoshinori (cartoonist), Ōshima Yōichi (president of Tōgin Research International), and Satō Seizaburō (professor at Saitama University)—publicly supported the objective of the group. The group sought to revise the current "masochistic" modern Japanese history and to offer in its place "a history of which the nation can be proud."[123]

Fujioka and his allies also sternly criticized the creation of national peace museums that include Japan's role as a victimizer. To these revisionists, war memorials such as the Ōkunoshima dokugazu shiryōkan (Ōkunoshima Poison Gas Museum), the Hiroshima heiwa kinen shiryōkan (Hiroshima Peace Memorial Museum), the Nagasaki genbaku shiryōkan (Nagasaki Atomic Bomb Museum), the Ōsaka kokusai heiwa sentā ("Peace Osaka"), the Ritsumeikan daigaku kokusai heiwa myūjiamu (Ritsumeikan University International Peace Museum), the Saitama ken heiwa shiryōkan (Saitama Prefecture Peace Museum), and the Kawasaki shi heiwakan (Kawasaki City Peace Museum), all of which exhibit materials depicting Japanese aggression in Asia, unfairly highlight Japanese wartime atrocities and contribute to eroding national pride and cultivating national shame among domestic visitors, many of whom are elementary, junior high, and high school students.[124]

Although the revisionist attacks were intense, progressives and their allies, from scholars to civic organizations, mobilized to refute their challenges. The year 1993 saw the opening of the Center for Research and Documentation on Japan's War Responsibility (Nihon no sensō sekinin shiryō sentā) and publication of the first issue of the Center's quarterly journal, *Kikan sensō sekinin kenkyū*. The journal published issues devoted to wartime Japan's biological warfare units (known as Units 731 and 1644), Japanese chemical warfare, military sex slaves in the Pacific, the Nanjing Massacre, postwar compensation and the ongoing trials, the annexation of Korea, violence against women in wartime, criticism of Fujioka Nobukatsu and his allies, and more.[125] The Center also organized open seminars on these issues in order to provide public education.

While some groups worked to promote scholarship and education, others sought direct redress for Japan's wartime atrocities. Between 1990 and 1995, Japanese lawyers supported twenty-seven lawsuits against the government by non-Japanese demanding compensation for their sufferings during the Asia-Pacific War. For instance, these lawyers helped the Koreans who fought for Japan during World War II and were later charged with war crimes, but who were denied money and benefits by the Japanese government after the war because of their Korean nationality. Lawyers also represented women who had been forced to provide sex to the Japanese soldiers during the war. Laborers who had been forced to work under inhumane conditions during the war and POWs and civilians who had been interned during the war received legal assistance as well. Lawyers also came to the aid of individuals and families who sought compensation for suffering resulting from the Nanjing Massacre and human experiments performed by Unit 731.[126] As of May 1998, more than two hundred lawyers were working on legal cases brought on behalf of Chinese war victims.[127]

Public education spread beyond textbooks, courtrooms, war memorials and lectures, and "ordinary people" were central in organizing circulating exhibitions of Japan's wartime past. An exhibition about Unit 731, including a panel discussion and film screening, began a nationwide tour beginning in Tokyo's Shinjuku district. Within three months, the exhibition had been held in fourteen locations and had attracted approximately forty thousand visitors. The organizing committee attributed its success to the people's desire to clarify historical facts, to foster alliances with other Asian nations, to promote an awareness of peace, to view biological warfare from the victim's side, and to understand national responsibility for the Asia-Pacific War. The reason organizers became interested in publicizing the issue was the unwillingness of the Ministry of Health and Welfare to investigate massive human bone deposits discovered in 1989 beneath the site of the now-demolished Army Medical School.[128]

These ordinary people who considered it important to face Japanese wartime aggression were not limited to the Tokyo area. They may not have been the overwhelming majority of society, but they were sufficiently numerous to confront revisionist challenges. It was they who encouraged war memorials in their communities to exhibit not only Japanese wartime suffering but also Japanese wartime aggression and who did not give in to revisionists' calls for the removal of all such "masochistic" exhibits. In late April 1996 approximately three hundred right-wing extremists gathered in Nagasaki. Using loudspeakers mounted on trucks, they demanded that all references to Japanese wartime atrocities be withdrawn from the atomic bomb museum. Although the museum agreed to remove some photographs that lacked clear documentation, these photographs were replaced with others of more certain authenticity. Thus the nature of the museum, which was meant to represent Japan as both victim and villain, was maintained.[129] Similarly, although conservative forces have been accusing Peace Osaka of being "masochistic" since the summer of 1996, some twenty local peace organizations that have supported the museum ever since it was planned have shown no sign of giving in.[130]

In 1995 a "no-war resolution" failed to win the Diet's support until it had been diluted by revisions that destroyed its original objective. However, thirty civic groups and approximately fifteen hundred people sponsored an open letter declaring their version of a "no-war resolution"—the Promise of No War among Citizens (Shimin no fusen sensei). The Promise, published on the anniversary of Japan's surrender, emphasized the urgency of taking the following actions: apologizing as a nation to other Asian countries for Japan's aggression; providing compensation to victims of Japanese wartime policies such as forced labor and military service; preventing Japan from becoming a military power once again; and destroying the world's supply of nuclear weapons.[131]

Progressive intellectuals, as well as ordinary people, were active in confronting revisionists. Whereas revisionist articles frequently appeared in journals such as *Shokun!* and *Seiron,* progressive accounts often appeared in journals such as *Shūkan kin'yōbi* (weekly) and *Sekai* (monthly). *Shūkan kin'yōbi,* for instance, carried articles by Honda Katsuichi, Fujiwara Akira, and Tawara Yoshifumi, all of whom challenged the revisionist movement. In response to the revisionist cartoonist Kobayashi Yoshinori, who often made fun of progressives' research on Japanese wartime atrocities, the journal included a cartoon and made fun of die-hard revisionists such as Etō Jun.[132] The journal *Sekai*, on the other hand, tended to publish more academic articles.[133] In the outrage with Fujioka and his allies, many books refuting the revisionists have been published as well.[134]

The events of the Massacre have continued to draw the attention of both revisionists and progressives. Whereas revisionist claims in recent books have not been new and have echoed the revisionist works of the 1980s,[135] progressives have forged ahead by publishing another collection of historical documents and three new major works about the Massacre that take original approaches and offer detailed histories. In 1992 the two volumes of *Nankin jiken shiryōshū* (A Collection of Historical Materials on the Nanjing Incident) were published. This 964-page collection of documents included different documents than those included in Hora's collection of 1985. It included massive translations of both English and Chinese documents that had been newly compiled by the members of the Study Group on the Nanjing Incident. Newly discovered documents in the United States, from sources such as the National Archives of the United States, Harvard's Houghton Library, the Library of the Yale University Divinity School, and Columbia's Rare Book and Manuscript Library, were included in the first volume. For the first time, items ranging from diplomatic and personal correspondence to newspaper and journal articles on the issue of the Massacre were translated into Japanese. Readers were even able to find Madame Chiang Kai-shek's personal letters asking for help from her friends in the United States. Regarding Chinese materials, translations of historical documents published in Mainland China and Taiwan, such as *Qin-Hua Rijun Nanjing datusha shiliao* (Historical Materials on the Nanjing Massacre by the Japanese Troops Who Invaded China) and *Qin-Hua Rijun Nanjing datusha dang'an* (Archival Materials on the Nanjing Massacre by the Japanese Troops Who Invaded China) were included.[136]

In 1995 one of the editors of *Nankin jiken shiryōshū*, Kasahara Tokushi, took a new approach and analyzed the Nanjing

Massacre from the viewpoints of Japanese soldiers, Chinese civilians and soldiers, and foreign bystanders in his *Nankin nanminku no hyakunichi* (One Hundred Days in the Nanjing Safety Zone). For this book, Kasahara used oral histories of foreign bystanders, such as Robert Wilson, Minnie Vautrin, Miner Searle Bates, Lewis Smythe, James McCallum, and John Magee, who stayed in the Nanjing Safety Zone and witnessed the Massacre in Nanjing. He juxtaposed these accounts of bystanders with diaries and memoirs by Japanese soldiers and interviews of Chinese survivors in order to portray the lives of more than two hundred thousand Chinese people living in the Nanjing Safety Zone.[137] Kasahara's use of such rich documentation allowed for an analysis of Nanjing in 1937–38 from the viewpoint of the people who experienced the mass atrocities, and his main concern in this book was not the number of the victims but the actual lives of the people in Nanjing.

Another major progressive contribution was *Nankin daigyakusatsu o kiroku shita kōgun heishitachi* (The Soldiers Who Recorded the Nanjing Massacre), edited by Ono Kenji, Fujiwara Akira, and Honda Katsuichi in 1996. Ono, a chemical company employee and a member of the Study Group on the Nanjing Incident, visited World War II veterans and their families during his free time and collected diaries written by Yamada's troops in the Thirteenth Army, soldiers who participated in the battle of Nanjing. Most of the soldiers were then in their thirties and drafted from the reserves. As Fujiwara Akira argued in the book's commentary, such diaries showed how ordinary Japanese men became transformed into looters and killers on the way from Shanghai to Nanjing. In addition, these diaries of Yamada's troops provided new information about the number of killings. They portrayed the killings of more than ten thousand Chinese POWs who were captured on December 14, 1937, near Mount Mufu (Mufu Hill). In the book, Ono encouraged local persons to collect diaries from former soldiers who fought in Nanjing in order to explore the Massacre in even greater depth.[138]

The third major work was yet another book by Kasahara

Tokushi. His *Nankin jiken* (The Nanjing Incident) included a discussion of the death toll in the city of Nanjing and six neighboring counties, all of which were under the jurisdiction of the Nanjing Special Municipality and in all of which atrocities occurred. Kasahara defined the Massacre as an event that took place between December 4, 1937, when Japan's Central China Expeditionary Army entered the area, and March 28, 1938, when the puppet Nanjing Government was established.[139] Based on his nearly fifteen years of research on Chinese, Japanese, and American sources, Kasahara concluded that many more civilians were killed in the vicinity of Nanjing than in the city. He estimated that more than two hundred thousand Chinese soldiers and civilians were killed during the Massacre.[140] His purpose in including such an estimate was not to refute the official Chinese figure of three hundred thousand but to dismiss the revisionist claim that the Nanjing Massacre was a fabrication because the death estimate produced by the Chinese government and the Tokyo Trial had been unreliable and inflated.[141] Moreover, partly because it is an inexpensive paperback, the book has been commercially successful. It sold approximately fifty thousand copies in less than six months; by contrast, Kasahara's *Nankin nanminku no 100 nichi* sold only about two thousand copies and is now out of print.

Other significant breakthroughs took place in courtrooms during the 1990s. In October 1993 the Tokyo High Court ruled that the education ministry's Textbook Authorization Research Council unlawfully requested that Ienaga rewrite references to the Nanjing Massacre as well as to Japanese military troops' crimes against women. On August 29, 1997, the Supreme Court ruled for the first time that the government had broken the law by forcing Ienaga to rewrite references to wartime Japanese atrocities. In addition to the Nanjing Massacre and wartime military sex slaves, the court now acknowledged that experiments on humans by Unit 731 were "beyond denial." Although the court ruled that the system of textbook authorization was constitutional and ordered the government to pay Ienaga only a small amount of compensation for the mental anguish he suffered, it was significant that the reference to Unit 731 would also be included in Japanese history textbooks along with accounts of the Nanjing Massacre and military sex slaves.[142]

Schoolteachers have continued to teach Japanese wartime history from the viewpoint of both victim and perpetrator. Indeed, they have probably emphasized the latter more than the former in reaction to increasing revisionist challenges. Numerous articles on their classroom experiences of teaching episodes of victimization such as the Nanjing Massacre, the use of "comfort women," the deployment of chemical and biological weapons, and the dragooning of forced labor have appeared in *Rekishi chiri kyōiku*. Yet teaching this kind of history has not always produced the responses that teachers have expected: some sensitive students have even joined the revisionist camp. For example, an eighth-grade girl who was probably still too immature to read the memoirs of a former "comfort woman," which included accounts of rape and oral sex, later became a loyal supporter of Kobayashi Yoshinori by the time she was sixteen. Kobayashi, who has urged his readers to resist the messages of Left-dominated education and mass media, seemed a savior to that student.[143]

To the contrary were the reactions of students of Kusawake Kyōko, an elementary school teacher in Mie prefecture who spent one year teaching war and peace. Her sixth-grade children studied what had happened to people both in their village and in other parts of the wartime Japanese empire, learning about "comfort women," indiscriminate Allied bombings, and medical experiments on humans by Unit 731. Instead of being ashamed of their "Japaneseness," these students decided to build a monument so that they would not forget about the war, which had taken the lives of so many people from many nations. They wanted their monument to remind them to be humane and kind.[144] Kusawake's success may be attributed to her ability to transform these children into active participants—they actually interviewed elderly people in the village and discussed issues among themselves—rather than passive listeners like the eighth-grade girl mentioned above. As Yamada Akira has pointed out, merely forcing students to memorize a "correct conclusion"—that the Asia-Pacific War was an act of aggression and that Japan must apologize and compensate for it—would have little effect in the long run. Rote lessons, after all, can change dramatically. The idea that Japan had fought a holy war for Asian independence might reassert itself if students did not themselves participate in studying wartime history and issues of postwar compensation.[145]

Why They Fight

Although progressives have published many scholarly books that illustrate what happened in and around Nanjing in 1937–38, their works have not successfully displaced the revisionist view. After all, to most revisionists the empirical practice of history does not matter much. For instance, even after the disclosure that the prominent revisionist Tanaka Masaaki had misquoted and falsified more than nine hundred passages from Matsui's diary in 1985, Tanaka stood by his broader argument.[146] In his *Nankin jiken no sōkatsu* (A Summary of the Nanjing Incident), he still insisted that the Massacre did not occur and blamed progressives for perpetuating the supposed myth of the Massacre. Tanaka still claims that the Massacre, not his own work, is a fabrication.

In addition, the faulty logic and history written by revisionists in the past have taken on the character of received truth in new revisionist works. When formulating their arguments, new revisionists draw on already published revisionist accounts. Fujioka's argument that 200,000 or 300,000 Chinese could not possibly have been killed recapitulated the claims of earlier revisionists' accounts, such as those by Tanaka Masaaki, Itakura Yoshiaki, and Higashinakano Osamichi (a professor at Asia University). For instance, Fujioka argued that the Nanjing International Committee specifically protested to the Japanese Embassy that only forty-seven civilians were killed by Japanese soldiers.[147] Higashinakano wrote his account of the Massacre using this same source, and he cited the figure of forty-seven civilians from Itakura Yoshiaki's "Zoku Nankin daigyakusatsu no sūjiteki kenkyū" (A Study of the Numbers Killed in the Nanjing Massacre, Part II), which appeared in the journal *Zenbō* (October 1984).[148] Another prominent revisionist, Watanabe Shōichi, argued in *Sore de mo "No" to ieru Nihon* (A Japan That Can Still Say "No") that John G. Magee, who testified at the Tokyo Trial, grossly exaggerated Japanese atrocities since he had only witnessed three Japanese atrocities with his own eyes, a point also made by Tanaka Masaaki in his *"Nankin gyakusatsu" no kyokō*.[149] Thus, later revisionists have adopted a pattern of repeating the statements of their predecessors without pausing to question whether those statements were empirically accurate in the first place.

Moreover, in order to refute works that they do not wish to accept, revisionists often pursue a strategy of discrediting entire accounts by stressing partial inaccuracies. For instance, Itakura attempted to discredit Sone's personal experience during the Massacre as detailed above. Other revisionists, such as Tanaka and Watanabe, have used Magee's testimony at the Tokyo Trial to support their claims that the Trial exaggerated the incident in Nanjing as a whole.[150] In 1993 Itakura and his allies sponsored a libel lawsuit against Azuma Shirō, the author of *Waga Nankin puratōn: ichi shōshūhei no taiken shita Nankin daigyakusatsu* (My Platoon: The Experience of the Nanjing Massacre by a Conscripted Soldier), and its publisher, Aoki shoten, in order to discredit the entire account given in Azuma's work.[151]

In all of their activities and writings, what is most at stake for revisionists is not the memory of the Chinese who were killed by Japanese soldiers, but the issue of "Japan" and "Japaneseness." The revisionists have engaged in their activities to promote an idea of "a Japanese national history for the Japanese people." Revisionists deny established accounts of wartime and prewar Japanese history, especially as they appear in history textbooks; revisionists claim that these historical narratives are full of masochism, darkness, and apology. To revisionists such as Fujioka, progressive views have deeply and unfairly discredited "Japan" and destroyed national pride. Fujioka and Nishio Kanji have even claimed that "progressive views were a Comintern [Communist International] version of Japanese history." They have been incredulous that their fellow Japanese, the progressives, have chosen to highlight such shameful parts of the Japanese past as the Nanjing Massacre, military sex slaves, and chemical and biological warfare. To revisionists such as Fujioka and Nishio, progressives are an incomprehensible psychological aberration.[152]

Fujioka and the revisionists have criticized the progressive accounts found in textbooks as overly emotional and flawed because they ignore international power politics. Fujioka insisted that war was merely a game played by nation-states pursuing their national interests.[153] He even argued that the American decision to drop atomic bombs on Japan was correct. He expressed gratitude for President Truman's decision to do so because "it saved Japan from experiencing a more horrible national tragedy"—a division of Japan between the Soviet Union and the United States.[154] One of Fujioka's allies, Ogasawara Mikio, a professor at Sakuyō Music University, also endorsed the view that Truman's decision was strategically correct in order to save the lives of American soldiers fighting in the Pacific. Ogasawara criticized protests by Japanese peace activists in 1995 against the Smithsonian Institution's decision not to exhibit photos of the devastation caused by atomic bombs. He argued that such protests went against Japan's national interest because they would not achieve anything except wounding the national pride of Americans. Equating the Smithsonian's stand with the position of all Americans, Ogasawara praised the healthy American nationalism evinced by "America's decision" not to exhibit its own atrocities caused by the bombs.[155]

Other prominent revisionists have also conceived of their mission as rewriting wartime and prewar Japanese history—a history they see as having been demonized. Tanaka Masaaki emphatically stated that he would argue for the rest of his life that the Nanjing Massacre was a fabrication.[156] The journalist Kitsukawa Manabu, who also condemned the Massacre as a fabrication, decided after the war to devote himself to reconstructing Japan instead of succumbing to a strong suicidal impulse he experienced at the time. In 1983 he completed his fourteenth book, titled *Nihon wa shinryaku koku de wa nai* (Japan Was Not an Aggressive Nation). During its writing, he was hospitalized three times because of the advancing infirmity of old age, but his passion to finish the book in order to teach the "true" Japanese history was said to have kept him alive.[157] By the time he had completed his book, he had lost most of his vision to a cataract. According to Kitsukawa, one motive for writing the book was to destroy the version of Japanese imperial history written by the Allied-sponsored Tokyo Trial, or "the monkey show," as he called it. Another objective was to promote national pride among Japanese nationals by teaching them that the "*dai tō-A sensō* [the Greater East Asian War] was a defensive war whose sacred purpose was to emancipate Asians from more than two hundred years of white slavery."[158]

Moreover, for politicians such as Fujio Masayuki, Okuno Seisuke, Nagano Shigeto, and others, the revision of the "untrue" wartime and prewar Japanese history was even worth the risk of forfeiting their professional careers. It was, for instance, during his second appointment to the cabinet in 1986 (in a political career that had begun in 1963) that Fujio Masayuki publicly announced his views regarding wartime Japanese history, including his denial of the Massacre. He refused to withdraw what he had said or to apologize for it, a stance that led Prime Minister Nakasone to fire him. Although this incident marked the end of his political career, Fujio claimed that he was proud of what he had done because he had succeeded in raising an important issue for his country and for future generations about the necessity of reconstructing Japan's past.[159] Okuno Seisuke, too, chose to leave office rather than withdraw his controversial 1988 remarks on wartime Japan, including his denial of the Massacre. He stressed that his attitude and comments would contribute to the future of Japan by helping Japanese youth to reconsider Japan's wartime history, since his comments generated widespread attention from the press and would be kept permanently in the record of the Diet.[160]

On the other side of these debates, the issues of "Japaneseness" and "Japan" are also important to the progressives, although they see these ideas differently. Kasahara Tokushi, for instance, would not have disputed that national self-respect is at stake in the debate over the Massacre. However, he argued that real self-respect as a nation would come only from an honest treatment of the past that included Japanese aggression as a part of national history. Moreover, he opposed the revisionist view, saying that it ignores the rights of the people who had to submit to the atrocities committed by the Japanese soldiers. Since the revisionist narrative was no longer credible in the eyes of the world, Kasahara argued, revisionists must face the negative aspects of the nation's history in order to avoid repeating dreadful mistakes such as the Massacre in the future.[161]

Similarly, another prominent scholar, Yoshida Yutaka, who has worked on the history of the Massacre for decades, stressed a collective responsibility among the Japanese for solving the unresolved issues resulting from fifty years of Japan's unwillingness to face its own war crimes during the Fifteen-Year War. He argued that although those who were born after the war did not have to bear the blame for waging the aggressive war, they were still responsible for leading society to acknowledge its past wrongdoings.[162] Yoshida insisted that the failure of the people to speak out against army misdeeds during the war was one of the reasons for massive wartime Japanese atrocities.[163]

Whereas Yoshida agreed that Japanese born after the war were not responsible for Japanese aggression during the war, Ienaga Saburō went further. He argued that insofar as one was born "Japanese," one was responsible for the past war crimes that one's fellow Japanese had committed. He asserted that an individual "Japanese" as a part of the larger "Japan" would continue to bear responsibility for the war since the "Japanese" comprise "Japan." He stressed that Japan's war guilt would never disappear. As a constituent component of "Japan," a "Japanese" would remain responsible for the past misconduct during the war, though Ienaga conceded that ethnic Japanese who have assimilated into other national societies would be exempt from such responsibility. Ienaga argued that acknowledging Japanese war crimes would prevent the mother country from committing another such sin, and that these efforts should be regarded as another kind of patriotism that could also contribute to human peace on earth.[164]

Although "Japaneseness" and "Japan" did not carry the same meanings for all progressives battling the revisionists, these progressives at least seemed to agree on the following points. They all agreed on their responsibility as Japanese citizens for facing national wrongdoings in the past and for deterring the people from committing the same errors that wreaked devastation both on Japan and beyond. They stressed that protecting national interests would never justify war atrocities and that war was not a game among states, but mass murder by a state in the name of national defense. The progressives' most crucial difference from the revisionists was that they felt the same kind of remorse for "non-Japanese" victims of Japanese aggression as they did for the "Japanese" who lost their lives during the Asia-Pacific War.

Beyond the debates over nationality, nationalism, and the nation, the telling of the history of the Tokyo Trial has remained highly contested between these two camps. Revisionists have all claimed that the Massacre was fabricated by the Trial and that the Trial actually established the demonized imperial Japanese history of the postwar period. Revisionists, from Tanaka Masaaki to Fujioka Nobukatsu, judged the Trial to be unfair and marred by distortions of the historical evidence; they considered it victors' justice. They stressed, for example, that the dissent of the Indian judge, Pal, who found each of the accused not guilty, was not only denied a reading at the court but was also deliberately excluded from publication during the American occupation.[165] According to Tanaka Masaaki, the Trial had three objectives: to denounce Japanese history prior to 1945 so that patriotism among the Japanese could be destroyed; to cultivate war guilt among the Japanese by claiming that Japan had waged an "aggressive war" and that the Japanese military was cruel and brutal; and to retaliate against Japanese wartime leaders by creating new "crimes against peace" and "crimes against humanity."[166] Thus, Tanaka concluded that "a nonpatriotic and masochistic Japanese people was created in this postwar period."[167]

Other criticism has focused on proving that the Trial was void under international law, as seen in the works of another prominent revisionist, Satō Kazuo, who praised the revisionist works by Suzuki Akira and Tanaka Masaaki highly. According to Satō, the Trial had no jurisdiction to prosecute Japanese wartime leaders. He argued that Japan's surrender was not unconditional but rather conditional, because Japan accepted the Potsdam Declaration, which allowed the occupation forces to prosecute Japanese only for conventional war crimes. The Trial, therefore, applied ex post facto law in prosecuting crimes against peace and crimes against humanity—neither of which had been in existence before 1945. He argued that individuals had never been criminally responsible for waging war under international law because war was regarded as a legitimate act of state, and that Allied war crimes, either conventional or newly created, had never been prosecuted before.[168]

Similarly, Fujio Masayuki contributed to the argument that the Trial was a "dark trial"—unfair and illegitimate. To him, the atrocity that should have been judged at the Trial was not the alleged Nanjing Massacre, but the dropping of atomic bombs by the United States.[169] To Okuno Seisuke, the Trial was absolutely illegitimate in terms of international law and was the victors' punishment of the defeated. According to Okuno, the American firebombing of Japanese cities and dropping of atomic bombs, as well as the Russian atrocities in Manchuria at the very end of the war, were more serious war crimes than any committed by the Japanese. Okuno contended that the Trial succeeded in imposing on Japan an "American version" of the history of World War II. In Okuno's eyes, the Trial "brainwashed" the Japanese, who, as a result of the Trial, started to think that Japan had conducted an aggressive war. This demonizing of Japan—

characterizing Japan as an "aggressor" and the Allies as "just"—fostered a demoralizing legacy by eroding any sense of national pride not only in Japanese of the time, but in Japanese of today as well.[170]

Historians who have fought for a more open history of the Massacre have also acknowledged the shortcomings of the Trial. In contrast with the revisionists, however, progressive historians have seen a positive side to the Tokyo Trial. According to them, the Trial benefited Japanese history by disclosing evidence that the Japanese alone might not have been able to pursue. These historians, however, asserted that the Trial's process was flawed because it did not go far enough in prosecuting all Japanese wartime leaders, such as Hirohito, politicians, bureaucrats, and businessmen, for their complicity in war crimes. Fujiwara Akira, for instance, argued that the Trial's inadequate pursuit of responsible wartime leaders fostered the active revisionist attacks in the 1980s, since such leaders were never charged with war crimes and thus could maintain a public presence.[171]

These progressive historians also proposed that the Trial was flawed because it did not thoroughly prosecute atrocities committed by the Japanese military. Although the Trial prosecuted atrocities against "subjects" of the Allied powers, those atrocities against "unpatriotic Japanese" *(hikokumin),* Taiwanese, and Koreans, as well as against the Chinese who lived in the areas controlled by Communist forces were never prosecuted.[172] In addition, even though substantial evidence existed regarding Japanese chemical and biological warfare in China, which should have been considered a crime against humanity, the Trial ignored this conduct for a political reason: To bring this evidence before the Tribunal, the Allies would have had to publish the data obtained from the more than three thousand human experiments performed in China. The Allies determined that the strategic value of controlling this data and preserving its secrecy outweighed its value as evidence.[173]

Moreover, in the eyes of progressive historians, too, the Trial was "victors' justice" because it did not prosecute war crimes committed by the Allied powers, such as the American bombing of major cities with atomic and conventional bombs that killed not only Japanese noncombatants but also non-Japanese residents, including Allied POWs, Koreans, and Chinese who had been forcibly taken to Japan. The Trial also disregarded Soviet atrocities against Japanese noncombatants—murder, looting, rape—in Manchuria and Northeast China. To historians such as Ienaga, such Allied war crimes should not have been exempted from censure.[174]

Despite the shortcomings of the Trial, though, progressive historians recognized its contribution to history. The Trial prosecuted war criminals and acknowledged, however imperfectly, their responsibility for killing citizens of other nations. These historians also concluded that the Trial was meaningful for the future of humanity because it treated aggressive war as a crime in terms of international law.[175] These historians opposed revisionists who ignored this significance and merely focused on the Trial's limitations. As Ienaga argued, in spite of what the revisionists contended, Japan's war with China was a war of aggression, and this fact must not be overlooked. Although Ienaga fully agreed with some of Judge Pal's dissenting arguments, he criticized the revisionists who tried to use Pal's minority opinion in order to deny the legality of the Tokyo Trial.[176]

The historiographical controversy regarding the Massacre has called into question the integrity of the craft and authority of historians. Historians who fought against revisionist interpretations of the Massacre stressed that it was essential to show their respect to the victims of the Massacre and to their survivors by keeping alive the story of their tragedy. People such as Fujiwara Akira, Honda Katsuichi, Hora Tomio, Kasahara Tokushi, Yoshida Yutaka, and others strongly agreed that the candid reporting of historical events was far more important than preserving a tidy image of the Japanese nation.[177] By contrast, people such as Fujioka Nobukatsu, Okuno Seisuke, Tanaka Masaaki, Watanabe Shōichi, and others seem to have been preoccupied with preserving "a national history" of which "the Japanese" can be proud and with silencing any history that would detract from their ideal of wartime Japan.

After all, the greatest defect of the revisionist arguments continues to be their insularity and internal contradictions. Instead of justifying Japan's wartime past by arguing that other nations do not admit their historical atrocities, it would be more productive for revisionists to argue that other nations should also have school textbooks that include their own war crimes and atrocities as Japanese textbooks currently do. Instead of arguing that the Tokyo Trial was unfair and void because of its shortcomings, it would be more productive to seek an international system that would, in the future, prosecute war crimes committed by both victors and losers equally according to the same global standard. Instead of looking for national pride by justifying Japanese wartime aggression that caused tens of millions of deaths among several nationalities, it would be more productive for them to think about how human beings would best be able to avoid the destruction that the world can no longer afford.

Conclusion: The Internationalization of the History and Memory of the Nanjing Massacre

How has this lengthy debate affected the history of the Nanjing Massacre? Are revisionists damaging the practice of empirical history? On the contrary, by insisting so strongly on their position, the revisionists have done more harm than good to their own cause. Their attempt to revise the history of the Massacre has not only motivated Japanese progressive historians, but it has also outraged non-Japanese scholars and concerned laypeople, prompting them to research and document the Massacre in further detail. A movement toward an internationalization of the history and memory of the Massacre has been taking place since the mid 1980s, and the revisionists have contributed to the increase in the discussion of the Massacre around the globe. By the early 1990s, Japanese progressive historians had located significant numbers of non-Japanese documents, mostly in China and the United States, and made them available to the

Japanese public.[178] In 1996, during her research on the Massacre, Iris Chang located the diary of John Rabe, who was chairman of the International Committee for the Safety Zone and who sheltered 650 Chinese in his mansion. The diary portrayed the everyday life of the Chinese refugees in Nanjing. It has already been partially translated into Japanese and has been available to Japanese readers since October 1997.[179] International conferences on the Massacre such as the panel held at the Association for Asian Studies in March 1997 and the meeting held in China in August 1997 have been an effort to share a common history and memory of the Massacre.[180] Since the early 1990s, war memorials in Japan, such as the Hiroshima Peace Memorial and the Nagasaki Atomic Bomb Museum, have incorporated accounts of the Massacre as a reminder of Japanese wartime aggression. As of 1995, the Memorial Hall in Nanjing had been visited by four million people, of whom sixty thousand were Japanese and ten thousand were other non-Chinese nationals.[181] In the UnitedStates, the Global Alliance for Preserving the History of World War II in Asia and the Pacific (founded in 1994), a Chinese-American activist organization that has approximately thirty member organizations, has been actively involved in facilitating the writing of the history of the Massacre by distributing documentary films regarding the Massacre, sponsoring a national tour of photography exhibits of the Massacre, and sponsoring the publication of books on the Massacre.[182]

Although revisionists' challenges have undoubtedly contributed to the development of the study of the Massacre and the internationalization of its history and memory, these challenges also have produced detrimental side effects. The attempt by Japanese revisionists to minimize the inhumanity of the Massacre and the death toll has led their critics across the world to respond by engaging in graphic, ever-escalating accounts of the cruelty of the Massacre. Non-Japanese writers, who are often outraged by Japanese revisionists, tend to use photos that few, if any, could stand to look at in order to stress the uniqueness of the cruelty and inhumanity of the Massacre in world history.[183] In addition, these non-Japanese accounts of the Massacre tend to choose a greater figure for the death toll than that which was pronounced by the Tokyo War Crimes Trial: 200,000 civilians and soldiers. For instance, after Ishihara Shintarō denied the Massacre in 1990, an open letter by the Chinese Alliance for Memorial and Justice stated that 340,000 were killed during the Nanjing Massacre. In her recent book, Iris Chang erroneously claimed that the judges of the Tokyo War Crimes Trial concluded that "260,000 noncombatants" were killed during the Massacre.[184] Actually, the Trial rejected the death toll of 260,000 deaths of both civilians and soldiers, which was submitted by the prosecutor to the court, and ruled that "over 200,000" civilians and prisoners of war were killed during the six weeks of the Japanese occupation.[185]

Such a competition to state in ever more graphic terms the ferocity and the death toll of the Massacre is understandable in light of revisionist challenges. And this competition may continue to intensify indefinitely, because Japanese atrocities in China were ferocious, and the death toll could be expanded to more than ten million, depending on how the space and scope of the Massacre are defined.[186] Unfortunately, no matter how much international accounts of the Massacre stress its cruelty and violence, Japanese revisionists will not stop claiming that the Massacre has been a "fabrication." The Nanjing Massacre is a battle over history in which the revisionists refuse to surrender. They have already risked their professional careers and even their lives. Although members of the Study Group on the Liberal View of History, such as Fujioka Nobukatsu, Kobayashi Yoshinori, and Nishio Kanji, have received threatening messages, including death threats, they continue to speak out.[187]

Since Japanese revisionists will not be complacent, the future of this competitive discourse over the cruelty and the death toll seems obvious: it will only escalate. Armed with ugly photos and stern rhetoric, revisionists will focus their attack on America's or China's own atrocities and war crimes, while non-Japanese accounts may further stress human suffering in Nanjing and other parts of Asia. These historical competitors will fight in order to "prove" which race— "the Japanese" or "the

Chinese"—suffered most.[188] Symptoms of such an escalation have already become visible. Fujioka's Study Group on the Liberal View of History has decided to send to the American media a report that denounces as inaccurate propaganda photographs used in Chang's *Rape of Nanking.*[189] Nakamura Akira, one of Fujioka's allies, has claimed that it was "the Chinese" who perpetrated racial atrocities and that the Massacre is a fabrication because "the Japanese" do not by nature behave in the way claimed.[190] Iris Chang, who has been outraged by the revisionist challenge, now calls the Massacre "the Pacific holocaust" and has stressed the necessity of fully revealing to the world Japanese wartime atrocities and crimes.[191]

Accounts of the Massacre enmeshed in this battle are limited in the contribution they can make to human society because they play this game according to their opponents', the revisionists', rules. Such history tends to be very simple; it emphasizes reductive phrases such as "the Japanese" and "the Chinese." In such accounts, the unit of measurement of sufferings is "race" and "nationality," and accounts like these often do not leave any room for any other atrocities, especially ones "the Japanese" may have suffered. After all, they pay almost exclusive attention to the Nanjing Massacre, and their single concern is to make "Japan" acknowledge its past crimes and the sufferings of the people in Nanjing. Such accounts do not seem to be seriously interested in studying the Massacre to prevent similar atrocities from happening, atrocities that are indeed still occurring today.

It is true that the revisionist challenges are powerful. It is also true, however, that the voices refuting revisionists in Japan are strong and powerful. Unfortunately, these voices have received little attention, especially outside Japan. Although high-ranking Japanese politicians' remarks denying the Massacre have been closely covered by the foreign media, the efforts of politicians such as Motooka Shōji (a member of the House of Councilors) and Tanaka Kō (a member of the House of Representatives), who have been trying to introduce a bill that would make Japan responsible for researching the damage caused by the Japanese involvement in the war, have not been publicized outside Japan.[192] Rabe's diary has received much attention in the foreign press,[193] but Kasahara Tokushi's *Nankin nanminku no hyakunichi* (1995), which examined the Massacre through oral histories of Westerners who witnessed the Massacre just as Rabe did, has received scant notice from the non-Japanese media. Although it is known that Fujioka Nobukatsu has sold more than eight hundred thousand copies of his *Kyōkasho ga oshienai rekishi*,[194] the Japanese and non-Japanese media do not report that books refuting Fujioka have also been successful. *The Diary of John Rabe* sold forty thousand copies in two months and Kasahara's *Nankin jiken* sold more than fifty thousand copies in six months.[195] Although a total sales figure is not available, Fujiwara Akira's *Kingendai shi no shinjitsu wa nanika* has gone through nine print runs. Ienaga's *Kyōkasho kara kesenai sensō no shinjitsu* has completed its sixth print run.[196] In addition, more than thirty books and numerous articles aimed at countering Fujioka and his supporters were published in 1997.[197]

Writers of the history and memory of the Massacre in countries other than Japan should realize that Japan, like other democratic countries, contains various different views within its society, and that these views vie with one another for the status of a master narrative. In the Japanese public memory, both progressive and revisionist viewpoints have coexisted in the past, and they will continue to coexist into the future as well. In history textbooks and in the historical academy in Japan, the progressive view will probably preserve its dominant position. Nevertheless, precisely because revisionist views present a challenge to established history and because they spark emotional reactions, the revisionists will continue to receive more media coverage, both at home and abroad. In addition, the media will continue to welcome revisionist voices, at least in part for commercial reasons.

As the internationalization of the Massacre has proceeded, those writing about the Massacre around the world have faced the challenge of transforming the study of the Massacre into a project that can preserve lives instead of promoting hatred toward "the Japanese." As Zbigniew Brzezinski once estimated, between 167 million and 175 million lives have been "deliberately extinguished through politically motivated carnage" in the twentieth century.[198] Places such as Bosnia—where approximately 200,000 people have been killed, 750,000 are missing, millions have become refugees, and 30,000 to 60,000 Muslim women have been raped—remind us that peoples are still spurred to hate and kill each other by primal motivations, including questions of ethnic, religious, racial, national, and regional identity.[199] The history and memory of the Nanjing Massacre can teach human beings about the dreadful experiences of people who had to go through atrocities like those that are still going on around the world today. War is, after all, a human disaster, not a natural one, and peoples can prevent such basic violations of human rights by sharing the history and memory of such events internationally. The Nanjing Massacre is not "their" problem, but "our" problem. The German diplomat P. Scharffenberg, who returned to Nanjing during the Massacre, wrote: "We Germans in Nanjing, including Mr. Rabe, all think that the war in Asia is fundamentally different from ones with which we are familiar. . . . [I]t seems as if we are back in the Thirty Years War."[200] Scharffenberg thought that Germans could never descend to the kind of cruelty that he witnessed in Nanjing. He failed to learn the obvious lesson of the Massacre, and the Holocaust would soon show that no part of humanity is immune to such pathological violence.

Notes

1. Pritchard, *The Tokyo War Crimes Trial,* vol. 20, pp. 49604–5.
2. Ibid., p. 49606.
3. Ibid., p. 49608.
4. Gluck, "The Past in the Present," p. 70. As Gluck notes, progressive intellectuals disagreed mightily among themselves and formed no single group or community. In fact, their primary concerns have not been the same throughout the postwar period. Therefore, in this chapter the term *progressives* is used rather loosely. Regardless of their po-

litical and ideological stances, however, progressives have joined in strong support of Japan's so-called Peace Constitution and rejection of the values of wartime Japan.

5. These figures are based on table 107—"Suggested Changes for Japan"—in the United States Strategic Bombing Survey, *The Effects of Strategic Bombing on Japanese Morale,* p. 152. Because some people had more than one suggestion for change, the percentage total is 106 percent. About 3,150 carefully selected interviews were conducted between November 10 and December 29, 1945. When asked about their emotional response, many gave more than one answer, yielding a percentage total of 125 percent. Approximately 30 percent felt regret, misery, or disappointment; 23 percent felt surprise, shock, or bewilderment; 22 percent felt relief or happiness; and 13 percent felt anxiety or worry when they heard that Japan had surrendered.

6. Yoshimi, *Kusa no ne no fashizumu,* p. 274.

7. When asked about their dissatisfaction, respondents often gave more than one response, yielding a percentage total of 186 percent. According to the poll, 85 percent mentioned inadequate food as a cause of dissatisfaction in their lives in November and December 1945. See United States Strategic Bombing Survey, *Effects of Strategic Bombing on Japanese Morale,* pp. 151, 154.

8. *Nihon keizai shinbun* reported May 4, 1946, on the anger felt by the public toward wartime leaders. According to the newspaper, people often made comments such as: "If these politicians had not gone to war, we would not be in our present miserable condition," and "If there had been no war, our husbands and sons would not have been killed, and our houses would not have been burned." *Mainichi shinbun* wrote in an editorial section on May 1, 1946: "We strongly feel that JAPAN was spoiled by these same poor actors [twenty-eight class A war criminals]. . . . The people now feel strong antipathy toward the irresponsible attitudes of these war leaders." See General Headquarters, Supreme Commander for the Allied Powers, Allied Translator and Interpreter Section, *Press Translations and Summaries—Japan,* Reel # 12, May 6, 1946, and May 3, 1946. Hereafter cited as GHQ.

9. A monthly summary for May written by the Supreme Commander for the Allied Powers mentions, "Most newspapers were pleased with the indictment as it was in full accord with the Potsdam Declaration."

10. GHQ, Reel #12, May 2, 1946.

11. Ibid.

12. Ibid. Newspaper articles and editorials that supported the trial are easy to find. See, for instance, "Civilization Is the Plaintiff," *Asahi shinbun,* April 30, 1946; "Let's Expose War Crimes for Ourselves,"

Minpō, May 1, 1946; "Serial Publication of Biographies of War Criminals: Tōjō Hideki and Minami Jirō," *Nishi Nippon shinbun* (Fukuoka), April 30, 1946; and "National Character and Pride," *Yomiuri shinbun*, May 13, 1946. See GHQ, Reels #12 and 13.

13. "Children, Too, Were Massacred; Revealed Massacre at Nanjing," *Asahi shinbun*, July 26, 1946, p. 2. See GHQ, Reel #17.

14. "Tokyo Trials," *Mainichi shinbun*, July 30, 1946. See GHQ, Reel #17.

15. "Our Gratitude to the Chinese People," *Yomiuri shinbun*, July 31, 1946. See GHQ, Reel #17.

16. Akazawa et al., *Tōkyō saiban handobukku*, p. 234.

17. Ibid., p. 166.

18. Tōyama, "Sengo no rekishigaku to rekishi ishiki," p. 21.

19. Tawara, "Kyōkasho no 'Nankin daigyakusatsu' kijutsu wa dō kawatta ka," pp. 170–71.

20. Tōyama, "Sengo no rekishigaku to rekishi ishiki," pp. 28, 29, citation on p. 24.

21. Inumaru, "Sengo Nihon Marukusushugi shigaku ni kansuru oboegaki: 1945–50 nen o chūshin ni," p. 101.

22. Tōyama, "Sengo no rekishigaku to rekishi ishiki," p. 72.

23. See, for instance, Imai Seiichi et al., *Shōwa shi*, p. 268; Tōyama, "Sengo no rekishigaku to rekishi ishiki," p. 3; and Inumaru, *Rekishi kagaku no kadai to Marukusushugi*, p. 5.

24. Miyata, "Reddo pāji."

25. "Nihon bōeijō no seiyaku, Beigawa kakunin, enjo o yakusu," *Asahi shinbun*, October 25, 1953, p. 1.

26. Nihon minshutō, *Ureubeki kyōkasho no mondai*, p. 18.

27. Tōyama, *Kyōkasho kentei no shisō to rekishi kyōiku*, p. 253.

28. Kyōkasho kentei soshō o shien suru zenkoku renrakukai, *Kyōkasho kara kesenai sensō no shinjitsu*, pp. 63–64.

29. The original treaty was signed in 1951 (before Japan's independence) and allowed the United States wide powers in using bases in Japan. Although the new treaty gave Japan a more equal relationship with the United States, progressives saw it as unconstitutional and dangerous because the treaty could drag Japan into an American war. See Rekishi kagaku kyōgikai, *Shiryō Nihon kingendai shi III*, p. 165.

30. Ibid., p. 260.

31. These figures are based on Kanda, *Shōwa shi nenpyō*, p. 76.

32. Ueyama, "Dai tō-A sensō no isan," pp. 358, 364–65.

33. Hayashi, *Dai tō-A sensō kōteiron* was published in July 1964, and Hayashi, *Zoku dai tō-A sensō kōteiron* in June 1965, both by Banchō shobō.

34. Hayashi, *Dai tō-A sensō kōteiron,* pp. 155, 194; Hayashi, *Zoku dai tō-A sensō kōteiron,* p. 486.
35. "Aka kara no rekishi no kaihō."
36. "Kyō no mondai."
37. "Meiji 100 nen o iwau igi to riyū."
38. Shimono and Gotō, *Nankin sakusen no shinsō.* According to Gotō, the objective of publishing the book was to tell the truth of the Massacre to children and to remove the disgrace that had been attached to the Sixth Army.
39. These figures are taken from NHK hōsō seron chōsajo, *Zusetsu sengo seron shi,* p. 179.
40. Reischauer, *Japan: The Story of a Nation,* p. 258.
41. In 1965, 33 percent answered that the United States was wrong regarding the Vietnam conflict; in 1966 and 1967, 31 percent; in 1968, 43 percent; and in 1972, 43 percent. In 1952, 66 percent chose the United States as their favorite country to visit, whereas 9 percent made that choice in 1973. Figures are from NHK hōsō seron chōsajo, *Zusetsu sengo seron shi,* p. 179.
42. Ienaga, *Taiheiyō sensō.* His postscript written in 1967 shows that the Vietnam War offered him an opportunity to ponder Japan's own war crimes during the Asia-Pacific War (pp. 423–25).
43. Shirota, "Sensō taiken o dō oshieru ka."
44. Ōta, "Dai niji sekai taisen go no Nit-Chū kankei."
45. Ikei, *Nihon gaikō shi gaisetsu,* pp. 302–3.
46. *Shōwa niman nichi no zen kiroku,* vol. 15, pp. 88–89.
47. Honda, *Chūgoku no tabi.*
48. Ibid., pp. 4–5.
49. Honda, *Chūgoku no Nihongun,* pp. 12, 290.
50. Honda, *Chūgoku no tabi,* p. 263.
51. Yamamoto, "Honda Katsuichi sama e no henshin."
52. Honda, "Zatsuon de ijimerareru gawa no me," pp. 162.
53. Yamamoto, *Watashi no naka no Nihongun,* vol. 2, pp. 324–26.
54. Suzuki, *"Nankin daigyakusatsu" no maboroshi,* pp. 11, 15, 22–23, 43.
55. See, for instance, ibid., chapters 2 and 4, pp. 53–111 and 143–202.
56. Hora, *Nankin jiken.*
57. Hora, *Nankin daigyakusatsu: "maboroshi" ka kōsaku hihan,* pp. ii–iv, 28, 49–50, 156, 176.
58. Hora, *Nankin daigyakusatsu no shōmei,* p. 2. Revisionists such as Watanabe Shōichi, however, came to a different conclusion. To Watanabe, it was Honda who lost the battle.
59. Ienaga, for instance, characterized the Fifteen-Year War (1931–

45) as "reckless" in the textbook, but the Ministry of Education insisted that the description was inappropriate and demanded that Ienaga rewrite it. See Tokutake, *Kyōkasho no sengo shi,* pp. 151–52.

60. Kyōiku shuppan and Nihon shoseki accounted for 30 percent of all junior high school textbooks in 1975. See *Kyōkasho repōto '97,* p. 68.

61. Tawara, *Kyōkasho kōgeki no shinsō,* pp. 158–70.

62. See, for instance, Oda, "Jūgonen sensō o dō oshieru ka"; Arai et al., "Jūgonen sensō o dō toraeru ka"; and Terada, "Chūgoku kingendai shi de nani o oshieru ka."

63. Tōyama, *Kyōkasho kentei no shisō to rekishi kyōiku,* p. 255.

64. Tokutake, *Kyōkasho no sengo shi,* pp. 192–93.

65. Tōyama, *Kyōkasho kentei no shisō to rekishi kyōiku,* p. 256.

66. Tawara, *Kyōkasho kōgeki no shinsō,* pp. 119–20. However, as conservatives point out, it is true that there were no reports of changes from *shinryaku* (aggression) to *shinshutsu* (advance) regarding Japan's aggression in north China. By 1982, many textbooks had already been replacing *shinryaku* with *shinshutsu* since the 1950s.

67. See "Kyōkasho sara ni 'senzen' fukken e."

68. Tokutake, *Kyōkasho no sengo shi,* pp. 201–2.

69. Hora et al., *Nankin jiken o kangaeru,* p. 12.

70. Tokutake, *Kyōkasho no sengo shi,* pp. 202–3.

71. Ibid., p. 206.

72. As discussed above, *aggression* was replaced with *advance* long before the 1982 textbook authorization, and there was not any direct revision from *aggression into northern China* to *advance into northern China* as reported by national newspapers. It is, however, undeniable that the government tried to tone down the aggressive nature of the Asia-Pacific War in history textbooks.

73. Watanabe Shōichi, "Manken kyo ni hoeta kyōkasho mondai."

74. Tanaka Masaaki, *"Nankin gyakusatsu" no kyokō,* p. 27.

75. Ibid., pp. 355–56.

76. Watanabe Shōichi, "Maegaki," in ibid., pp. 5–6.

77. Tanaka Masaaki, *"Nankin gyakusatsu" no kyokō,* p. 355.

78. See, for instance, Itakura, "Shinbun ga ōkiku sodateta chiisa na gohō"; Kobori, Hasegawa, and Watanabe, "Eiga 'Tokyō saiban' ni monomōsu"; Tanaka Masaaki, "'Nankin gyakusatsu' Matsui Iwane no jinchū nisshi"; "'Nankin gyakusatsu' sansensha no shōgen" (a roundtable discussion by Tanaka Masaaki, Itakura Yoshiaki, and three former officers who served in the battle in Nanjing); Tanaka Masaaki, "'Nankin daigyakusatsu kinenkan' ni monomōsu."

79. Tanaka and his allies continued their fight. They sued the ministry again in 1991 and insisted that the references to the atrocities in

Nanjing in seven junior high school textbooks were inaccurate. The case was dismissed in 1992 by the Tokyo District Court. See Hata Ikuhiko, *Shōwa shi no nazo o ou,* vol. 1, pp. 130–31.

80. Hora et al., *Nankin jiken o kangaeru,* pp. 5–6.

81. Hora, *Nit-Chū sensō: Nankin daigyakusatsu jiken shiryōshū,* 2 vols.

82. Tanaka Masaaki, *"Nankin gyakusatsu" no kyokō,* pp. 309–11.

83. Hora, *Nankin daigyakusatsu no shōmei,* pp. 20–22.

84. Honda, *Sabakareta Nankin daigyakusatsu.*

85. Members of Chūgoku kikansha renrakukai, all of whom were prosecuted and imprisoned because of their war crimes, had been active long before the 1980s in writing about their experiences of atrocities in China, such as medical experiments on human beings, the massacre of a village, the "three alls" operation (kill all, burn all, loot all). See, for instance, Chūgoku kikansha renrakukai, *Shinryaku: Chūgoku ni okeru Nihon senpan no kokuhaku.*

86. Sone, *Shiki Nankin gyakusatsu,* pp. 1–3; Azuma, *Waga Nankin puratōn: ichi shōshūhei no taiken shita Nankin daigyakusatsu,* pp. 2–3.

87. Sone, *Shiki Nankin gyakusatsu,* p. 203.

88. Azuma, *Waga Nankin puratōn,* pp. 8–9.

89. Hata Ikuhiko, *Shōwa shi no nazo o ou,* pp. 133–34.

90. See, for example, Itakura, "'Nankin gyakusatsu' no zangeya Sone Kazuo no shōtai."

91. Fujio, "'Hōgen daijin' ōi ni hoeru." He claimed that the truth of the Nanjing Massacre was unknown. According to Fujio, "killing people in war was not murder in terms of international law" (p. 123). Fujio's comments were in response to the Chinese protest against Prime Minister Nakasone's visit to the Yasukuni Shrine, where approximately 2.5 million war dead dating back to 1853 were enshrined, including class A war criminals.

92. Okuno, "'Shinryaku hatsugen' doko ga warui." Okuno thinks that it was impossible for the Japanese military to have killed three hundred thousand people in Nanjing during the event, as claimed by the Chinese government (p. 119).

93. Fujio, "'Hōgen daijin' futatabi hoeru."

94. Okuno, "'Shinryaku hatsugen' doko ga warui," pp. 112–13.

95. Yang, "A Sino-Japanese Controversy: The Nanjing Atrocity as History." Yang cites (p. 33), for instance, Zou et al., "Nanjing datusha de lishi shishi burong cuangai" (The Historical Facts of the Nanjing Massacre Will Not Allow Tampering), p. 85.

96. Tōkyō shoseki, the largest publisher of elementary school social studies *(shakaika)* textbooks, did not mention the Massacre in the

1980s; see Tawara, *Kyōkasho kōgeki no shinsō,* pp. 166–68. Its share was 35.3 percent of the total market in 1986; see Nakamura Kikuji, *Kyōkasho no hensan, hakkō kyōkasho seido no hensen ni kansuru chōsa kenkyū,* p. 95.

97. The share was 32.4 percent of the total market.

98. Tawara, *Kyōkasho kōgeki no shinsō,* pp. 158–66.

99. Adachi, "Sensō ni katan saserareta minshū," pp. 8–9. See also his "Kodomotachi to tomo ni mirai o kirihiraku tame ni."

100. Komatsu, "Kagai no men o chūshin ni sueta 15 nen sensō no gakushū," p. 15.

101. See *Rekishi chiri kyōiku,* nos. 505 and 512. These two issues are indexes of the journal. They cover all the issues from no. 1 (November 1953) through no. 500 (March 1993). See pp. 76–87 of no. 512 for a section listing titles and volume numbers of articles on the Asia-Pacific War.

102. See, for example, the following articles by Kasahara Tokushi: "'Nankin daigyakusatsu' to rekishi kenkyū," "'Nankin daigyakusatsu' wa nakatta no ka," and "Saisho no Nankin daigyakusatsu hōdō." Kasahara has also written a series of articles titled "Nankin daigyakusatsu no zenbō wa naze hōdō sarenakatta no ka."

103. See *Rekishi chiri kyōiku,* nos. 505 and 512.

104. See, for instance, Fujio, "'Hōgen daijin' ōi ni hoeru," p. 123.

105. "Nihon o yurugashita 100 yo nichi," pp. 2–3.

106. Ibid., pp. 5–6.

107. Ad Hoc Committee on the Case against Hirohito, "Unmasking Hirohito: The Other Hitler." This was a full-page advertisement.

108. Ministry of Foreign Affairs, Japan, *Diplomatic Blue Book 1990: Japan's Diplomatic Activities,* p. 2.

109. "Taisen no kōi 'kibishiku hansei.'"

110. *Gekkan keidanren* (April 1992), quoted in Yoshida, *Nihonjin no sensō kan: sengo shi no naka no henyō,* p. 175.

111. "Saki no sensō 'shinryaku sensō' to meigen."

112. Kisaka, "Ajia, taiheiyō sensō no rekishiteki seikaku o megutte," p. 3.

113. Kasahara, "Sensō kōteiron, menzairon no kiseki to genzai," pp. 7–8.

114. See, for instance, Uesugi Chitoshi, "Nagasaki genbaku shiryōkan no mondai bubun"; Satō, *Kenpō kyūjō, shinryaku sensō, Tōkyō saiban.*

115. "Backgrounder: Chronology of Japanese Politicians' Denial of Japanese Aggression History."

116. Kristof, "Many in Japan Oppose Apology to Asians for War."

117. Kasahara, "Sensō kōteiron, menzairon no kiseki to genzai," pp. 2–3.

118. Fujioka, "Sōkan no ji."

119. Shōji, "Senjika no Nihon wa 'fashizumu?'"; Satō, "Rekishi no naka no kokusaihō: 'shinryaku' 'shinryaku sensō'"; Andō, "'Sensō o torae naosu bunken annai."

120. Fujioka and Nishio, *Kokumin no yudan: rekishi kyōkasho ga abunai,* p. 1.

121. Tawara, *Kyōkasho kōgeki no shinsō,* pp. 170–72.

122. Fujioka and Nishio, *Kokumin no yudan,* pp. 212–14.

123. Regarding the debate about history guidelines for teachers in the United States, see Gluck, "History according to Whom: Let the Debate Continue."

124. Regarding war memorials and museums in Japan, see Rekishi kyōikusha kyōgikai, *Heiwa hakubutsukan, sensō shiryōkan handobukku.* This book discusses eighty-six war memorials in Japan and thirteen abroad. These war memorials are often visited by elementary, junior high, and high school pupils on field trips. For example, approximately twenty-five thousand students visit the Ōkunoshima Poison Gas Museum every year (Murakami, *Dokugasutō no rekishi,* p. 2). More than half a million students visit the Nagasaki Atomic Bomb Museum annually (Kamata, "Nagasaki genbaku shiryōkan no kagai tenji mondai," p. 22). For revisionist challenges, see Tawara, *Dokyumento "ianfu" mondai to kyōkasho kōgeki,* pp. 87–88. The Ōkunoshima Poison Gas Museum was opened on Ōkunoshima Island, Hiroshima, in 1988. The museum exhibits documents and photographs proving Japan's use of chemical weapons on the Chinese front. In 1991 the three-story "Peace Osaka" was founded and began showing exhibits that included Japanese atrocities in China, Korea, and other parts of Asia. Ritsumeikan University's International Peace Museum opened in Kyoto in 1992. In 1994 an east wing was added to the Hiroshima Peace Memorial Museum to house artifacts from the Meiji period to the Shōwa period, including evidence of Japanese aggression in China. Two years later the renovated Nagasaki Atomic Bomb Museum opened; its exhibits include a section called "The War between China and Japan and the Pacific War."

To understand why Fujioka was offended by these museums that included Japanese atrocities, see his "GHQ ni wasuresaserareta 'Tōkyō daikūshū.'" Fujioka urged readers to mourn victims of the Allied air raids on Tokyo rather than spending tax money to build "masochistic" museums. Ian Buruma discusses the museum of the Yasukuni Shrine, Peace Osaka, and Ristumeikan University's International Peace Museum in his *Wages of Guilt,* pp. 202–38.

125. Leading scholars, mostly Japanese and Chinese historians, and peace activists have contributed articles to the journal. Back issues are

available from the Center. As of March 1999 twenty-two issues have been published. Each issue has a particular focus: no. 1, the "comfort women"; no. 2, Unit 731; no. 3, inhumane treatment of POWs; no. 4, the "comfort women"; no. 5, chemical and biological warfare; no. 6, Germany and war responsibility; no. 7, war compensation by foreign countries; no. 8, the Fifteen-Year War; no. 9, Japanese POW policies during the war; no. 10, postwar compensation and reparation; no. 11, the world and the fiftieth anniversary of the end of World War II; no. 12, the annexation of Korea; no. 13, war and violence against women; no. 14, freedom of historical documents and war exhibitions; no. 15, the critique of "Liberal Historical View," part 1; no. 16, the critique of "Liberal Historical View," part 2; no. 17, the critique of "Liberal Historical View," part 3; no. 18, the "comfort women"; no. 19, the "comfort women"; no 20, recent lawsuits demanding compensation; no. 21, antiwar movements by Japanese soldiers in China during the Japan-China War; no. 22, war museums and monuments.

126. Aitani, "Sengo hoshō saiban no genjō to kadai," pp. 2–3.

127. Onodera, "Sengo hoshō saiban tōsō no kadai to tenbō," p. 12.

128. Watanabe Noboru, "Sensō, sengo sekinin o tou 731 butaiten o kaisai shite," p. 57.

129. Kamata, "Genbaku shiryōkan de nani o manabu ka," p. 63. Kamata is aware of the criticism that the museum exhibits too little about Japanese aggression in China compared to other museums such as Peace Osaka and Ritsumeikan University's International Peace Museum. Yet he disagrees with the view that the devastation of Nagasaki and the sufferings elsewhere in Asia should be seen on completely equal terms. He believes that it is cruel for residents of Nagasaki to be singled out as representatives of Japanese aggression rather than as living testimony to the inhumanity of the atomic bomb (p. 67). Kamata notes that it was the wartime Japanese government and military—not the people of Nagasaki, including Koreans, Chinese, and Allied POWs—who made the decision to go to war and who destroyed the lives of people in Asia as well as in Japan. He argues that it is the Japanese government, not the people of Nagasaki, who should be held responsible for Japanese wartime aggression and atrocities in Asia (p. 67).

130. Koyama, "Piisu Ōsaka e no uyoku no kōgeki," pp. 42–43. Peace Osaka was opened to the public in 1991.

131. See its op-ed piece titled "Heiwa ga miemasu ka."

132. See, for instance, Kariya, "Kōmori o ute!" The cartoon claims that Etō's brain became feeble and that he repeated the same thing over and over through an entire decade. By contrast, Kobayashi Yoshinori, also a cartoonist, often makes fun of progressives such as Yoshimi Yoshiaki, Nishino Rumiko, and others in his *Shin gomanizumu sengen 3.*

133. See, for example, Yoshimi and Suzuki, "Kōshōron ni hantai suru: Nihongun 'ianfu' mondai no honshitsu to wa"; Komagome, "'Jiyū shugi shikan' wa watashitachi o 'jiyū' ni suru no ka?"

134. See, for instance, Kasahara, *Ajia no naka no Nihongun: sensō sekinin to rekishigaku, rekishi kyōiku;* Fujiwara et al., *Kingendai shi no shinjitsu wa nanika;* Ienaga et al., *Kyōkasho kara kesenai sensō no shinjitsu: rekishi o yugameru Fujioka Nobukatsu shi ra e no hihan;* Tawara, *Dokyumento "ianfu" mondai to kyōkasho kōgeki;* Yoshida, *Gendai rekishigaku to sensō sekinin.* All of these books are specifically aimed at refuting Fujioka and his allies.

135. See, for instance, Fuji, *"Nankin daigyakusatsu" wa kōshite tsukurareta.* For articles or book chapters see, for instance, Itakura, "'Nankin daigyakusatsu 20 man' setsu e no hanshō"; Higashinakano Osamichi, "Rekishi no kenkyu ka rekishi no waikyoku ka: Nankin daigyakusatsuron no kansei"; Fujioka, "'Nankin daigyakusatsu 30 man' no uso."

136. Nankin jiken chōsa kenkyūkai, *Nankin jiken shiryoshū,* 2 vols.

137. Kasahara, *Nankin nanminku no hyakunichi,* p.71.

138. Ono et al., *Nankin daigyakusatsu o kiroku shita kōgun heishitachi,* pp. xvii, 378–82.

139. Kasahara, *Nankin jiken,* p. 215.

140. Ibid., p. 228. The death toll recorded in battlefield reports kept by the Japanese army divisions and in the official navy reports are included in the book (pp. 224–25).

141. Daqing Yang discusses this point in the next chapter.

142. See the summary of Ienaga's lawsuits in *Yomiuri shinbun,* August 30, 1987, p. 11. The court ordered the government to pay Ienaga 400,000 yen (approximately $3,400).

143. Kobayashi, "Shin gomanizumu sengen," p. 74.

144. These children collected recyclable materials valued at 134,000 yen in order to finance the monument. See Kusawake, "'Tannaka heiwa no hi' wa watashitachi no atarashii dai ippo."

145. Yamada, "Arata na kyōkasho kōgeki no haikei ni aru mono," p. 29.

146. Hata Ikuhiko, *Shōwa shi no nazo o ou,* p. 132.

147. Fujioka and Nishio, *Kokumin no yudan,* p. 213. Fujioka does not provide the sources from which he cites.

148. Higashinakano Osamichi, "Rekishi no kenkyū ka rekishi no waikyoku ka," pp. 44–45. See especially p. 45, n. 27.

149. Watanabe, "Nankin daigyakusatsu wa nakatta," p. 183;Tanaka Masaaki, *"Nankin gyakusatsu" no kyokō,* p. 314.

150. See, for instance, Tanaka Masaaki, *"Nankin gyakusatsu" no kyokō,* pp. 312–14.

151. Aoki shoten and Azuma lost the case in the Tokyo District Court in 1996, and the case has been appealed. In his book Azuma portrayed the plaintiff as putting a Chinese person in a mail bag, pouring gasoline on him, and burning him. Azuma failed to convince the court that the reference was accurate.

152. See, for instance, Fujioka and Nishio, *Kokumin no yudan,* pp. 1–2, 241–44.

153. Ibid., p. 174.

154. Fujioka, *Ojoku no kingendai shi,* pp. 140, 144.

155. *"Kingendai shi" no jugyō kaikaku* 1 (September 1995): 120.

156. Interview with Tanaka Masaaki on June 16, 1996.

157. Kitsukawa, *Nihon wa shinryaku koku de wa nai,* pp. 280–82.

158. Ibid., pp. 278–79.

159. Fujio, "'Hogen daijin' futatabi hoeru," pp. 110, 124.

160. Okuno, "'Shinryaku hatsugen' doko ga warui," pp. 112–13.

161. Kasahara, *Ajia no naka no Nihongun,* pp. 252–53.

162. Yoshida et al., *Haisen zengo: Shōwa tennō to gonin no shidōsha,* pp. 8–10.

163. Yoshida, *Gendai rekishigaku to sensō sekinin,* pp. 247–49.

164. Ienaga, *Sensō sekinin,* pp. 309–11, 396.

165. See, for instance, Satō, *Kenpō kyūjō, shinryaku sensō, Tōkyō saiban,* p. 94.

166. Tanaka Masaaki, *Tōkyō Saiban to wa nanika,* pp. 5–7.

167. Ibid., pp. 8–14.

168. Satō, *Kenpō kyūjō, shinryaku sensō, Tōkyō saiban,* pp. 84, 86–87, 89.

169. Fujio, "'Hōgen daijin' ōi ni hoeru."

170. Kristof, "Many in Japan Oppose Apology to Asians for War"; Okuno, "'Shinryaku hatsugen' doko ga warui," pp. 120–21.

171. Fujiwara, "Rekishi no bōkyaku wa yurusarenai," pp. 250–53.

172. Awaya, *Tōkyō saiban ron,* p. 158.

173. Awaya, *Miketsu no sensō sekinin,* p. 42. Sheldon Harris's *Factories of Death: Japanese Biological Warfare, 1932–45, and the American Cover-up* provides detailed analysis of this matter.

174. Ienaga, "The Historical Significance of the Tokyo Trial," p. 168.

175. Awaya, "'Tōkyō saiban shikan' to wa," p. 165.

176. Ienaga, "The Historical Significance of the Tokyo Trial," pp. 168–69.

177. See, for instance, Kasahara, *Ajia no naka no Nihongun,* p. 252; Hora, Fujiwara, and Honda, *Nankin daigyakusatsu no kenkyū,* pp. 3–6.

178. See, for instance, Nankin jiken chōsa kenkyūkai, *Nankin jiken shiryōshū.*

179. Regarding Chang's outrage at the revisionist denials, see, for

instance, Chang, *The Rape of Nanking,* pp. 12–13. Rabe, *Nankin no shinjitsu,* includes Rabe's diaries from September 21, 1937, through February 28, 1938.

180. Some sixty scholars from China, Japan, and the United States attended the latter conference and visited the sites where the massacres took place.

181. Yang, "A Sino-Japanese Controversy," p. 25.

182. For instance, films such as *Magee's Testament* and *In the Name of the Emperor,* as well as a pictorial book titled *The Rape of Nanking* are available from the organization.

183. See, for instance, Yin and Shi, *The Rape of Nanking: An Undeniable History in Photographs;* Hong, *Riben zai Hua baoxing lu,* pp. 239–67.

184. Chang, *The Rape of Nanking,* p. 4.

185. Pritchard, *The Tokyo War Crimes Trial,* vol. 20, p. 49608.

186. According to Japanese school textbooks, a total of ten million people died in China during World War II. See, for instance, International Society for Educational Information (ISEI), *Japan in Modern History: Primary School,* pp. 216–17; ISEI, *Japan in Modern History: Junior High School,* pp. 352–23. According to the Chinese official figure prior to May 1995, 21.6 million casualties (9.325 million deaths, 9.47 million wounded, 2.89 million missing) occurred between 1937 and 1945. After 1995, when Prime Minister Murayama Tomiichi visited China, the figure of 35 million casualties (the number of deaths is unknown) between 1931 and 1945 replaced the former figure. See Ishii, "Sengo Nit-Chū kankei no kiseki," p. 96.

187. Kobayashi, "Shin gomanizumu sengen," chap. 37, p. 73.

188. Fujioka Nobukatsu stressed that neither China nor the United States was using textbooks that emphasized its own atrocities. See Fujioka and Nishio, *Kokumin no yudan,* p. 2.

189. "Jijitsu gonin o Eibun de shiteki," *Sankei shinbun,* evening edition, April 13, 1998. The *Sankei* carried many articles that stressed Chang's "distortions" of the Nanjing Massacre and her use of the incident as a political tool for extracting an apology and compensation from Japan. See, for instance, "Nihon seifu e no hoshō motomeru hōan o shiji," *Sankei shinbun,* May 9, 1998; "'Reipu obu Nankin' . . . shōko nashi? sōsaku? arata ni 3 mai giwaku shashin," *Sankei shinbun,* May 15, 1998; "'Reipu obu Nankin' 2 nen mae, dō taitoru shashinshū," *Sankei shinbun,* evening edition, May 25, 1998.

190. Nakamura, *Dai tō-A sensō e no michi,* pp. 452–56.

191. Iris Chang's speech at the Gun Tong Gung restaurant, Flushing, New York, on June 28, 1998. Chang was a guest speaker at the welcoming dinner for the Delegation of 21 from Japan, including lawyers,

scholars, and World War II veterans, who were supporting ongoing lawsuits in Japan with regard to Unit 731, the Nanjing Massacre, and forced labor and relocation, among other matters.

192. Uesugi Satoshi, "'Ianfu' mondai no shinkyokumen," p. 36.

193. See, for instance, David Chen, "Nazi Was Humanitarian to Chinese, War Diary Reveals"; David Chen, "At the Rape of Nanking: A Nazi Who Saved Lives."

194. Efron, "Defender of Japan's War Past."

195. Hata Ikuhiko, "Nankin daigyakusatsu 'Rābe kōka' o sokutei suru," p. 80.

196. Uesugi, "'Ianfu' mondai no shinkyokumen," p. 33.

197. Information acquired from Tawara Yoshifumi on January 4, 1997. Also see ibid.

198. Brzezinski, *Out of Control,* p. 17.

199. Hirsch, *Genocide and the Politics of Memory: Studying Death to Preserve Life,* p. 5.

200. Rabe, *Nankin no shinjitsu,* p. 246.

4

The Challenges of the Nanjing Massacre

Reflections on Historical Inquiry

DAQING YANG

More than a decade ago, a debate about the Nazi Holocaust broke out in West Germany. The "historian's debate"—known as *Historikerstreit*—began when the noted philosopher Jürgen Habermas challenged the attempts by several historians to compare and even link the Nazi crimes with other mass atrocities. Even though largely confined to West Germany, the *Historikerstreit* drew considerable attention from historians and commentators abroad. Because the controversy took place in a politically charged atmosphere, in part because of President Ronald Reagan's controversial visit to the German military cemetery at Bitburg where some SS soldiers were also buried, many were quick to grasp its political and moral implications.[1] A number of historians even regarded it as a political battle that has generated "more heat than light."[2]

The *Historikerstreit* and the new wave of writings on the Holocaust in recent decades have paralleled an ongoing discussion among historians and literary theorists in the United States about the nature of historical consciousness and historical judgment. The title of Peter Novick's 1988 book, *That Noble*

Dream: The "Objectivity Question" and the American Historical Profession, aptly captures the essence of historians' struggle in recent decades to redefine their professional inquiry, especially after the so-called linguistic turn.[3] The Holocaust historian Saul Friedländer was among the first to perceive a critical link between these two different debates. To him, the debate about the new interpretations of Hitler's Final Solution in history seems to test implicit boundaries and raise not only aesthetic and intellectual issues, but moral ones as well.[4] Indeed, as a number of recent works on the *Historikerstreit* point out, this contentious debate has also raised serious questions about writing history, especially the history of major traumatic events.[5] Bringing together specialists from two hitherto largely unconnected fields, Friedländer convened a three-day conference in 1990 to explore, among other themes, the "limits of representation" regarding the Holocaust. As many of the conference participants have demonstrated, the Holocaust poses an intellectual as well as a moral challenge for the entire historical profession, which has been searching for a new identity.

In recent years the Asia Pacific region has also been witnessing a number of bitter debates about the events of World War II. For example, the so-called military comfort women—a euphemism for forced wartime sexual slavery in the Japanese military—became the subject of a heated controversy that has engulfed activists, politicians, and historians alike. The equally contentious debate about the Japanese atrocities in Nanjing, which first erupted in the 1970s, has become the one of the longest-running historical controversies in East Asia. Such a contentious and prolonged debate about recent history has often been described as another old politico-ideological battle between the progressives (or the Left) and the conservatives (or the Right) in Japan, or as a conflict between Japan and its Asian neighbors. Such characterizations are not wrong. Indeed, the political and ideological aspects of these controversies are extremely important and deserve careful analysis in their own right, a task the other chapters in this volume as well as my own earlier work have all tried to accomplish.[6]

There are also other important issues at stake, however, that cannot be addressed by political analysis alone. The debate about the Nanjing Massacre has raised urgent questions about historical methodology and the nature of historical knowledge, about the place of politics and moral judgment within historical inquiry, and, at the level of practice, about the possibility of a shared historical understanding that transcends national divisions. In this sense, the event known as the Nanjing Massacre also poses great challenges that no serious historian can afford to ignore.

This chapter is part of an ongoing attempt to confront these problematic issues as reflected in the recent Japanese, Chinese, and, to a lesser extent, American writings on the Nanjing Massacre. My examination is not limited to the works of professional historians, since many influential writers on this subject are journalists and freelance writers. I do believe that we who are professional historians have a greater responsibility, however, not just because our work tends to carry an aura of authority, but also because our professional craft is at stake. Therefore, what concerns me most here is not so much individual writers or the specific politico-ideological stance they represent but the historical agendas and approaches, both explicit and implicit, in the contending positions as well as their implications for historical inquiry in general.

To discuss the Nanjing Massacre in connection with the Holocaust, it should be made clear at the outset, is neither to conflate the two fundamentally different historical events nor to suggest that the two debates parallel each other. Instead I contend that the debate about the Nanjing Massacre has raised many issues similar to those encountered in studying the Holocaust.[7] To better understand the debate about the Nanjing Massacre, it is therefore necessary to situate it in the wider discourse about the nature and function of historical inquiry. Even though there may not be easy solutions to the challenges discussed in this chapter, a fruitful way of working toward some answers, I would suggest, is to learn from the ongoing efforts of historians wrestling with the Holocaust and its representations. Likewise, the debate about the Nanjing Massacre should be of concern to historians elsewhere because, like the debate about the Holocaust in Europe, it has implications beyond the narrow confines of regional history.

The Methodological Challenge

At the methodological level the event known as the Nanjing Massacre poses a considerable epistemological challenge for historians. Even a casual observer cannot fail to notice the ubiquitous presence of terms such as *historical facts* or *truth* in nearly every piece of Japanese and Chinese writing on the subject.[8] If "facts" and "truth" are indeed everyone's concern in this debate, why are they so hard to come by? Despite the proliferation of publications on the Nanjing Massacre in Japan and China over the past decades, few historians involved have paused to ponder the more fundamental questions: What is historical truth? Who is entitled to such truth? What is the relationship between the historian, historical evidence, and historical event?[9] Significantly, it is Ueno Chizuko, a noted sociologist and feminist scholar in Japan, who has made the sharpest critique of the prevailing positivist historical methodology in her analysis of the controversy about the so-called military comfort women. As protagonists on both sides of the "comfort women" debate argue about the level of empirical research, she contends, the collapse of an ideologically inspired historical inquiry seems to be followed by a return to "foolish historical empiricism."[10]

By contrast, questions concerning historical evidence and truth have engaged many historians in the West. Some claim that there is no such thing as even a bare minimum of incontrovertible historical facts and, as a result, there are no "facts" but only "interpretations." This view is certainly not wrong, in the sense that historical facts, even if they exist, cannot speak for themselves; historians (in the broadest sense) do. As R. G. Collingwood paraphrased Benedetto Croce more than half a century ago, events in the past become historically known only when they "vibrate in the historian's mind."[11] In recent decades the characterization of historical inquiry has undergone profound changes, in large part because of the influence of postmodernism. Historians are reminded that language itself imposes a limit on the representation of any experience in the past. Casting profound doubts on the commonly assumed unproblematic correspondence between evidence (text) and reality, the postmodernist critique of positivist historiography has raised many legitimate questions about historians' often privileged claim to truth in history.

The tendency to deny any correspondence between history and reality, however, as Friedländer and other participants at the 1990 conference have pointed out, can have disturbing implications, especially when applied to an event like the Holocaust. An extreme case of mass criminality such as the extermination of the Jews in Europe, they argue, challenges theoreticians of historical relativism to face the corollaries of positions otherwise too easily dealt with on an abstract level. Namely, if an event in history is open to any kind of "emplotment," as has been suggested, does that mean that Holocaust denial, in the theoretical sense, is just as valid as other interpretations? An interpretation falls into the category of a lie Hayden White has in fact argued "when it denies the reality of the events of which it treats, and into the category of untruth when it draws false conclusions from reflection on events whose reality remains attestable on the level of 'positive' historical inquiry."[12] It is significant that even White, arguably the most important historian under the influence of postmodernism, not only recognizes the reality of historical events but also accepts positive historical inquiry as of some use in attesting to them. At the same time, many others have come to emphasize the need to problematize the process of historical inquiry itself before we can reach a better understanding of past events. In the words of James E. Young, a literary scholar who has studied various forms of Holocaust representations, historical inquiry should be made into "the combined study of both *what happened* and *how it is passed down to us.*"

> In this way, historical inquiry might remain a search for certainties about substantial realities, even as it is broadened to encompass the realities of history's eventual transmission. Extended backward into the notion of history "as it happened," such a conception includes as part of its search for veritable fact the search for veritable, yet highly contingent, representations of these facts as they unfolded.[13]

Thus, before we answer those questions concerning the truth of the Nanjing Massacre, historians need to take a harder look at the much reified process of empirical research itself. Both the evidence itself and the ways historians represent the event should be subject to critical examination.

Problems of Evidence

History is a discipline whose very existence depends on evidence. Even when there is no doubt that an event itself was real, historical inquiry requires historians to gain knowledge of such a historical reality through reconstruction based on their evidence. This is as true of the realities of the Nanjing Massacre as of other historical events. For instance, exactly how many Chinese—both civilians and soldiers—were in Nanjing and its vicinity when the city fell on December 13, 1937, is both real and definite, but this reality is not easily intelligible to a historian.[14] In an ideal situation in the Rankean tradition, the historian gathers all evidence, sifts through it, and draws the most logical conclusion. This is rarely how it works in practice. In studying the Nanjing Massacre, historians have to work under less than perfect conditions as far as sources are concerned. To illustrate this point, it is helpful to see that the evidence on the Nanjing Massacre generally originates from three main sources: bystanders, victims, and perpetrators. Each category poses a different kind of epistemological challenge to the historian.

Accounts by bystanders—foreign correspondents who broke the news to the world and foreign nationals in the International Safety Zone in Nanjing who kept records of the Japanese atrocities—were the earliest source. Although the reports by A. T. Steele and Tillman Durdin appeared in the *Chicago Daily News* and *New York Times* less than a week after the Japanese troops occupied the city, some records by bystanders came to light only recently, as in the case of John Rabe's diary.[15] Many reports filed by Rabe's International Safety Zone Committee to the Japanese authorities in Nanjing as well as the private correspondence of its members were published in 1938 by *Manchester Guardian* correspondent Harold Timperley.[16] It is essentially through this early body of information that the world came to know of the widespread Japanese atrocities in Nanjing. As third-party observers these individuals provided convincing reports of the brutality and damage inflicted by the Japanese troops, and in some cases by Chinese soldiers. But this type of evidence also has its limitations: Durdin and other foreign journalists had departed from the city by December 15. The remaining two dozen or so Westerners—largely confined to the Safety Zone—witnessed only a fraction of what actually happened afterwards in a larger area with hundreds of thousands of residents.[17]

Next came the victims' accounts. Here the historian is confronted with a major difficulty: in a strict sense, many victims by definition have left no voices, if we are talking about those men and women who perished in and around Nanjing. Only a few survivors made it out of Nanjing in the next several months, and some of their hellish experiences became the first Chinese accounts that appeared in Chinese-language newspapers.[18] The majority of the survivors of the Nanjing Massacre, however, had to remain in the occupied city for nearly eight years before it was no longer dangerous to openly talk of Japanese atrocities. The Military Tribunals in Tokyo and Nanjing after the war made it possible for the first time for the surviving victims to bear witness in public. Even then, not all surviving victims were eager to recount their sufferings, even when called upon by the Nationalist government to provide evidence in support of the prosecution of several Japanese officers for crimes in Nanjing. Rape victims and their relatives, in particular, were reluctant to come forward. An October 1946 government survey of Japanese crimes committed in the Nanjing Massacre recorded only thirty-six cases of rape and rape-murder, compared to more than 2,700 cases of other crimes.[19]

In the People's Republic of China, although a few survivors were interviewed in the 1950s and 1960s, the government largely kept their stories out of the public domain. Significantly, one of the early efforts to gather victims' accounts was the extensive interviews with the survivors of the Nanjing Massacre and other Japanese war crimes in China by the Japanese reporter Honda Katsuichi in 1971. Having made the pursuit of Japanese war crimes a life mission, Honda went on to publish another book in 1987, presenting more Chinese accounts of Japanese atrocities based on his additional interviews in the lower Yangtze River area along the route of the Japanese attack.[20] Systematic collection of victims' accounts as historical evidence in the PRC did not begin in earnest until the 1980s, more than forty years after the event. Two citywide surveys in Nanjing, conducted in 1984 and 1990 respectively, located more than 1,700 survivors.[21] Among them, 176 were reported to have survived Japanese atrocities with scars still on their bodies, 514 lost relatives, and forty-four women were raped by Japanese soldiers.[22] Some of this testimony was published in 1985 for the first time as part of the *Source Material Relating to the Horrible Massacre Committed by the Japanese Troops in Nanjing.*[23] In 1994, a greater number of victims' accounts—642 in all—were published as a separate book edited by the director of the Nanjing Massacre Memorial.[24]

Last, with few exceptions the perpetrators' own stories did not appear until well after the war.[25] Japan's strict wartime censorship prevented first-hand information on the Japanese army's brutal behavior from trickling back into Japan, although some returning soldiers bragged about their exploits in Nanjing. Although the Allied forces collected a vast number of the Japanese documents spared from destruction immediately after the war for the Military Tribunal in Tokyo, few of them pertained directly to the Japanese operations in Nanjing. During the 1950s and 1960s, a few Japanese veterans who had been in Nanjing began to recount their experiences, sometimes in an effort to discredit the verdicts of the Military Tribunals.[26] In fact, the appearance of written accounts by Japanese officers and soldiers as well as military documents is a relatively recent and perhaps the most significant development in terms of historical evidence since the postwar Tribunals.

Even long after the event, evidence does not always emerge automatically, but often as a result of the unrelenting efforts of citizen groups and concerned individuals. For instance, Ono Kenji, a factory worker who became interested in the subject, spent several years locating diaries and journals among Japanese veterans in the Fukushima area who had participated in the battle of Nanjing.[27] Many such newly unearthed Japanese accounts provide important insight into the behavior and psychology of the ordinary rank-and-file soldiers and, in some cases, of high-ranking commanders.[28] However, even the best efforts have so far located less than 30 percent of all the military records of the various Japanese battalions that had participated in the battle in Nanjing.[29] Certain key officers such as Colonel Chō Isamu, who is believed by some to have issued the order in the name of General Matsui Iwane to kill all Chinese prisoners, left no paper trail. Published sources say almost nothing about whether Prince Asaka, one of the highest-ranking Japanese commanders in Nanjing, knew about these atrocities being perpetrated by troops under his command or whether he issued the order.

Written evidence is therefore far from complete. Moreover, in attempting to reconstruct and to understand traumatic events in recent history, historians have to acknowledge a major limitation of their enterprise—our still-poor understanding of how human memory functions. The historical profession, especially since the late nineteenth century, has emphasized the centrality of written records. Political and military historians, in particular, often revere official documents as the "primary sources," considering them more faithful and closer to the "historical reality" than other types of historical evidence. Although the development of oral history methods in recent decades has corrected such a disciplinary bias to some extent, the inherent problems in such new methodology are by no means easily resolved.

Here historians need to confront the issue of how to evaluate human memory as credible historical evidence, since it has cast a shadow over the debates about World War II in Asia. Inevitably, much of the Chinese evidence of the Nanjing Massacre was reminiscences of survivors. Not surprisingly, Honda's shocking presentation of Chinese survivors' accounts in 1972 invited immediate attacks on his methodology. He was accused of presenting the Chinese side of the story uncritically. Since then, any discrepancies in these postwar testimonies have been seized upon by some in Japan as evidence of the fabrication of the Nanjing Massacre. Such accusations are not all without factual merit: the count of 57,418 victims in one mass execution in Nanjing by a single Chinese survivor may raise legitimate doubts in the minds of inquisitive historians. However, Honda's accusers often fail to acknowledge that many other survivors have more than just words to tell of their experiences. Li Xiuying, who was pregnant in December 1937, resisted rape by Japanese soldiers and for that she suffered multiple stab wounds and was left for dead. Her condition was recorded on film by one of the American missionaries in Nanjing. Miraculously, she not only survived but, with scars all over her body, also became one of the most effective living witnesses to the Japanese atrocities in Nanjing. Li's case may be exceptional, for she had film footage and scars to support her credibility as a witness. But how can the thousands who had neither withstand the accusation of fabrication?

Quite a few Japanese authors writing on this subject are well aware of the problems involved and have been struggling with this issue as well. When his historian colleagues pointed to the limits and fluidity of oral testimonies, Honda reminded them of the bias of written records and proposed that the investigator should start with a "blank sheet" instead of some kind of logical assumption in order to recreate a certain historical scene. Even with this method, he noted, at best it was the "subjective fact" from the perspective of the witness. While there may be a "correct fact"—which cannot be refuted and does not contradict itself—ultimately there is no such thing as a purely "objective fact."[30] Others have pointed out that the issue here is not whether the testimonies of Chinese victims were all iron-clad "facts." Emphasizing the difference between the event, language of the event, and human language, one Japanese writer points out that human language—namely, the language of the testimonies—is woefully inadequate in representing an event such as the Nanjing Massacre. In this sense, survivors speak not to historians of the present, but toward events in the past.[31]

The problem of memory for historical inquiry is far from being unique to the study of the Nanjing Massacre. Ueno Chizuko rightly considers the evaluation of victims' testimony of central importance in the discussion of the "comfort women" question, since written evidence, if any still remains, sheds little light on whether or not these women were taken by force. Western scholars have found memory is often quite resilient after years of repression, but it also is subject to distortion, both willful and unconscious. Historian Michael Kammen further notes that not all distortions are cynical in nature, emphasizing that distortion or even manipulation does not always, or inevitably, occur for cynical or hypocritical reasons.[32] Many Holocaust scholars are wrestling with similar issues in historical methodology. At Friedländer's conference, historian Carlo Ginsburg made a passionate plea for truth and reality by evoking the scenario of "just one witness." Citing different rules and epistemological foundations, he pointed out the danger of transferring legal principles into historical research. Unlimited skepticism toward historical narratives, even if they are based on one sole survivor, he argued, is therefore groundless.[33] Others are searching for a place for the understanding of the witness, as subjective and skewed as it may be, for a larger historical understanding of events. Rather than dismiss personal reminiscence on the grounds of factual discrepancy or incoherence, James E. Young calls upon historians to "integrate both the *factual truths* of the historian's narrative and the *contingent truths* of the victims' memory, both deep and common." In this way, he suggests, "no single, overarching meaning emerges unchallenged; instead, narrative and counter-narrative generate a frisson of meaning in their exchange, in the working through process they now mutually reinforce."[34] In other words, historians need to reconsider the nature of historical reality: without abandoning their critical stand toward all historical evidence, they need to give a voice to those who experienced it first-hand.

Burden of Proof

Even the access to all available evidence does not automatically guarantee the most accurate representation, Reconstructing a historical event is not the same as simply adding up all available evidence like a jigsaw puzzle, since the historian needs to create a structure to make sense of the evidence. Here, too, historians must look at the constraints on their enterprise.

Historians' ability to reconstruct past realities is severely limited by language itself. In fact, this lies at the heart of the postmodernist critique of positivist historiography. Historical reality is inherently infinite and opaque, just as experience of that reality is always complex. Representation of reality and experience through the historian's narrative, however well crafted, is bound to be incomplete and to have a distorting effect. The lack of agreement on what the events of 1937 should be called is one reflection of the linguistic problem. The term *Nanjing Massacre,* primarily used in China but also in Japan and elsewhere, reveals as much as it limits the event in Nanjing. Does a massacre slight rape, pillage, or arson? Was it a massacre or a Great Massacre?[35] The term *Nanjing Incident,* on the other hand, has been used in Japan by writers of different persuasions, but it invites much criticism elsewhere for making the horror of 1937 sound mundane.

Moreover, the historian faces the problematic relationship between the fragmentary evidence and the holistic truth, between historical details and master narratives. Some historians would adopt a precise narrative description of the unfolding events so that it carries its own interpretation. Christopher Browning's mind-numbingly detailed study of one murderous German police unit during the Holocaust, as has been pointed out, is meant to intuitively substantiate an interpretative framework that extents far beyond the history of one particular event.[36] Not everyone can be satisfied with such a strategy, however. Those who deny the Nanjing Massacre may insist that even if all evidence "demonstrate[s] individual atrocities, no one can prove the 'great massacre.'"[37]

On the other hand, many Chinese writings tend to emphasize the Nanjing Massacre as an act of Japanese militarism and aggression in a sort of "master narrative" without defining all of its necessary elements or paying careful attention to historical particularities.[38] Faithfully accounting for every bit of historical detail is no easy task, if it is possible at all. The historian may happen to believe that the truth of an event is bigger than the sum of its parts. Raoul Hilberg, who wrote the first documentary history of the Holocaust, poignantly asks the rhetorical question: "Is it not equally barbaric to write footnotes after Auschwitz?"[39] In some cases, the individual piece of evidence may lose its centrality to the master narrative. For instance, one may feel perfectly justified in using a photograph of a similar execution scene in another part of China or of victims of Japanese aerial bombing in a different city as evidence of the Nanjing Massacre in exhibitions, on the ground that the message about the brutality of Japanese aggression remains the same. Such a practice, however, brings about the danger of misinterpreting actual historical evidence.

Even photographic evidence, as many professional historians have come to realize, can be especially fraught with danger if its origins cannot be ascertained. Kimijima Kazuhiko, a Japanese historian studying the Nanjing Massacre, has included a cautionary note about the use of photographic evidence in a textbook on historical sources for Japanese college students. The photograph in question, depicting Japanese soldiers beheading a Chinese, was among those taken by Japanese soldiers themselves and developed in a photo shop in Nanjing sometime between 1937 and 1939. Almost incredibly, a Chinese clerk working in the shop secretly made an extra set of prints, which were hidden until the end of the war and then admitted as evidence no. 1 at the Nanjing Tribunal. The story of these pictures as well as the photographs themselves were featured in many recent Chinese publications. Kimijima and his Japanese colleagues who have long argued that the Massacre did happen doubt whether this particular photograph actually depicted a scene of the Japanese atrocities in Nanjing during the winter of 1937–38, since all the Japanese soldiers in the photograph were in their summer uniforms. Kimijima used this example to emphasize that before a photograph can be used as reliable historical evidence, its photographer, location, and time must be ascertained.[40] Kimijima's caution may seem excessive to some, but it is more understandable in view of the contentious debate within Japan. By contrast, such scrupulousness is often lacking in many photographic works on the Nanjing Massacre published in China and the United States. In fact, it is only recently that a few historians in China have taken up the somewhat thankless task of pointing out factual mistakes or discrepancies in some Chinese publications.[41]

Although responsible historians should not give up empirical assiduousness or abdicate their duty to expose falsehood, a simple positivist approach can produce a fetish of facts. A form of misguided empiricism among some historians is the unquestioned privileging of official—in many cases Japanese—documents. In extreme cases, it develops into what David Fischer has called "the fallacy of negative proof."[42] Watanabe Shōichi, a professor and frequent commentator on the subject, is one such practitioner. The fact that he did not learn about the Nanjing Massacre during the war and that the Shōwa emperor did not refer to it in his famous 1946 soliloquy, Watanabe argues, were both proofs that the Massacre was fabricated at the postwar trials.[43] Ara Ken'ichi's book is another example of taking denials by some Japanese witnesses or participants as proof that large-scale atrocities did not happen at all.[44] Such an erroneous assumption is also the underlying logic in the writings of Higashinakano Osamichi, a professor of intellectual history and the author of the most recent attempt to prove that the Nanjing Massacre is a latter-day fabrication. For example, he reasoned that since some fourteen Americans in Nanjing did not mention incidents of Japanese soldiers shooting Chinese civilians in one report to the American embassy, such alleged acts must not have happened. Similarly, the fact that the Nanjing Massacre was not mentioned in many contemporary English or Chinese publications in 1938 can lead to only one conclusion, according to him: "It was not recorded because it did not happen."[45] It is a legitimate question to ask why an event was not recorded or known at the time, and many historians have analyzed, among other things, Japanese censorship.[46] It is puzzling, however, how a scholar of intellectual history can refuse to acknowledge the existence of overwhelming incriminating evidence.

How do historians cope with the burden of proof, then? No easy solution seems available. The dialogue initiated by Saul Friedländer seems to have convinced many historians that despite the inherently literary quality of history-writing, history is not literature, in that history tries to deal with something that is real, not fictional.[47] In fact, many students of history are seeking a new and possibly consensual grounding for the already fragile historical venture. They strive to establish a stable truth of events in a decidedly unstable literary form. Although this has not produced consensus on the issue of historical methodology, most historians realize that there is no substitute for vigorous empirical research, a critical evaluation of the evidence, and responsible reappraisal. Because their professional craft is recognized as fragile, a critical awareness of methodology is becoming indispensable. As one of the most observant historians of the Holocaust, Saul Friedländer has called for "the simultaneous acceptance of two contradictory moves: the search for ever closer historical linkage and the avoidance of a naive historical positivism leading to simplistic and self-assured historical narration and closures."[48] Historians studying the Nanjing Massacre would do well to listen to such advice.

Whither Revisionism?

Even if historians have strictly followed the rules of evidence and proof, the historical knowledge they produce is unlikely to remain unchanged forever. It is noteworthy that not all sources became available to all historians or all at once. Inevitably, the availability as well as the nature of these various kinds of evidence have influenced both the historiography and the course of the debate about the Nanjing Massacre. For one thing, the perpetrators' history was delayed, and early histories of the incident produced up to the 1970s almost invariably relied heavily on the evidence presented at the Tokyo Military Tribunals by foreign eyewitnesses or Chinese survivors.[49] For historians to understand how the atrocities took place, there is no alternative but to look closely at perpetrators as well. Such investigation only became truly possible in the 1980s, with the publication of works by Fujiwara Akira, Yoshida Yutaka, and Hata Ikuhiko, among others. By examining Japanese records, incomplete as they were, these historians offered in-depth analysis of the causes of the Japanese atrocities.[50] On the other hand, lack of access to most such Japanese evidence (partly because of language barriers) and a general reliance on Chinese and Western sources have until recently made it difficult for Chinese historians to understand the complexities of Japanese military institutions.

If historical inquiry must be regarded as a process of knowledge, there seem to be three major moments when the Nanjing Massacre became known, though not necessarily to the same audience. This is a consequence not only of the availability of evidence, but also of the dominant concerns of the day—the problematic of historians. The first moment was during the war (1937–45), when Western journalists and others broke the news to the world and wrote about it in their publications. The second was during the postwar Military Tribunals held in Tokyo and Nanjing between 1946 and 1948, at which several Japanese officers were charged with and convicted of atrocities in Nanjing. The third moment, which we are still experiencing, began in Japan more than two decades ago and has now engulfed

China and even many in the United States, largely in response to the growing controversy in Japan.

The point is not which of these moments yields more authentic truth. It is an illusion to consider the wartime version more authentic simply because of its proximity to the event itself. For instance, the "Rape of Nanking" was described at the time as largely confined to the walled city itself. Must historians restrict ourselves to the same geographical area despite more recent discovery of similar atrocities in the vicinity of the city, or if we do not, will the event we describe become something other than the "Rape of Nanking"? It is also naive to privilege the most recent version simply because of the accumulation of new evidence, since all evidence has limits and may yield different answers if historians ask different questions.

The point here is that the process has an effect on our knowledge of the event. It is a truism that all historical writing is the product of a particular moment in time that shapes historians' decisions about what needs to be explained. The postwar Military Tribunals, a major moment for the unfolding knowledge of the Nanjing Massacre, have been criticized for distorting the postwar view of the event. There may well be grounds for such allegations. For example, the fact that the Japanese atrocities in Nanjing have been known in China as the Nanjing Massacre is partly explained by the process of the war crimes investigations conducted by the Nationalist government. There are indications that the Chinese Nationalist regime encountered less difficulty in gathering sufficient evidence to prove massacre than to prove rapes.[51] In the meantime, because only a few Japanese officers were put on trial for the atrocities in Nanjing, the behavior of ordinary soldiers was not subject to close examination. These trials were indeed severely flawed from the perspective of historical inquiry.[52] As Kasahara Tokushi, a leading Japanese scholar with many critical works on the subject, puts it, the Tribunal's case against division commander Tani Hisao, the only high-ranking officer prosecuted in Nanjing, was not entirely convincing on the basis of the evidence presented. If a full investigation of the whole incident were carried out, he rightly suggests, higher-level commanders, army leaders, and even the emperor would have been implicated. Kasahara thus draws a careful distinction between accepting the entire verdict of the Tribunal, on the one hand, and recognizing the facts of the atrocities brought out by the Tribunal, on the other.[53]

Historical understanding is never static. The pool of evidence is unstable. Just as new evidence may appear, some old evidence may prove flawed or even false. New questions have to be asked, and earlier conclusions may need to be challenged, modified, or even reversed. All of this requires that the historian keep an open mind and be prepared to revise his or her presumptions and hypotheses, especially in the face of new evidence. Moreover, the meaning of the past event is not always a constant. In this sense, there is some truth in the saying that each generation writes a different history.

These are the basic tenets of historical training. In the media coverage of the debate, however, the term *revisionism* has usually been associated with those who seek to deny or minimize Japanese atrocities in Nanjing and wartime transgression in general. Indeed, these self-styled "revisionists" are fond of portraying their critics whose works confirmed the atrocity as dogmatic guardians of some outdated "truth." However, such use of the term *revisionism* is misleading. As historian Arno Mayer reminded us, "critical and scrupulous revision is the lifeblood of historical reflection and inquiry."[54] In her work on Holocaust denial, Deborah Lipstadt also pointed to the fundamental difference between revisionism and denial.[55]

Revisionism has received a mixed reception in China. On the one hand, recent research by some Chinese historians shows that some reappraisal is at work. For instance, although they still consider Japanese militarism the most fundamental cause of the massacre, they now recognize that there were also direct and indirect causes that accounted for the particularly massive scale of the atrocities. Among them was the fact that Nanjing was the political center of China, which increased the stakes for both attackers and defenders, and thus the intensity of the battle. In addition, they admit that the poorly organized retreat under the

Chinese commander, General Tang Shengzhi, stranded in Nanjing nearly one hundred thousand Chinese troops, many of whom disappeared into the civilian population.[56] This is an encouraging step in the right direction, but it is just a beginning.

On the other hand, often in an understandable reaction to attempts—both real and perceived—by "revisionists" to whitewash Japan's war crimes in recent history, many Chinese writers have uncritically equated previous conclusions with "historical facts." The verdicts of the Military Tribunals in Nanjing and Tokyo are often quoted in China as confirmation of the crime committed. In particular, the total Chinese death toll in the Nanjing Massacre remains a most guarded subject. The verdict of 300,000 victims, reached by the Military Tribunal in Nanjing in 1946, has become the official Chinese estimate and was inscribed on the wall at the Memorial to the Victims of the Japanese Massacre in Nanjing in 1985. A recent sculpture added to the memorial features the figure in more abstract forms—three columns of six circles. Although figures and symbols are common to all collective remembrance, many have pointed out that the number has been turned into a symbol of the legitimacy of the postwar Tribunals.

From a historiographical point of view, all aspects of the event known as the Nanjing Massacre have to be constantly re-examined, just like any other event in history. Even if a certain conclusion seemed most plausible half a century ago, the new evidence that has come to light in the past several decades should form the basis for re-evaluation. Needless to say, it is much easier to revise the history of seventeenth-century peasant uprisings than that of a recent traumatic event, but there is no alternative to responsible, constant reappraisal. Even with the Holocaust, as Mayer noted, "after fifty years the question is no longer whether or not to reappraise and historicize . . . but rather how to do so responsibly."[57] At the same time, professional historians should be aware that their discipline, by demanding and rewarding constant revision and reinterpretation, might well be subversive to the purpose of commemoration.[58] This logic of historical inquiry can destabilize the much-desired certainty in remembrance.

Given the obvious tension between revision and remembering, historians need to approach such areas with great sensitivity and caution in view of memory's real assailants. This in turn raises the issue of the moral implications of historical inquiry.

The Challenge of Politics and Morality

Critical empirical research remains an indispensable tool of historical scholarship. Contrary to what some historians hope to see, however, it cannot reduce the Nanjing Massacre to a body of incontrovertible facts. Although many historians like to believe that their mission is simply digging up new evidence and ascertaining historical facts, perhaps more important is their task of helping to make sense of the past. Ultimately, veritable facts and pure interpretations do not belong to distinct and separate categories, but evidence and interpretation exist in a continuum in the historian's reconstruction of the historical event. Here the historian does not merely encounter epistemological difficulties, but also faces a moral challenge.

It is now customary to speak of the "politicization of history," by which is usually meant the manipulation of history-writing and memory-making for overt political or ideological purposes. Many historians and critics have expressed repugnance at the fact that the debate about the Nanjing Massacre has become so politicized. The journalist Ian Buruma, who has written about Japanese and German efforts to deal with the wartime past, described the memory of the Nanjing Massacre as "drenched in politics."[59] A prominent Japanese historian of modern China wrote that the debate now reeks of "political odor."[60] However, such apparent indignation, though understandable, should not create an illusion that politics is external to the enterprise of history-writing and memory-making. Indeed, one may ask, is it ever possible to completely purge historiography and memory of politics? In particular, can there ever be a neutral environment to work through the apparently painful memories of a major traumatic event?

In his important analysis of the *Historikerstreit,* historian

Charles Maier addresses the issue of politics as a factor not outside historical inquiry but instead inherent in it. As he puts it, "[Historical] interpretations must simultaneously be *political* interpretations in that they support some beliefs about how power works and dismiss others. But they need not be *politicized* interpretations; they need not be weapons forged for a current ideological contest."[61] This is an important insight, for even if there is value-free science, there is no such thing as value-free historical scholarship. There is more than a kernel of truth in Hayden White's argument that "'pure' interpretation, the disinterested inquiry into anything whatsoever, is unthinkable as an ideal without the presupposition of the kind of activity that politics represents."[62] The purity of any interpretation, as White suggests, can be measured only by the extent to which it succeeds in repressing any impulse to appeal to political authority in the course of earning its understanding or its explanation of its object of interest.[63] As is widely recognized, historical interpretation can be of grave importance in contemporary debates about political choices. As Ralph Darendorf put it at a 1988 conference on the *Historikerstreit,* "Purists may not like this; they may pursue the old mirage of what actually happened; but it is a mirage. The past comes to life by the way in which it relates to the present and to plans for the future. The relationship is complex."[64] Self-styled positivist scholarship in the antiquarian tradition of "facts for facts' sake" can still be useful, but it is inadequate at best. Acknowledging some validity in the belief that scholarship should be tested independent of its origins, motives, and consequences, Maier nonetheless concludes that "even for the process of understanding historical arguments, of learnng to live with a plurality of truths, one cannot avoid inquiries into historians' starting points."[65] Thus, politics can exist in the most seemingly apolitical sites of scientific inquiry.

Perpetrators and Victims

If politics is inherent in historical inquiry, then making the distinction between the victim and the perpetrator in the investigation of an atrocity is a necessary moral obligation. In fact, such a distinction is crucial to our understanding of a historical event such as the Nanjing Massacre. At a fundamental level, the event is an atrocity committed by the Japanese troops against Chinese civilians and disarmed soldiers. It is true that such a simplification tends to leave out many important aspects of the event and may even be used to promote nationalistic projects of history-writing. However, the failure to acknowledge this basic distinction can produce grave consequences.

It is worth remembering that the Nanjing Massacre took place in the context of Japan's military invasion of China. The kind of brutality seen in Nanjing—wanton killing, raping, and looting—was by no means isolated, but rather characteristic of the war Japan was waging in China. Nor can this brutality be separated from the contempt for other Asians that had permeated prewar Japanese society. Whatever historians may theorize about construction of identity, being Chinese in Nanjing at the height of the terror was extremely hazardous. To illustrate how ethnic prejudice often made a difference, Japanese author Tsuda Michio cites the following example: During the war in south China, a Japanese sergeant who had raped and killed numerous Chinese women became "impotent" as soon as he found out to his shock that one of his victims was actually a Japanese woman who had married a Chinese and emigrated to China.[66] All these conditions point to the fundamental question of unequal power relationships that existed between the Chinese and the Japanese in Nanjing in 1937 and in other occupied areas during the rest of the war.

Taken out of the context of Japan's aggression in China, the Nanjing Massacre would become a mere accident or an anecdote in the annals of military operations. It has been portrayed precisely thus. For example, in a five-hundred-page history of the army operations in China during the first seven months of the conflict, historians of Japan's Self-Defense Agency relegated the "Nanjing Incident" literally to a footnote, albeit one more than two pages long.[67] Ignoring the importance of political contexts can produce skewed interpretations, which sometimes can be found among the writings of more learned historians. For instance, historian Hata Ikuhiko has on more than one occasion suggested that had the Chinese commander surrendered his troops in an orderly fashion in Nanjing, as the Russian general did at Port Arthur in 1905 and the British did in Singapore during the Pacific War, "the Nanjing Incident would not have taken place, or perhaps at a much smaller scale even if it did happen."[68] Although this statement seems quite reasonable from the perspective of military operations, it ignores the fact that the Chinese defense of their own capital against an invasion was *politically* different from Russian or British troops holding on to essentially colonial outposts against Japanese attacks. Here, sensitivity to the political aspect of the event is more than just a virtue on the part of the historian; lack of it can easily create further misunderstandings.

Perhaps equally important to historians is the fact that the perpetrator-victim distinction often has direct implications for the evidence upon which they reconstruct history. It would be naive to believe that the field of historical evidence is ever a neutral playground. In the case of war atrocities, as many have pointed out, the nature of written evidence tends to privilege the powerful and disfavor the vanquished. Those Chinese men and women killed in Nanjing—overwhelmingly though not exclusively at the hands of the Japanese troops—could not bear witness in the same way Japanese soldiers and officers could after the war. Surviving victims' shame can prevent them from speaking out. That perpetrators tend to conceal any incriminating evidence of their crime is hardly a novel idea. Incriminating evidence at the scene of the atrocities was either destroyed or suppressed. Bodies of killed Chinese POWs had to be burned or thrown into the river, not only for sanitary reasons but to leave no trace of the massacre. At the lowest level, it was common for Japanese soldiers to kill their Chinese rape victims so that they could not live to lodge complaints. A few Japanese soldiers were indeed tried by their own military court, but the existing court martial records of the Japanese Tenth Army, which had taken part in the operations in Nanjing, show that only a small fraction of cases was actually brought to its attention.[69] Even if the Japanese army or the military police had conducted an investigation of the entire incident, it is highly questionable that it would have offered the "definitive evidence" that some historians had hoped.[70] There were good reasons for the wartime Japanese authorities to exercise strict control over both foreign correspondents and their own writers at home. *Manchester Guardian* correspondent Harold Timperley was prevented by Japanese censors in Shanghai from sending reports about Japanese atrocities in Nanjing and elsewhere. Japan's prize-winning writer Ishikawa Tatsuzō was given a four-month sentence for writing a work of fiction with references to brutal killings by the Japanese soldiers in the Nanjing area. The March 1938 issue of the monthly journal *Chūō kōron,* which published an already sanitized version of his novel, was immediately withdrawn.[71]

Moreover, politics and moral judgment continue to influence how evidence is produced, if it is produced at all, even well after the war. As many historians of the subject have pointed out, those who believed they were guilty tended to remain silent while those who believed in their innocence spoke out. Even those who admitted guilt would talk about killing POWs or looting, but hardly anyone admitted to raping and killing rape victims.[72] One researcher told of a Japanese captain who recorded the details of critical events in Nanjing in his diary but insisted on taking his diary to his grave with him.[73] Even the indefatigable Ono Kenji, who recovered many former soldiers' wartime diaries, encountered quite a few who refused to disclose theirs. Under such circumstances, a historian can only feel exasperation at the loss of important evidence. At the same time, those Japanese soldiers who did come forward to tell their stories of the event or provide evidence of the atrocities faced enormous pressure from their former comrades or veterans' associations.[74] Many were derogatorily dubbed "*zangeya*" (habitual confessors) or liars, and some were even physically threatened.[75] In one case, the widow of a former soldier whose diary recorded brutal killings of innocent Chinese in Nanjing was compelled to claim that the diary had been burned so as to ward off possible harassment.[76] Several veterans' groups even brought libel suits against individuals or newspapers that published incriminating accounts on the grounds of factual discrepancies.

The victim-perpetrator distinction is also highly relevant as historians try to understand the post-traumatic experiences of those who survived, a subject that deserves to be studied on its own. A study conducted by two scholars involved in a Jewish-German seminar at Yad Vashem—the Heroes and Martyrs Memorial in Israel—is quite revealing. They found that the Israelis and the Germans approach the Holocaust quite differently. The former tend to seek responses from Germans on a political level, namely "responses deriving from elements of deep soul-searching and the resolve to take a moral stand, such as combating contemporary anti-Semitism or increasing sensitivity to Jewish forms of memory." On the other hand, pacifism is the code of contemporary behavior many Germans deduce from their understanding of the past.[77]

The parallel to how many Chinese and Japanese look at the war and at the issue of Nanjing Massacre is striking. Most Chinese accounts of the Nanjing Massacre have ended with a simple political message: the revival of militarism in Japan must be stopped and the Japanese government has to atone for the country's past aggression against China. Although the majority of Japanese do consider the moral implications of an atrocity like the Nanjing Massacre, many do so only in a universal way, to the extent that perpetrators and victims became indistinguishable. Much has been made of the fact that General Matsui Iwane, upon returning to Japan, built an altar dedicated to the fallen Japanese and Chinese soldiers in Nanjing.[78] When this mode is applied to historical inquiry, however, it can lead to what Charles Maier calls Bitburg History. Such an approach, as Maier describes it, "unites oppressors and victims . . . in a common dialectic," and makes it difficult to pin down any notion of collective responsibility.[79]

Many Japanese ex-soldiers who testified to the atrocity in Nanjing put the blame squarely on the war. Former sergeant Ide Junji, who recalled witnessing brutal killings in Nanjing by the Japanese troops, put it as well as anyone else: "Human beings are capable of being god and demon. It is war that induces human beings to become demons."[80] There is certainly truth in such a statement, and sentiments like this are genuine and have contributed to the strong pacifism in postwar Japan. War is indeed responsible for many human excesses. However, blaming everything on the war is at best inadequate and at worst can be used as an excuse to avoid confronting the crucial issue of agency, for even in the most brutal of wars not everyone killed or raped civilians.[81] Acknowledgment of the dehumanizing impact of war, although highly important, cannot replace a critical analysis of the individual decisions as well as the particular political institutions.

Commonality and Comparison

Indispensable as it is, the distinction between the perpetrator and the victim is not without problems. Because it simplifies a complex, multifaceted event, reducing it to black and white, such a binary prism is inadequate for understanding the historical process, which necessarily includes shades of gray. For instance, the fact that more than a few Chinese collaborators assisted Japanese troops in sorting out Chinese soldiers in the Safety Zone demonstrates that the perpetrator-victim distinction is not always drawn along purely national lines. Simply making the distinction between perpetrators and victims does not explain why the atrocity took its particular form or why the perpetrators behaved as they did. Although most Chinese studies of the Nanjing Massacre have placed the responsibility squarely on the Japanese side, as some recent Chinese work has recognized, General Tang Shengzhi's failure to bring about an orderly retreat was a major contributing factor to the massive loss of Chinese lives. Some writers even acknowledge that the Chinese resistance may have intensified Japanese revenge, although they are at pains to point out that this can in no way justify the atrocity.[82] At the same time, as many Japanese historians have demonstrated, the causes of Japanese brutality also have to be sought in the institutionalization of terror against surrendered soldiers within the Japanese military. Therefore, an understanding of the Nanjing Massacre and its implications must go beyond simply condemning it as the product of Japanese militarism.

Perhaps more important, making such a distinction does not automatically make the status of victim or perpetrator absolute or eternal, nor can these categories be easily equated with an entire people or nation-state. Necessary as they are, politically determined ethical yardsticks are not the final criteria for judging events such as the Nanjing Massacre in human history. In this sense, the Nanjing Massacre is not simply a Japanese atrocity against the Chinese, but also a human catastrophe, for it took place in a brutalized (though still undeclared) war that escalated the brutality on all sides, albeit to different degrees. The Massacre was also fueled by ethnic hatred and contempt, and sanctioned by male domination of women. Unfortunately, even if there can be said to have been a distinctively Japanese configuration of these factors in 1937 and during the rest of the war, no single country or people can claim total immunity in its history.[83] Indeed, neither the history of the West nor the history of China, with their own share of imperial expansions and barbarity, can serve as a final point of reference to condemn Japanese aggression and atrocity in World War II. The ultimate moral judgment should be anchored in a common ideal of humanity. As genocide and mass brutality have continued to take place long after World War II, often justified by demonizing the ethnic "other," historians have all the more responsibility to prevent the categories of victim and perpetrator from being misused.[84]

Here the historian has to confront the question of comparison, an important tool in historical inquiry. But not all comparisons are equally justified, as Charles Maier astutely puts it, since to control the terms of comparison "is to control the parameters of historical—and sometimes political—discourse."[85] For this very reason, analogy and comparison lie at the heart of the *Historikerstreit,* as the philosopher-historian Ernest Nolte attempted to compare and thus link the Nazi Final Solution with the Bolshevik policy of eliminating domestic class enemies in the 1930s.[86] Comparison, even if executed in a subtle form in the discussion of the Nanjing Massacre, has to be scrutinized.

In a recent piece on the issue of death figures in Nanjing, historian Hata Ikuhiko, who has written a well-researched monograph on the subject, began with brief but poignant references to several earlier "Nanjing Incidents." The first one took place during the Taiping takeover of the city in 1853, in which allegedly more than thirty thousand people were killed. The second was the massacre of one thousand students by the warlord Zhang Xun in September 1913. There was yet another "Nanjing Incident": During the Northern Expedition in March 1927, the KMT troops led by Jiang Jieshi (Chiang Kai-shek) attacked foreign legations including the Japanese embassy. One indignant Japanese navy officer even attempted *seppuku* (ritual suicide), Hata noted, because Japanese guards offered no resistance.[87] In a somewhat different context, Japanese intellectual historian and critic Matsumoto Ken'ichi has argued that the earlier Nanjing massacres, especially the Taiping massacre, have informed the Chinese perceptions of the 1937 Japanese atrocities in Nanjing.[88] Although these many "Nanjing Massacres/Incidents"—all of which are real historical events—may illustrate the confusion of nomenclature, their inclusion in the study of the 1937 Japanese atrocity can also serve the purpose of a subtle comparison. Readers are left with the unmistakable impression that the Chinese were quite capable of inflicting carnage upon themselves and causing injuries to foreigners.

On the face of it, few would deny this. The Chinese indeed have a lot of accounting to do themselves, especially with regard to what one American scholar has termed "China's bloody century."[89] A simple juxtaposition of the Japanese atrocities in Nanjing with earlier killings at the hands of the Chinese can perhaps demonstrate that what happened in 1937 was not *uniquely* Japanese behavior, but how it advances our understanding of the particular atrocities in 1937 is unclear. Worse, such practices by reputable historians lend credence to apologetics, since casual references to Chinese or other atrocities in recent history can work as thinly masked pretexts for those who seek to minimize or altogether deny Japan's war crimes. In fact, it has become standard practice for a number of Japanese writers to argue that mass killing has been commonplace throughout Chinese history but was uncharacteristic of the Japanese people, and hence the 1937 massacre was a Chinese fabrication.[90] A comparative examination of the wrongs committed by others may deepen our understanding of human conditions in war, but it should not exonerate perpetrators of particular atrocities.

If such a "comparative criminology" can be misleading, we also need to be careful about what might be called "comparative victimology." Although it is understandable that victims themselves may see their experiences as unique and more painful than those of others, it becomes problematic when some start ranking the Nanjing Massacre as a bigger calamity than other well-publicized calamities such as the bombing of Hiroshima and Nagasaki. In an effort to raise the profile of an atrocity that has been relatively underacknowledged in the West, Iris Chang in her bestseller makes the claim that in Nanjing the Japanese "outdid the Romans of Carthage (*only* 150,000 died in that slaughter [emphasis added]), the Christian armies during the Spanish Inquisition, and even some of the monstrosities of Timur Lenk."[91] In order to prove that the Nanjing Massacre was one the worst instances of mass destruction, she compares its intensity, proportion, and cruelty with those of other well-known wartime catastrophes. Such an exercise is morally misguided in that it unfairly slights the suffering of other peoples and thus prevents genuine compassion and understanding of what war does to individuals. "It makes me uneasy," historian Laura Hein wrote recently on the same issue, "that they [who establish a hierarchy of horror] can make the imaginative leap to one group of humans so much more easily than to another."[92] Moreover, such a comparison is methodologically sterile, as it does not advance our true understanding of either Nanjing or Hiroshima. Worse, by according one set of death figures such centrality in the discussion of the Nanjing Massacre, this approach not only precludes necessary historical reappraisal but in fact falls perilously close to the logic of the argument that if the figures of 300,000 or 400,000 cannot be substantiated, the massacre either must not have happened or was not so bad after all.

To be sure, historians are not primarily acting as political or moral advocates. Writing history in order to score ideological or political points, however justifiable that may seem at the time, often ends up compromising the scholarship itself.[93] Writing a history of war atrocities such as the Nanjing Massacre, however, has all manner of moral implications. Although a historian should strive to be fair and objective, it is highly doubtful whether s/he can be completely impartial on issues of massive human criminality. As historian Omer Bartov has observed in his thoughtful piece on the Holocaust historiography, "[if] historians, as intellectuals, concede their moral neutrality, then they will finally concede their intellectual, political, and moral irrelevance. Thereby they will also abuse their function as educators, reconstructors of the past, and serious critics of the present."[94] One British historian has even warned that if historians shun all the moral aspects and write "objective" or nonmoral history, "the best intention of historians may result in what they would not desire; namely, a slide from a non-moral attitude in historians to attitudes in their readers that are, first, amoral, and then, perhaps, immoral."[95] Above all the historian must be aware of both the particular aspect of the atrocity as well as its universal implications. This is all the more necessary given the efforts of those who have no qualms about using history for overt political or ideological gain.

The Challenge of Transnational History

Highly emotional and controversial subjects such as the Nanjing Massacre also raise an increasingly urgent question for practicing historians: Is it still possible to achieve shared historical understanding that transcends national boundaries? Needless to say, national boundaries are not the only fault lines to cross, as historians within the same country can be just as deeply divided along ideological or even methodological lines. In the post–Cold War world, the conflict of nationalism, many have argued, has replaced the old conflict of ideology. Consequently, it is in the realm of international or interethnic politics that this need for a shared understanding of history has become most urgently felt. The debate about the Nanjing Massacre provides a timely opportunity for historians to consider this proposition.

A Desirable Objective?

Before we face this question, we should note that today there is no consensus on whether such a shared understanding is even desirable. Indeed, some would question its desirability because a transnational historical understanding would undermine a nation-centered narrative and might be injurious to national pride and identity.

In Japan, once considered by many as the model of a postindustrial society, a vocal segment within intellectual circles is demanding that historical education should serve to instill "pride in Japan" in the country's young people. Members of the Society for New History Textbooks—many of them professional historians—celebrate the formation of national consciousness and the state in Japan as the most important theme in modern history education. Most of them see little good in sharing a view of Japanese history with other countries and instead are calling for a Japan-centered perspective in historical education to replace what is called "historical views of Japan based on the interests of foreign countries" (or former enemy countries). Consequently, those Japanese who strive to bring attention to Japan's war crimes in Asia or other darker sides of its past are branded "masochistic," while non-Japanese who do so are branded "anti-Japanese."[96] In China, although the idea of universality based on historical materialism still has considerable influence among the country's historians, the government has increasingly stressed using historical education to strengthen the patriotic feelings of its citizens. One lesson to be learned from the Nanjing Massacre, we are told, is that "backwardness invites aggression" *(luohou jiuyao aida)* and "if the country is not wealthy and strong, its people suffer" *(guojia bu fuqiang, renmin jiu zaoyang)*.[97] The national orientation in such statements is quite unmistakable. Tendencies toward nation-centered views of history are thus alive and well in both Japan and China.

Despite, or perhaps because of, such trends in both countries, a common historical understanding has become not just desirable but all the more timely. Economic and technological forces are bringing the societies closer together, for better or for worse. The historical records of human interactions—war and colonialism among them—have become common property, belonging to neither the perpetrator nor the victim alone.[98] If in the past one could afford to ignore what people in a neighboring country thought about such historical experience, that is no longer the case. Often the differences become heightened by the transnational media, so that even history (in the broad sense) produced primarily for a national audience (such as history textbooks) or even for a local audience can have international repercussions. The waves of protest from Asian capitals following various "misstatements" by Japanese cabinet officials in the past decade or so is a case in point. In March 1996, when the city of Nagasaki succumbed to demands of conservative and right-wing groups and replaced photographs that depicted the Nanjing Massacre in the city's new Atomic Bomb Museum, the Chinese press fired rounds of their own criticism.[99] The Chinese and Japanese pronouncements on the Nanjing Massacre are no exception to this transnational phenomenon. Through translations, journal articles, and newspaper editorials, both countries have begun to affect each other's discourse on the subject in unmistakable ways.[100]

Moreover, understanding of history can have a real impact on current perceptions of the "other," especially as the nation-states involved in past conflicts have not withered away. Given the widely recognized "gaps" in historical understanding between Japan and its Asian neighbors over issues related to World War II, as one American current affairs analyst has pointed out, any new confidence-building initiative in the region will be predicated on addressing issues from the past.[101] Many Japanese have also come to the realization that the unresolved issues of history are damaging Japan's potential to play a more active role in the region.[102] In practical terms, therefore, promoting a shared historical understanding would bring the benefits of reducing tension and facilitating international cooperation.

A Feasible Goal?

Even if we can agree that a shared historical understanding is desirable, many historians would think it nothing more than a "noble dream" that is impossible in practice. In one sense this may well be true. As Ueno Chizuko has pointed out, it is naive to speak of the same historical understanding shared between victims and perpetrators. Those caught in an unequal power relationship are bound to have drastically different views of the same event.[103] For historians the most fundamental question concerns our own subjectivity—what is termed the transferential relationship between the author and the subject. If at the beginning of this century Lord Acton could confidently declare that "our [history of] Waterloo must be one that satisfies French and English, German and Dutch alike,"[104] the prevailing view among many Western historians seems much less sanguine today. The declining popularity of positivism in Western historiography and the consequent fragmentation of a "universal truth" acceptable to all parties have given rise to the phenomenon in America described by one observer as "every group its own historian."[105] As the history of the Holocaust presents historians with transference in the most traumatic form conceivable, the intellectual historian Dominick LaCapra has stated the problem most forcefully:

> Whether the historian or analyst is a survivor, a relative of survivors, a former Nazi, a former collaborator, a relative of former Nazi or collaborators, a younger Jew or German distanced from more immediate contact with survival, participation, or collaboration, or a relative "outsider" to those problems will make a difference even in the meaning of statements that may be formally identical. Certain state-

ments or even entire orientations may seem appropriate for someone in a given subject position but not to others.[106]

In other words, meaning can never exist independent of the historian, but is always contextual. To make this point, in LaCapra's view, is not to deny an important role for objectivity, but objectivity does become a more difficult and problematic undertaking when it comes to such an emotional and politicized subject. Because the historian cannot claim total detachment from his or her subject, the problematic relationship between the analyst and the subject has to be honestly acknowledged.

However, such a relationship is neither as simple nor as absolute as LaCapra suggests. A historian is by no means condemned to a singular identity defined in ethnic terms. When Takahashi Tetsuya, a Japanese scholar of philosophy born after the war, addresses the issue of responsibility of the Japanese of his generation, he has offered a useful suggestion. For Japanese to accept the responsibility of war, he has concluded, does not necessarily mean an unqualified acceptance of nationalism or the nation-state of Japan, because individual Japanese can claim membership in a nation, but also in other forms of community that include locality, profession, and gender.[107] These multiple identities in turn provide a plurality of vantage points from which one may relate to an event in the past.

The painting career of two Japanese artists offers an encouraging example that it is possible to free oneself from the iron cage of national consciousness. For many years after World War II, Maruki Iri and Toshi devoted themselves to painting the sufferings caused by the atomic bombings of Hiroshima and Nagasaki. In fact, their names became associated with their famous *Hiroshima Murals,* which were shown around Japan and even in the United States. During their American tour in the early 1970s, they were confronted with questions about the Nanjing Massacre. This was around the time when the debate in Japan had just begun. After much soul-searching, the Marukis decided to create another mural of human suffering titled *The Nanjing*

Massacre depicting Japanese as brutal killers. The painting was based on their own extensive research of the subject. Underlining her gender identity, Mrs. Maruki made a special point of painting Chinese women rape victims herself. The painting had a powerful impact on Japanese viewers, including many schoolchildren.[108] Since then, the Marukis have supported efforts to redress Japan's wartime wrongs and have staged exhibitions in Japan on the Nanjing Massacre with Chinese artists.[109] The important message they convey is highly relevant to historians: the possibility of overcoming a narrow victim consciousness by becoming a true humanist who faces up to the dark episodes in one's own national history. In doing this, the Marukis help bring down the barrier of national narrative of history without completely skirting the issue of identity and subjectivity of being Japanese.

Although historians need to be aware of the problem of transference in studying an event such as the Nanjing Massacre, they should strive to, and can indeed, transcend a predetermined position of national identity. Indeed, being Japanese has not prevented many historians in Japan from producing some of the most critically acclaimed works on the Nanjing Massacre in any language. The national and linguistic divide notwithstanding, history-writing remains a collective enterprise, and historians also belong to what is called "the interpretive community" that is ultimately transnational. Given the rules and codes to which members can and must be held rationally accountable, some would even argue that truth, if it does exist, is established by growing rational consensus. Thus, in historical interpretation it is "not so much the subjective *imposition* of meaning, but rather the inter-subjective *judgment* of meanings that matters."[110] Although these rules and codes may themselves have biases and therefore should not be exempt from critical examination, "a community of critical discourse" offers the best hope that extends beyond any one local group trapped in its subjectivity.

All of this is not to say that the remaining differences over the particular aspects as well as interpretations of the Nanjing

Massacre will disappear anytime soon. The historical event known as the Nanjing Massacre cannot be reduced to a body of "facts" beyond any contention. Even among historians with perfectly good intentions, inevitably different individuals with different values and viewpoints, looking at the same phenomenon, may draw different conclusions at different times even from the same body of evidence. The fragmentary nature of available evidence causes further divergence in interpretive tendencies. Moreover, even if scholars can resolve their differences over historical methodology, they still may disagree over issues such as ethics and morality.

Some of the differences, however, can be narrowed to pave the way for a transnational common understanding of traumatic events such as the Nanjing Massacre. I would argue that a common historical understanding is possible, if by that we do not mean one unified version of history imposed on all groups, but rather a constructive framework of historical inquiry. To transcend a singular, fixed, and flattening view of an event such as the Nanjing Massacre, what is needed is a framework that addresses the historical-empirical as well as the moral-political dimensions of the event, a framework that recognizes both particular as well as the universal aspects of the experience. Such a framework requires historians to navigate the uncertain terrain of historical research without abandoning high standards of scholarship; it should enable historians to maintain much-needed sensitivity to the moral and political implications of their enterprise without appealing to national or other political authorities. Such a framework is the first step toward a meaningful dialogue across national divides.

Toward Dialogue

In this way, an analysis of the Nanjing Massacre is not simply an academic exercise, but has implications for practice. Indeed, although history and memory may still be strongly linked to national identities, history-writing has already become increasingly transnational. For instance, historians from Japan and Korea have embarked on substantive discussions of their respective history textbooks.[111] In addition to translations of historical works and foreign research trips, international symposia on the Nanjing Massacre attended by both Chinese and Japanese historians have contributed to the cross-fertilization of ideas across linguistic boundaries.

Such processes of exchange can highlight the difficulties inherent in the transnational dialogue. The continued disagreement over the nomenclature is just one example. A number of observers have pointed out the difficulties in establishing a shared understanding of history between China and Japan in particular, the two close neighbors bound in a "special relationship." Japanese scholars active in the intellectual exchange with China have noted the "lack of a psychological condition among Chinese historians to accept even academic findings." Some even evoked the cultural difference between the Chinese and the Japanese as barriers to reaching a real common historical understanding.[112]

But difficulty in genuine scholarly dialogue is not always due to cultural difference, nor does it exist only between China and Japan. In 1995 a select group of Japanese, Chinese, and American historians gathered in Tokyo for three days for a candid discussion of war and atrocities. Witness the following exchange regarding the Nanjing Massacre. After two American historians raised the question of why it is so difficult for the Japanese to accept the Nanjing Incident and to admit the shameful behavior in Nanjing, their two Japanese counterparts responded:

Itō: For me, to apologize for things that can't be ascertained as facts is very difficult. What is it like to apologize for something that can't be ascertained like Japan having killed 300,000 or 400,000 people?

Kojima: I agree. One should admit the crimes committed, but it is inappropriate to be told to admit to crimes not committed.

Berger: The question about the Nanjing Incident at this point is not so much if Japanese apologize or not, but whether to recognize it. At the present, it

> is not necessary to admit whether there were 30,000 or 300,000 victims.[113]

Itō Takashi is a leading political historian highly respected for his own works and numerous compilation of primary documents; Kojima Noboru is a widely read writer who has published numerous popular nonfiction works on Japan's modern history. Neither can be faulted for what seems to be a preoccupation with empirical facts. The issue of Chinese death tolls is certainly one of the important issues that must be critically reexamined by historians, but the Nanjing Massacre defined solely or primarily in terms of numbers is historiographically wanting, as it overshadows other important aspects of the event itself. A reduction of the Nanjing Massacre to an issue of discrepant numbers, even if it can be justified on empirical grounds, as this episode demonstrates, makes it almost impossible to carry on a meaningful dialogue.

A number of Japanese politicians and academics have repeatedly called for setting up a joint Chinese–Japanese committee to investigate the Nanjing Massacre. So far they have been ignored by Chinese historians who are skeptical of the motives behind these suggestions. Such suspicions may be excessive but are not entirely unfounded. If joint empirical research is undertaken, one Japanese proponent predicted, the Chinese claim of 300,000 will collapse.[114] Fujioka Nobukatsu, the cofounder of the Society for Creating New History Textbooks, has reasoned that if the 300,000 figure could not be substantiated, then the Great Massacre must not have taken place, making it a Chinese and Allied fabrication like the Tokyo Trial's verdict that Japan committed aggression in Asia.[115]

To overcome such a stalemate and to start a genuine dialogue, empirical vigor alone, though indispensable, is not sufficient. Sensitivity to the political and moral implications of historical inquiry on the part of historians becomes crucial. As another popular history writer in Japan indicates, although joint Sino-Japanese investigation of this event may be useful, the Japanese should first of all admit that "the Nanjing Massacre did happen."[116] Such a recognition, though a minimal precondition, is likely to reduce the psychological barrier and bring the Chinese and Japanese researchers closer to genuine dialogue and meaningful collaboration on such an emotional and divisive subject. In fact, this is also what some Chinese historians have come to recognize. As Sun Zhaiwei, a leading Chinese historian of the subject, pointed out in a recent study of the Nanjing Massacre, even the sensitive subject of the Chinese death tolls in Nanjing can be discussed, as long as "one respects and recognizes the historical fact" that the invading Japanese troops wantonly slaughtered the Chinese people on a large scale.[117] Such a statement may appear to be a small step and Sun's is perhaps still a minority voice in China, but the fact that it has been endorsed by other Chinese historians offers hope that they, too, are prepared to move beyond their own obsession with numbers.[118] At a 1997 international conference held in Nanjing marking the sixtieth anniversary of the Massacre, the Japanese historian Kasahara Tokushi, who has published many critical studies of Japanese invasion in China, introduced his tentative estimate of Chinese victims, which was considerably lower than the conventional Chinese figure of 300,000. No objection was raised from the Chinese participants, and his paper was published in China together with some sixty essays presented at the conference.[119] Such developments in both Japan and China indicate that a genuine dialogue among historians is ideed possible, even if the obstacles to meaningful collaboration remain formidable.

Today, a genuine dialogue among historians working on the Nanjing Massacre is more urgent than ever. New research has been carried out in Japan over the past decade or so that has advanced our understanding in particular of the causes of the atrocities in Nanjing.[120] Historians elsewhere can benefit enormously from such historical scholarship rather than clinging to previous interpretations based on the idea of *bushidō,* or an abstract notion of Japanese militarism. Seen in a wider context, a better understanding of the Nanjing Massacre may have much to contribute to the ongoing studies of war atrocities still taking place in different parts of the world.

This analysis of some of the works on the Nanjing Massacre has highlighted several theoretical difficulties and problems involved in approaching the history of a recent traumatic event. As it has demonstrated, the challenges facing historians are as much about evidence and knowledge in historical inquiry as about justice and morality in history. In this sense the debate about the Nanjing Massacre has profound implications for all historians.

The Nanjing Massacre will not be reduced to a subject of dispassionate scholarship to be left to professional historians alone. Like other major traumatic incidents in recent history, the Nanjing Massacre has several irreducible aspects: individual experience, collective symbolism, and historical event, bound in a symbiotic relationship.[121] What historians consider their subject of inquiry is made up of individual experience that has been invested with collective symbolism. These three elements may overlap but cannot replace each other. Although often considered custodians of the past, historians alone cannot adequately cope with such an event or bring an end to the divergence of views or the emotional content of this subject—nor need they do so. Dominick LaCapra made a valid point when he reminded historians that "[historical] understanding is not furthered by routine oppositions between 'scientific history' and the 'other,' which often appears in the form of myth, ritual, or memory." Ultimately, he suggests, historians are involved in a dialogue with the past that has implications for the present and future. They must articulate the relationship between the requirements of their professional expertise and the less easily definable demands placed on the use of language by the difficult attempt to work through transferential relations.[122] Historians need not be deterred by the difficulty of this task. A heightened awareness of the methodological issues and the moral implications involved as well as a more self-reflexive view of our own subjective positions constitutes the best preparation possible not only for approaching a subject such as the Nanjing Massacre, but also for embracing the historical profession in the new millennium.

Notes

An earlier version of this chapter was published in Japanese translation in *Shisō* (August 1998): 83–109. I would like to thank Takashi Fujitani, Carol Gluck, and Kojima Kiyoshi as well as the other essayists in this volume for sharing their ideas with me. Some of the same materials have appeared in my essay "Convergence or Divergence? Recent Historical Writings on the Rape of Nanjing," *American Historical Review* 104.3 (June, 1999): 842–65.

1. My understanding of the German *Historikerstreit* is primarily based on the following works: Gina Thomas, *The Unresolved Past: A Debate in German History;* Baldwin, *Reworking the Past: Hitler, the Holocaust, and Historians' Debate; Forever in the Shadow of Hitler? Original Documents of the Historikerstreit, the Controversy Concerning the Singularity of the Holocaust.*

2. Evans, *In Hitler's Shadow: West German Historians and the Attempt to Escape from the Nazi Past,* provides helpful background to the debate.

3. Novick, *That Noble Dream: The "Objectivity Question" and the American Historical Profession.* See especially part 4, "Objectivity in Crisis," pp. 419–629.

4. Friedländer, *Probing the Limits of Representation: Nazism and the "Final Solution,"* p. 2.

5. See especially Maier, *The Unmasterable Past: History, Holocaust, and German National Identity,* and the continuous stream of articles published in the journal *History and Theory: Studies in the Philosophy of History.*

6. Yang, "A Sino-Japanese Controversy: The Nanjing Atrocity as History." For an expanded version of this paper that discusses the Nanjing Massacre in the context of postwar Sino-Japanese relations, see Yang, "Contested History: The Nanjing Massacre in Postwar Japan and China."

7. On a different level, Ian Buruma's *Wages of Guilt: Memories of War in Germany and Japan* has already connected the European and East Asian efforts to come to terms with the wartime past.

8. To give but one recent example, the diary of John H. Rabe, chairman of the International Safety Zone Committee in Nanjing, was published in Japan under the title *Nankin no shinjitsu* (The Truth about Nanjing). An example of Chinese historians guarding the "historical facts" from tampering is Zou et al., "Nanjing datusha de lishi shishi burong cuangai," p. 88.

9. One of the few previous attempts regarding the Nanjing Massacre is a panel discussion about methods and problems of oral history. See "Zadankai II: Nyūginia kōchi kara Nankin e." For other discussions of

evidence and methodology, see Hata Ikuhiko, *Nankin jiken: 'Gyakusatsu' no kōzō,* pp. 107–111; Kasahara, Suzuki, and Watanabe, "Nankin gyakusatsu jiken," esp. pp. 88–100.

10. Ueno, "Posuto reisen to 'Nihonban rekishi shūseishugi,'" pp. 63–64. For a more detailed exposition of Ueno's views, see her "Kioku no seijigaku: Kokumin, kojin, watashi."

11. Collingwood, *The Idea of History,* p. 202.

12. *The Content of Form,* pp. 77–78.

13. Young, "Toward a Received History of the Holocaust," p. 41.

14. An example closer to home is the difficulty in reaching a definitive estimate of the number of participants in the Million Man March in Washington in 1995.

15. The publication of the John Rabe diary in Chinese, German, Japanese, and English reflects widespread interest in such a historical document.

16. Timperley, *Japanese Terror in China;* Hsu, *A Digest of Japanese War Conduct.*

17. For a sampling of the records kept by American missionaries in Nanjing, see Smalley, *American Missionary Eyewitnesses to the Nanjing Massacre.* For works largely based on these records, see Kasahara, *Nankin nanminku no hyakunichi;* Zhang Kaiyuan, *Nanjing datusha de lishi de jianzheng.*

18. Some of these accounts are reprinted in Nanjing datusha shiliao bianji weiyuanhui, *Qin-Hua Rijun Nanjing datusha shiliao,* pp. 1–155.

19. Zhongguo dier lishi dang'anguan et al., *Qin-Hua Rijun Nanjing datusha dang'an,* p. 542. For testimonies on rape, see pp. 331–53.

20. See Honda, *The Nanjing Massacre: A Japanese Journalist Confronts Japan's National Shame.*

21. Some 642 testimonies are included in Zhu, *Qin-Hua Rijun Nanjing datusha xinchunzhe zhengyanji.*

22. Ting, "Nanjing Massacre: A Dark Page in History," p. 20.

23. See Nanjing datusha shiliao bianji weiyuanhui, *Qin-Hua Rijun Nanjing datusha shiliao,* pp. 399–487.

24. Zhu, *Qin-Hua Rijun Nanjing datusha xinchunzhe zhengyanji.*

25. For example, Shimada, "Nankin kōryakusen to gyakusatsu jiken"; Imai Masatake, "Nankin jōnai no tairyō satsujin"; Hata Kensuke, "Horyo no chi ni mamireta byakko butai." Strictly speaking, some of these were eyewitness reports by Japanese journalists rather than by soldiers.

26. For a useful survey of these materials, see Hora, *Nit-Chū sensō shi shiryōshū 9: Nankin jiken II,* pp. 297–36.

27. Ono et al., *Nankin daigyakusatsu o kiroku shita kōgun heishitachi.*

28. Examples include Iguchi et al., *Nankin jiken: Kyōtō shidan kankei shiryōshū;* Kaikōsha, *Nankin senshi.*

29. Fujiwara, "Nankin daigyakusatsu no giseisha sū ni tsuite," p. 68.

30. "Zadankai II."

31. Hosomi, "Dekigoto to kioku: 'Nankin daigyakusatsu' 60ka nen ni yosete," p. 76.

32. See, for example, Schudson, "Dynamics of Distortion in Collective Memory."

33. Ginsburg, "Just One Witness."

34. Young, "Toward a Received History of the Holocaust," pp. 23, 39. In fact, historian's truth may also be considered contingent, since it depends on the historian's evidence and interpretation, whereas victim's truth is more experiential.

35. The literal translation of the Chinese *datusha* and Japanese *daigyakusatsu* would be "great massacre." This has led some Japanese to play with semantics by arguing that they are simply denying that what happened in Nanjing was a "great massacre."

36. Browning, *Ordinary Men: Reserve Police Battalion 101 and the Final Solution in Poland.*

37. See, for example, Tanaka Satoshi, "Nachisu no bōrei ga sasayaku 'Nihon akudama ron,'" p. 248. The author is a university professor in Japan.

38. See, for example, Fu, "Nanjing datusha yu Riben diguozhuyi."

39. Hilberg, "I Was Not There," p. 25.

40. Kimijima, "Nankin jiken no gyakusatsu shashin."

41. An example of this is Gao, "Du *Nanjing datusha tuzheng.*"

42. Fischer, *Historians' Fallacies: Toward a Logic of Historical Thought,* pp. 47–48.

43. Watanabe Shōichi, "Higeki no shōchō: Shōwa tennō," translated as "The Emperor and the Militarists." See also Watanabe's forward to Tanaka Masaaki, *"Nankin gyakusatsu" no kyokō.* Watanabe continues to make the dissembling statement that no Westerner reported the atrocities at the time.

44. Ara, *Kikigaki Nankin jiken.* For an early criticism of this approach, see Hata Ikuhiko, "Shōwa shi no nazo o ou," pp. 234–35.

45. Higashinakano Osamichi, "Aratamete 'Rābe no nikki' o tettei kenshō suru," p. 289, and *"Nankin gyakusatsu" no tettei kenshō,* p. 337.

46. For a study of this subject, see Ishiko, "Nankin gyakusatsu jiken: hōdō sarenakatta jijitsu no imi."

47. For a recent assessment of Western historiographical trends that takes postmodernism into consideration, see Iggers, *Historiography in the Twentieth Century: From Scientific Objectivity to the Postmodern Challenge.* An admirable effort at presenting a new conception of his-

torical inquiry based on practical realism and pragmatism is Appleby et al., *Telling the Truth about History.*

48. Friedländer, "Trauma, Transference, and 'Working Through' in Writing the History of the Shoah," pp. 52–53.

49. For example, Hora Tomio, a Japanese historian who began publishing groundbreaking work in the late 1960s, largely used Tokyo War Crimes Trials documents.

50. Fujiwara, *Nankin daigyakusatsu;* Yoshida, *Tennō no guntai to Nankin jiken;* Hata Ikuhiko, *Nankin jiken: "Gyakusatsu" no kōzō.*

51. "Nanjing shi linshi canyihui guanyu xiezhu diaocha Nanjing datusha an jingguo" (November 1946), in Zhongguo dier lishi dang'anguan et al., *Qin-Hua Rijun Nanjing datusha dang'an,* pp. 554–57.

52. For a perceptive historical analysis of the Tokyo Trial, see chapter 15 in Dower, *Embracing Defeat: Japan in the Wake of World War II.*

53. Kasahara, *Nankin jiken,* pp. 233–34.

54. Mayer, *Why Did the Heavens Not Darken: The "Final Solution" in History,* p. xiii. I quote from this work with the full awareness that not all of its revisionist conclusions are accepted by many historians and might be misused by others.

55. Lipstadt, *Denying the Holocaust: The Growing Assault on Truth and Memory,* pp. 20–21.

56. Sun, *Nanjing datusha,* pp. 10–18.

57. Mayer, *Why Did the Heavens Not Darken,* p. ix.

58. Hans Kellner has made the same point in "'Never Again' Is Now," esp. p. 141.

59. Buruma, "War and Remembrance: Memories of the Nanjing Massacre Are Drenched in Politics."

60. Yokoyama, "Kaisetsu: Nankin no sanji to Rābe no nikki," pp. 323–24.

61. Maier, *The Unmasterable Past,* p. 32

62. White, *Content of the Form: Narrative Discourse and Historical Representation,* p. 59.

63. Ibid.

64. Gina Thomas, *The Unresolved Past,* p. xiii.

65. Maier, *The Unmasterable Past,* p. 13.

66. Tsuda, *Nankin daigyakusatsu to Nihonjin no seishin kōzō,* pp. 161–62.

67. Bōeichō bōei kenshūjo senshishitsu, *Shina jihen rikugun sakusen,* part 1, pp. 436–38. Although discussing it in greater detail, the official history of the battle of Nanjing by the veterans' organization of the Imperial Army Cadet Academy treated the event in similar fashion. See Kaikōsha, *Nankin senshi.*

68. Hata Ikuhiko, "Nankin daigyakusatsu 'Rābe kōka' o sokutei

suru," pp. 86–87. Hata made similar comments at the Princeton Conference in late 1997. Compare this with his important 1986 study, in which he attributed the Japanese atrocities to the characteristics of "fascist troops in a war of aggression." Hata Ikuhiko, *Nankin jiken,* pp. 234–35.

69. See *Zoku-Gendaishi shiryō (6): Gunji keisatsu,* pp. xxxi–xxxiv, 1–119.

70. Hata Ikuhiko, "The Nanking Atrocities: Fact and Fable," p. 50.

71. For a complete version with deleted passages restored, see Ishikawa, "Ikite iru heitai."

72. Hata Ikuhiko, *Nankin jiken,* pp. 108–9.

73. See "'Nankin daigyakusatsu' no kakushin," p. 76.

74. For an example of reactions to confessions by former soldiers, see Uesugi Chitoshi, "'Waga Nankin puratōn' o kokuhatsu."

75. This is not to say that everyone who confessed was telling the truth. One such case involved Sone Kazuo, a former Japanese soldier who published several books on his experience in Nanjing. He has been accused of faking his rank. A complete rejection of Sone's testimony is Itakura, "Hata Ikuhiko shi e no chūkoku: 'Zangeya Sone Kazuo' e no shinkō," p. 4.

76. On this episode, see Hata Ikuhiko, "Shōwa shi no nazo o ou," pp. 243–45.

77. See Lozowick and Millen, "Pitfalls of Memory: Israeli-German Dialogues on the Shoah," pp. 267, 270.

78. See, for example, Tanaka Masaaki, *"Nankin gyakusatsu" no kyokō.*

79. Maier, *The Unmasterable Past,* p. 14.

80. Ide, "Watashi ga mokugeki shita Nankin no sangeki," p. 276.

81. In a piece published during the war the Chinese writer He Qifang wrote about a Japanese soldier in Nanjing who chose not to rape. He, "Ribenren de beiju."

82. Sun, *Nanjing datusha.*

83. Attempts to look at both sides of a brutal conflict without relativizing the responsibility of either include Dower, *War without Mercy: Race and Power in the Pacific War,* and Tanaka Yuki, *Hidden Horrors: Japanese War Crimes in World War II.*

84. For a recent discussion of this issue, see the essay by Omer Bartov, "Defining Enemies, Making Victims: Germans, Jews, and the Holocaust," and its responses in the *AHR* forum "Genocide in the Twentieth Century."

85. Maier, *The Unmasterble Past,* p. 32.

86. On the issue of comparison in the *Historikerskreit,* see ibid., pp. 66–99.

87. Hata Ikuhiko, "Nankin gyakusatsu jiken: kazu no kōsatsu." For an English translation, see Hata Ikuhiko, "The Nanking Atrocities: Fact and Fable." See also Hata Ikuhiko, *Nankin jiken,* p. 242.

88. Matsumoto, "Shinwa to shite no Nankin daigyakusatsu," and "Nankin daigyakusatsu no shinwateki kōzō."

89. Rummel, *China's Bloody Century: Genocide and Mass Murder since 1900.* Using almost entirely secondary sources in English, Rummel concludes that the majority of the Chinese victims in the twentieth century died at the hand of their own government.

90. See Suzuki, *"Nankin daigyakusatsu" no maboroshi,* esp. pp. 31–43; Tanaka Masaaki, *"Nankin gyakusatsu" no kokyō,* and *Nankin jiken no sōkatsu,* pp. 12–15, 240–55.

91. Chang, *The Rape of Nanking: The Forgotten Holocaust of World War II,* pp. 5–6.

92. See "Doing the Really Hard Math."

93. When the Chinese monthly *Xinhua yuebao* in 1951 accused the "imperialists and fascists" in the International Safety Zone of colluding with the Japanese troops in massacring innocent Chinese, it went far beyond the interpretative possibilities offered by all the available evidence. See "Zhuiyi Rikou Nanjing datusha."

94. Bartov, "Intellectuals on Auschwitz: Memory, History, and Truth," p. 134.

95. Stanford, *The Nature of Historical Knowledge,* p. 178.

96. See, for example, the speech by Fujioka Nobukatsu at a recent symposium on the writing of new history textbooks. "Shinpojiumu: Atarashii rekishizō o motome," p. 78; "'Atarashii rekishi kyōkasho o tsukuru kai' shūisho."

97. See Chen Anji's preface to Zhu, *Qin-Hua Rijun Nanjing datusha xinchunzhe zhengyanji,* p. 4.

98. Norma Field has made the same point in "Kyōiku genba de no sensō: Higai to kagai no kioku tsunagaru mono," p. 269.

99. Kamata, "Nagasaki genbaku shiryōkan no kagai tenji mondai."

100. For example, Honda, *Chūgoku no tabi;* Hora, *Nankin daigyakusatsu no shōmei;* Tanaka Masaaki, *"Nankin gyakusatsu" no kyokō;* and Hata Ikuhiko, *Nankin jiken,* have all been translated into Chinese. In particular, Tanaka's work was translated into Chinese to serve as a reminder that "there are real deniers in Japan." In addition to Nankin shi bunshi shiryō kenkyūkai, *Shōgen: Nankin daigyakusatsu,* which is translated from the Chinese by Kakami Mitsuyuki and Himeta Mitsuyoshi, Gao Xingzu's *Rinjun qin-Hua baoxing: Nanjing datusha* has also been translated into Japanese.

101. Howell, "The Inheritance of War: Japan's Domestic Politics and International Ambitions," p. 97.

102. For an analysis of such shifts among Japanese politicians and business leaders, see Yoshida, *Nihonjin no sensō kan,* pp. 166–75.

103. Ueno, "Kioku no seijigaku," p. 167.

104. In such a history, Acton went on, "nobody can tell, without examining the list of authors where Bishop of Oxford laid down pen, and whether Fairbairn or Gasquet, Liebermann or Harrison took up." Quoted in Carr, *What Is History?*, pp. 6–7.

105. See Novick, *That Noble Dream,* pp. 469–521.

106. LaCapra, "Representing the Holocaust: Reflections on the Historians' Debate," p. 110.

107. See, for example, Takahashi Tetsuya, "Tasha no sensō no kioku o mizukara no kakushinbu ni kizamu."

108. Dower and Junkerman, *The Hiroshima Murals.* This statement is also based on the author's 1992 visit to the Maruki Gallery, located in rural Saitama.

109. *Asahi shinbun,* 25 April 1996 (Hyōgo). Mr. Maruki Iri passed away in 1995.

110. Jay, "Of Plots, Witnesses, and Judgments," pp. 105–6.

111. On this endeavor, see Nik-Kan rekishi kyōkasho kenkyūkai, *Kyōkasho o Nik-Kan kyōryoku de kangageru.*

112. See, for example, Amago, "Nit-Chū kankei—sengo sedai kara no teigen"; Hirayama, "Yūki o motte rekishi to mukiau," p. 196.

113. Kojima et al., *Jinrui wa sensō o fusegeru ka,* esp. pp. 292–94.

114. Sase, "Nagano hatsugen to kokusai kangaku," p. 168. One such Japanese advocate is Ishihara Shintarō, who considers the Nanjing Massacre a "fabrication." See Ishihara, "'Nankin daigyakusatsu' no kyokō: Rekishi no kaisan o haisu."

115. Fujioka, *Jiyūshugi shikan to wa nani ka,* p. 48.

116. For example, Hosaka, *Bōkyaku sareta shiten,* p. 107.

117. Sun, *Nanjing datusha,* pp. 9–10.

118. See the review of Sun's book by the Nanjing University historian Zhang Xianwen, "Guizai chuangxin."

119. See Kasahara, "Nanjing datusha de quanmao."

120. One recent example is Fujiwara, *Nankin no Nihongun.*

121. One can think of Paul Cohen's recent work, *History in Three Keys: The Boxers as Event, Experience, and Myth.*

122. LaCapra, "Representing the Holocaust," pp. 126–27.

Glossary

Agawa Hiroyuki	阿川弘之
akai kyōkasho	赤い教科書
Akihito	明仁
arashi	あらし
Asahi jānaru	朝日ジャーナル
Asahi kasei	旭化成
Asahi shinbun	朝日新聞
Atarashii kyōkasho o tsukuru kai	新しい教科書をつくる会
Bungei shunjū	文芸春秋
canku	残酷
Chō Isamu	長勇
Chūseiteki sekai no keisei	中世的世界の形成
Daiē	ダイエー
daigyakusatsuha	大虐殺派
Dai tō-A sensō	大東亜戦争
Dai tō-A sensō no sōkatsu	大東亜戦争の総括
Dashizhuang	大石庄
Deng Xiaoping	鄧小平
detarame	デタラメ
Diaoyu Islands (Senkaku Islands)	釣魚島

dogeza gaikō	土下座外交
Etō Jun	江藤淳
Etō Takami	江藤隆美
Fuji Xerox	富士ゼロックス
Gekkan keidanren	月刊経団連
Genshi heiki shiyō kinshi no Sutokkuhorumu apiiru shomei undō	原子兵器使用禁止のストックホルムアッピール署名運動
gongshi	共識
Gotō Kōsaku	五島広作
guojia bu fuqiang, renmin jiu zaoyang	國家不富强人民就遭殃
Guomindang	國民黨
Guo Moruo	郭沫若
Hani Gorō	羽仁五郎
Hashimoto Ryūtarō	橋本龍太郎
Hayashi Mariko	林真理子
heiwa no toride	平和のとりで
hikokumin	非国民
Hirohito	裕仁
Hiroshima heiwa kinen shiryōkan	広島平和記念資料館
Hirota Kōki	広田弘毅
Hosokawa Morihiro	細川護熙
Hu Yaobang	胡耀邦
hyōronka	評論家
Ikeda Hayato	池田勇人
Inoue Kiyoshi	井上清
iro no tsuita kyōkasho	色のついた教科書
Ishimoda Shō	石母田正
Itō Takashi	伊藤隆
Jiang Jieshi	蔣介石
jihen	事変
Jikkyō shuppan	実教出版
Jimintō kyōkasho mondai shō iinkai	自民党教科書問題小委員会
Jingji ribao	经济日报
Jinmu	神武
Jiyū minshutō	自由民主党

Jiyū shobō	自由書房
Jiyūshugi shikan kenkyūkai	自由主義史観研究会
kagai no mondai	加害の問題
kagaisha ishiki	加害者意識
Kaifu Toshiki	海部俊樹
Kaikō	偕行
Kamiya Fuji	神谷不二
Kangzhan sunshi diaocha weiyuanhui	抗哉损失调查委员会
Kase Toshikazu	加瀬俊一
Katogawa Kōtarō	加登川幸太郎
Kawasaki shi heiwakan	川崎市平和館
kenkoku kinenbi	建国記念日
kentei	検定
kigensetsu	紀元節
Kikan sensō sekinin kenkyū	季刊戦争責任研究
Kike wadatsumi no koe	きけわだつみのこえ
Kim Young Sam (Kim Yŭng-sam)	金泳三
kono Tōnan Ajia shinryaku	この東南アジア侵略
kono Tōnan Ajia shinshutsu	この東南アジア進出
Kōtō Nihon shi saishinban	高等日本史最新版
Kuni no ayumi (ge)	くにのあゆみ（下）
Kuni no ayumi hihan: tadashii Nihon no rekishi	くにのあゆみ批判 正しい日本の歴史
Kyōiku shuppan	教育出版
kyōtsū ninshiki	共通認識
Li Peng	李鹏
Lishi dang'an	历史档案
Li Xiuying	李秀英
Lu Su	鲁苏
luohou jiuyao aida	落後就要挨打
maiguo	卖国
Mainichi shinbun	毎日新聞
Manzhouguo (Manchukuo)	満洲國
Matsui Iwane	松井石根
Matsumura Kenzō	松村謙三
Mei Ruao	梅汝璈

Miki Takeo	三木武夫
minshū	民衆
Minshuteki shokenri o mamoru tatakai	民主的諸権利を守る戦い
Minshutō	民主党
Miyazawa Kiichi	宮沢喜一
Motooka Shōji	本岡昭次
Mufushan	幕府山
Mukai Toshiaki	向井敏明
Murayama Tomiichi	村山富市
Mutō Akira	武藤章
Nagano Shigeto	永野茂門
Nagasaki genbaku shiryōkan	長崎原爆資料館
Nakajima Kesago	中島今朝吾
Nakasone Yasuhiro	中曽根康弘
Nanjing datusha	南京大屠殺
"Nanjing datusha de lishi shishi burong cuangai"	南京大屠杀的历史史实不容篡改
"Nanjing datusha de quanmao"	南京大屠杀的全貌
Nanjing de xianluo	南京的陷落
"Nanjing shi linshi canyihui guanyu xiezhu diaocha Nanjing datusha an jingguo"	南京市临时参议会关于协助调查南京大屠杀案经过
Nankin daigyakusatsu	南京大虐杀
Nankin jiken chōsa kenkyūkai	南京事件調査研究会
Nankin jiken kenkyūka	南京事件研究家
Nihon bunkyō shuppan	日本文教出版
Nihon jinmin no rekishi	日本人民の歴史
Nihon keizai shinbun	日本経済新聞
Nihon no rekishi (ge)	日本の歴史（下）
Nihon no sensō sekinin shiryō sentā	日本の戦争責任資料センター
Nihon rekishi	日本歴史
Nihon shi kaiteiban	日本史改訂版
Nihon shoseki	日本書籍
Nikkeiren	日経連
Noda Tsuyoshi	野田毅

Nomura Shūsuke	野村秋介
Ogasawara Mikio	小笠原幹夫
Ogawa Heiji	小川平二
Ōkunoshima dokugasu shiryōkan	大久島毒ガス資料館
Ōsaka kokusai heiwa sentā	大阪国際平和センター
Ōsaka shoseki	大阪書籍
Ōshima Yōichi	大島陽一
Pingdingshan	平頂山
Qin-Hua Rijun Nanjing datusha dang'an	侵华日军南京大屠杀档案
Qin-Hua Rijun Nanjing datusha shiliao	侵华日军南京大屠杀史料
Qin-Hua Rijun Nanjing datusha shiliao bianji weiyuanhui	侵华日军大屠杀史料编辑
Qin-Hua Rijun Nanjing datusha yunan tongbao jinianguan	侵华日军南京大屠杀遇难同胞纪念馆
Rekishigaku kenkyūkai	歴史学研究会
Rekishi kentō iinkai	歴史検討委員会
Rekishi ka wa tennōsei o dō miru ka	歴史家は天皇制をどう見るか
Rekken	歴研
Riben qin-Hua yanjiu	日本侵华研究
Rijun qin-Hua baoxing: Nanjing datusha	日军侵华暴行：南京大屠杀
Ritsumeikan daigaku kokusai heiwa myūjiiamu	立命館大学国際平和ミュージアム
Saitama ken heiwa shiryōkan	埼玉県平和資料館
Sakurai Shin	桜井新
Sankei shinbun	三経新聞
Sankō	三光
Sanseidō	三省堂
Satō Seizaburō	佐藤誠三郎
Seiron	正論
seitō na mono de nai	正当なものでない

Sekai	世界
Sekai no rekishi	世界の歴史
Sekai shi	世界史
Senkaku Islands (Diaoyu Islands)	尖閣諸島
senryō	占領
seppuku	切腹
shakaika	社会科
Shimamura Yoshinobu	島村宜伸
shimatsu seyo	始末せよ
Shimin no fusen sensei	市民の不戦宣誓
Shimizu shoin	清水書院
Shina	支那
Shin Nihon shi	新日本史
Shin Nihon shi kaiteiban	新日本史改定版
shinryaku	進略
Shinshō sekai shi	新詳世界史
shinshutsu	侵出
Shin ureubeki kyōkasho no mondai	新うれうべき教科書の問題
Shokun!	諸君
Shūkan asahi	週刊朝日
Shūkan kin'yōbi	週刊金曜日
Shūsen 50 shūnen kokumin iinkai	終戦五十周年国民委員会
shūshin	修身
Sugamo	巣鴨
Suzuki Zenkō	鈴木善幸
taigai bōchō	対外膨張
Takahashi Kazuo	高橋一夫
Tamaki Hajime	玉城肇
Tanaka Kō	田中甲
Tang Shengzhi	唐生智
Tani Hisao	谷寿夫
Teikoku shoin	帝国書院
tennōsei	天皇制
Tian'anmen	天安門

Tōjō Hideki 東条英機
Tōkyō nichinichi shinbun 東京日日新聞
Tōkyō shinbun 東京新聞
Tōkyō shoseki 東京書籍
Tongzhou 通州
tucheng xuelei 屠城血泪
Ureubeki kyōkasho no mondai うれうべき教科書の問題
Wadatsumikai わだつみ会
Watanabe Michio 渡辺美智雄
Xinhua yuebao 新华月报
Yamakawa shuppan 山川出版
Yasukuni Shrine 靖国神社
yeman 野蠻
yōjinbōteki chishikijin 用心棒的知識人
Yomiuri shinbun 読売新聞
Yōsetsu sekai shi 要説世界史
Yuibutsu shikan Nihon rekishi nyūmon 唯物史観日本歴史入門
zaibatsu 財閥
zangyaku kōi 残虐行為
Zenbō ゼンボー
zesei 是正
Zhou Erfu 周而复
"Zoku Nankin daigyakusatsu no sūjiteki kenkyū" 続南京大虐殺の数字的研究
Zou Mingde 邹明德

Bibliography

Ad Hoc Committee on the Case against Hirohito. “Unmasking Hirohito: The Other Hitler.” *New York Times,* 16 February 1989, p. 9.

Adachi Yoshihiko 安達喜彦. “Kodomotachi to tomo ni mirai o kirihiraku tame ni” 子どもたちとともに未来を切りひらくために (Creating Our Future with Children). *Rekishi chiri kyōiku* 歴史地理教育 345 (December 1982): 16–27.

———. “Senso ni katan saserareta minshu” 戦争に加担させられた民衆 (The People Who Helped the War). *Rekishi chiri kyōiku* 歴史地理教育 339 (August 1982): 8–12.

Aitani Kunio 藍谷邦雄 “Sengo hoshō saiban no genjō to kadai” 戦後補償裁判の現状と課題 (The Present Condition and Tasks of Postwar Trials Concerning Government Reparations). *Kikan senso sekinin kenkyu* 季刊戦争責任研究 10 (winter 1995): 2–9.

“Aka kara no rekishi no kaiho” 赤からの歴史の解放 (Liberation of History from the Reds). *Yomiuri shinbun* 読売新聞, evening edition, 7 December 1963, p. 9.

Akazawa Shirō 赤澤史朗 et al., eds. *Tokyō saiban handobukku* 東京裁判ハンドブック (Handbook of the Tokyo War Crimes Trial). Tokyo: Aoki shoten, 1989.

Amago Satoshi 天児慧. “Nit-Chu kankei—sengo sedai kara no teigen” 日中関係：戦後世代からの提言 (Sino-Japanese Relations: A Proposal from the Postwar Generation). *Sekai* 世界 517 (July 1988): 258–70.

Ando Yutaka 安藤豊. "'Senso' o torae naosu bunken annai" 「戦争」をとらえ直す文献案内 (An Introduction to Books That Reconsider the "War"). *"Kingendai shi" no jugyo kaikaku* 「近現代史」の授業改革 1 (September 1995): 89–94.

Appleby, Joyce, Lynn Hunt, and Margaret Jacob. *Telling the Truth about History.* New York: Norton, 1994.

Ara Ken'ichi 阿羅健一. *Kikigaki Nankin jiken* 聞き書き南京事件 (Notes Based on Interviews on the Nanjing Incident). Tokyo: Tosho shuppansha, 1987.

———. "Nankin jiken 'jugun nikki' no maboroshi" 南京事件「従軍日記」のまぼろし (The Illusion of an "Army Diary" during the Nanjing Incident). *Shokun!* 諸君 28.7 (July 1996): 136–44.

Arai Shin'ichi 荒井信一 et al., eds. "Jugonen senso o do toraeru ka" 十五年戦争をどうとらえるか (How to Comprehend the Fifteen-Year War). *Rekishi chiri kyoiku*歴史地理教育 219 (December 1973): 42–61.

"'Atarashii rekishi kyokasho o tsukuru kai' shuisho" 「新しい歴史教科書をつくる会」趣意書 (Prospectus of the "Committee to Prepare a New History Textbook"). In *Atarashii Nihon no rekishi hajimaru* 新しい日本の歴史はじまる (A New Japanese History Begins), comp. Japanese Institute for Orthodox History Education, pp. 314–15. Tokyo: Gentōsha, 1997.

Awaya Kentaro 栗屋憲太郎. *Gendaishi hakkutsu* 現代史発掘 (Discovering Modern Japanese History). Tokyo: Otsuki shoten, 1996.

———. "In the Shadows of the Tokyo Tribunal." In *The Tokyo War Crimes Trial: An International Symposium,* ed. Hosoya Chihiro et al., pp. 79–89. Tokyo: Kōdansha, 1986.

———. *Miketsu no senso sekinin* 未決の戦争責任 (The Unsolved Responsibility for the War). Tokyo: Kashiwa shobo, 1994.

———. *Tokyo saiban ron* 東京裁判論 (Discussion of the Tokyo War Crimes Trial). Tokyo: Otsuki Shoten, 1989.

———. "'Tokyo saiban shikan' to wa" 東京裁判史観とは (The Tokyo Trial View of History). In *Kingendai shi no shinjitsu wa nanika: Fujioka Nobukatsu shi no "rekishi kyoiku, heiwa kyō-*

iku ron" hihan 近現代史の真実は何か：藤岡信勝氏の「歴史教育・平和教育論」批判 (Truths in Modern Japanese History: A Critique of Fujioka Nobukatsu's "Historical Education and Peace Education"), ed. Fujiwara Akira 藤原彰 et al., pp. 158–67. Tokyo: Ōtsuki shoten, 1996.

Azuma Shirō 東史郎. *Waga Nankin puraton: ichi shoshuhei no taiken shita Nankin daigyakusatsu* わが南京プラトーン：一召集兵の体験した南京大虐殺 (My Platoon: The Experience in the Nanjing Massacre of a Conscripted Soldier). Tokyo: Aoki shoten, 1987.

"Backgrounder: Chronology of Japanese Politicians' Denial of Japanese Aggression History." *Xinhua News Agency,* 16 August 1995.

Bai Wu 白芜. *Jinri zhi Nanjing* 近日之南京 (Nanjing Now). Chongqing: Nanjing wanbaoshe chubanbu, 1938.

Baldwin, Peter, ed. *Reworking the Past: Hitler, the Holocaust, and Historians' Debate.* Boston: Beacon Press, 1990.

Bartov, Omer. "Defining Enemies, Making Victims: Germans, Jews, and the Holocaust." *American Historical Review* 103 (June 1998): 771–816.

———. "Intellectuals on Auschwitz: Memory, History, and Truth." In *Murders in Our Midst: The Holocaust, Industrial Killing, and Representation,* pp. 115–36. New York: Oxford University Press, 1996.

Bates, Miner Searle. Papers. Yale Divinity School Library, Yale University, New Haven, Connecticut.

Bauman, Zygmunt. *Modernity and the Holocaust.* Ithaca, N.Y.: Cornell University Press, 1989.

Beasley, W. G. *The Rise of Modern Japan.* New York: St. Martin's Press. 1990.

Bōeichō bōei kenkyūjo senshishitsu 防衛庁防衛研究所戦史室. *Shina jihen rikugun sakusen* 支那事変陸軍作戦 (The Army's Strategy—The Sino-Japanese War). Tokyo: Asagumo shinbunsha, 1975.

Brackman, Arnold C. *The Other Nuremberg: The Untold Story of the Tokyo War Crimes Trials.* Glasgow: William Collins Sons, 1989.

Browning, Christopher R. "German Memory, Judicial Interrogation, History Reconstruction: Writing Perpetrator History from Postwar Testimony." In *Probing the Limits of Representation: Nazism and the "Final Solution,"* ed. Saul Friedländer, pp. 22–36. Cambridge, Mass.: Harvard University Press, 1992.

———. *Ordinary Men: Reserve Police Battalion 101 and the Final Solution in Poland.* New York: Aaron Asher Books, 1992.

Brzezinski, Zbigniew. *Out of Control.* New York: Charles Scribner's Sons, 1993.

Buruma, Ian. "The Afterlife of Anne Frank." *New York Review of Books* 45.3 (19 February 1998): 4–8.

———. *Wages of Guilt: Memories of War in Germany and Japan.* New York: Farrar Straus Giroux, 1994.

———. "War and Remembrance: Memories of the Nanjing Massacre Are Drenched in Politics." *Far Eastern Economic Review* (5 September 1991): 51–52.

Carr, Edward Halett. *What Is History?* New York: Vintage Books, 1961.

Chang, Iris. *The Rape of Nanking: The Forgotten Holocaust of World War II.* New York: Basic Books, 1997.

Chen Anji 陈安吉, ed. *Qin-Hua Rijun Nanjing datusha shi guoji xueshu taolunhui lunwenji* 侵华日军南京大屠杀史国际学术讨论会论文集 (Essays from an International Symposium on the History of the Nanjing Massacre by the Japanese Army of Invasion into China). Hefei: Anhui daxue chubanshe, 1998.

Chen, David. "At the Rape of Nanking: A Nazi Who Saved Lives." *New York Times,* 12 December 1996, p. 3.

———. "Nazi Was Humanitarian to Chinese, War Diary Reveals." *New York Times,* 15 December 1996, p. 4A.

Chi Jingde 遲景德. "Zhanhou Zhongguo xiang Riben suoqu peichang yanjiu" 戰後中國向日軍索取賠償研究 (Researching China's Post-war Reparation Demands to Japan). Paper presented at Guofu jiandang geming yibai zhounian xueshu taolunhui 國父建黨革命一百周年學術討論會 (Conference for the 100th Anniversary of Sun Yat-sen's Revolutionary Party). Taiwan, 19–23 January 1994.

China Weekly Review. 1938.

Chinese Alliance for Memorial and Justice, The. "The Nanking Massacre: A Message of Future to Japan." *New York Times,* 26 December 1990, p. D16.

Chūgoku kikansha renrakukai 中国帰還者連絡会 (The Group of Returnees from China). *Shinryaku: Chūgoku ni okeru Nihon senpan no kokuhaku* 侵略：中国における日本戦犯の告白 (Invasion: Confessions of Japanese War Crimes in China). Tokyo: Shindoku shosha, 1958.

Cohen, Paul. *History in Three Keys: The Boxers as Event, Experience, and Myth.* New York: Columbia University Press, 1997.

Collingwood, R. G. *The Idea of History.* Oxford: Oxford University Press, 1946.

"'Dai sanji Ienaga kyōkasho soshō' saikōsai hanketsu" 第三次家永教科書訴訟最高裁判決 (The Supreme Court's Judgment in Ienaga's Third Textbook Trial). *Yomiuri shinbun* 読売新聞, 30 August 1997, p. 11.

Dirlik, Arif. "'Past Experience, If Not Forgotten, Is a Guide to the Future'; or What Is in a Text? The Politics of History in Chinese-Japanese Relations." In *Japan in the World,* ed. Masao Miyoshi and H.D. Harootunian, pp. 29–58. Durham, N.C.: Duke University Press, 1993.

Dower, John W. *Embracing Defeat: Japan in the Wake of World War II.* New York: Norton, 1999.

———. *War without Mercy: Race and Power in the Pacific War.* New York: Pantheon Books, 1986.

Dower, John, and John Junkerman. *The Hiroshima Murals.* New York: Kodansha, 1986.

D'Souza, Dinesh. *The End of Racism: Principles for a Multiracial Society.* New York: Free Press, 1995.

Duan Yueping 段月萍. "Bo Rijun Nanjing datusha 'xugou' lun" 驳日军南京大屠杀「虚構」论 (Refuting the "Illusion" Theories of the Japanese Military's Nanjing Massacre). In *Kang-Ri zhanzheng shishi tansuo* 抗日战争史事探索 (Probing Historical Events in the War of Resistance against Japan), ed. Jiangsu sheng lishi xuehui 江苏省历史学会 (Historical Studies Association of Jiangsu Province), pp. 328–36. Shanghai: Shanghai shehui kexueyuan chubanshe, 1988.

Durdin, F. Tillman. "Japanese Atrocities Marked Fall of Nanking after Chinese Command Fled." *New York Times,* 9 January 1938, p. 38.

———. "US Naval Display Reported Likely unless Japan Guarantees Our Rights; Butchery Marked Capture of Nanking." *New York Times,* 18 December 1937, pp. 1, 10.

Efron, Sonni. "Defender of Japan's War Past." *Los Angeles Times,* 9 May 1997, p. A1.

Elias, Robert. *The Politics of Victimization: Victims, Victimology, and Human Rights.* New York: Oxford University Press, 1986.

Evans, Richard J. *In Hitler's Shadow: West German Historians and the Attempt to Escape from the Nazi Past.* New York: Pantheon Books, 1989.

Field, Norma. "Kyōiku genba de no sensō: Higai to kagai no kioku tsunagaru mono" 教育現場での戦争：被害と加害の記憶繋がるもの (War in Education: Memory Links between Victimized and Victimizer). *Sekai* 世界 641 (October 1997): 269–71.

Fischer, David Hackett. *Historians' Fallacies: Toward a Logic of Historical Thought.* New York: Harper & Row, 1970.

Fitch, George. Papers. Harvard-Yenching Library. Harvard University, Cambridge, Massachusetts.

Fogel, Joshua A. *The Literature of Travel in the Japanese Rediscovery of China, 1862–1945.* Stanford, Calif.: Stanford University Press, 1996.

Foreign Broadcast Information Service. *Daily Report: China.* 1975–95.

Foreign Broadcast Information Service. *Daily Report: East Asia.* 1995.

Forever in the Shadow of Hitler? Original Documents of the Historikerstreit, the Controversy Concerning the Singularity of the Holocaust. Trans. James Knowlton and Truett Cates. Atlantic Heights, N.J.: Humanities Press, 1993.

Frei, Norbert. *Vergangenheitspolitik: Die Anfänge der Bundesrepublik und die NS-Vergangenheit.* Munich: C. H. Beck, 1996.

Friedländer, Saul. "Trauma, Transference, and 'Working Through' in Writing the History of the Shoah." *History and Memory* 4 (spring/summer 1992): 39–59.

———, ed. *Probing the Limits of Representation: Nazism and the "Final Solution."* Cambridge, Mass.: Harvard University Press, 1992.

Fu Zeng 付曾. "Nanjing datusha yu Riben diguozhuyi" 南京大屠杀与日本帝国主义 (The Nanjing Massacre and Japanese Imperialism). *Jindai shi yanjiu* 近代史研究 16 (February 1983): 154–80.

Fuji Nobuo 富士信夫. *"Nankin daigyakusatsu" wa kōshite tsukurareta* 「南京大虐殺」はこうしてつくられた (This Is How "The Nanjing Massacre" Was Made Up). Tokyo: Tendensha, 1995.

———. *Watashi no mita Tōkyō saiban* 私の見た東京裁判 (The Tokyo War Crimes Trial That I Observed). 2 vols. Tokyo: Kōdansha gakujutsu bunko, 1988.

Fujio Masayuki 藤尾正行. "'Hōgen daijin' futatabi hoeru" 放言大臣再び吠える (The Outspoken Minister Barks Again). *Bungei shunjū* 文芸春秋 64.11 (November 1986): 110–24.

———. "'Hōgen daijin' ōi ni hoeru" 放言大臣大いに吠える (The Outspoken Minister Barks Loudly). *Bungei shunjū* 文芸春秋 64.10 (October 1986): 122–33.

Fujioka Nobukatsu 藤岡信勝. "GHQ ni wasuresaserareta 'Tokyō dai kūshū'" GHQに忘れさせられた「東京大空襲」 (The Tokyo Air Raids: Wiped from Our Memory by GHQ). *Shokun!* 諸君 30.7 (July 1998): 152–61.

———. *Jiyūshugi shikan to wa nani ka* 自由主義史観とは何か (What Is a Liberal View of History?). Tokyo: PHP bunko, 1997.

———. *Kyokasho ga oshienai rekishi* 教科書が教えない歴史 (History That Textbooks Do Not Teach). Tokyo: Sankei shuppan, 1996.

———. "'Nankin daigyakusatsu 30 man' no uso" 南京大虐殺三十万の嘘 (The Fabrication of 300,000 in the Nanjing Massacre). In *Kokumin no yudan: rekishi kyōkasho ga abunai* 国民の油断：歴史教科書が危ない (Negligence of the Nation: The Danger of History Textbooks), ed. Fujioka Nobukatsu and Nishio Kanji 西尾幹二, pp. 209–15. Tokyo: PHP kenkyūjo, 1996.

———. *Ojoku no kingendai shi: ima kokufuku no toki* 汚辱の近現代史：いま克服のとき (Modern Japanese History: The Time Has Come to Get Over the Disgrace). Tokyo: Tokuma shoten, 1996.

———. "Sōkan no ji" 創刊の辞 (Greetings at the Publication of the First Issue). *"Kingendai shi" no jugyō kaikaku*「近現代史」の授業改革 1 (September 1995): 1.

Fujioka Nobukatsu 藤岡信勝 and Nishio Kanji 西尾幹二. *Kokumin no yudan: rekishi kyōkasho ga abunai* 国民の油断：歴史教科書が危ない (Negligence of the Nation: The Danger of History Textbooks). Tokyo: PHP kenkyūjo, 1996.

Fujiwara Akira 藤原彰. *15 nen sensōshi* 十五年戦争史 (History of the 15-Year War), vol. 4. Tokyo: Aoki shoten, 1989.

———. *Nankin daigyakusatsu* 南京大虐殺 (The Nanjing Massacre). Tokyo: Iwanami shoten, 1985.

———. "Nankin daigyakusatsu no giseisha sū ni tsuite" 南京大虐殺の犠牲者数について (On the Number of Those Sacrificed in the Nanjing Massacre). *Rekishi chiri kyōiku* 歴史地理教育 530 (March 1995): 66–73.

———. *Nankin no Nihongun* 南京の日本軍 (The Japanese Army in Nanjing). Tokyo: Aoki shoten, 1997.

———. "Rekishi no bōkyaku wa yurusarenai" 歴史の忘却は許されない (The Oblivion of History Must Not Be Permitted). In *Tennōsei to kokumin shuken* 天皇制と国民主権 (The Emperor System and Popular Sovereignty), ed. Shin Nihon shuppansha henshūbu 新日本出版社編集部, pp. 243–54. Tokyo: Shin Nihon shuppansha, 1989.

Fujiwara Akira 藤原彰 et al., eds. *Kingendai shi no shinjitsu wa nanika: Fujioka Nobukatsu shi no "rekishi kyōiku, heiwa kyōiku ron" hihan* 近現代史の真実は何か：藤岡信勝氏の「歴史教育・平和教育論」批判 (Truths in Modern Japanese History: A Critique of Fujioka Nobukatsu's "Historical Education and Peace Education"). Tokyo: Ōtsuki shoten, 1996.

Gaimushō 外務省. *Gaimushō Shōwa 12-nendo shitsumu hōkokusho* 外務省昭和12年度執務報告書 (Report on the Execution of Duties for 1937 by the Foreign Ministry), vol. 2. Tokyo: Kuresu, 1995.

Gao Xingzu 高兴祖. "Du *Nanjing datusha tuzheng*" 读《南京大屠杀图证》 (Reading the *Illustrated Proof of the Nanjing Massacre*). *Kang-Ri zhanzheng yanjiu* 抗日战争研究 23 (February 1997): 22–29.

———. *Rijun qin-Hua baoxing: Nanjing datusha* 日军侵华暴行: 南京大屠杀 (Japanese War Atrocities: The Nanjing Massacre). Shanghai: Shanghai renmin chubanshe, 1985.

Gao Xingzu 高兴祖 et al. "Riben diguozhuyi zai Nanjing datusha" 日本帝国主义在南京大屠杀(Japanese Imperialism in the Nanjing Massacre). Trans. Robert Gray. China News Digest. Global News #GL96-039 (http://www.cnd.org/njmassacre/njm-tran), 21 and 23 March 1996.

General Headquarters, Supreme Commander for the Allied Powers, Allied Translator and Interpreter Section. *Press Translations and Summaries—Japan.* Reels #12, 13, 17.

Ginsburg, Carlo. "Just One Witness." In *Probing the Limits of Representation: Nazism and the "Final Solution,"* ed. Saul Friedländer, pp. 82–96. Cambridge, Mass.: Harvard University Press, 1992.

Giordano, Ralph. *Daini no tsumi* 第二の罪 (The Second Crime). Trans. Nagai Kiyohiko 永井清彦 et al. Tokyo: Hakusuisha, 1990.

———. *Die zweite Schuld oder Von Last Deutscher zu sein.* Hamburg: Rasch und Rohring Verlag, 1987.

Gluck, Carol. "History according to Whom: Let the Debate Continue," *New York Times,* 19 November 1994, p. 23.

———. "The Idea of Shōwa." In *Shōwa: The Japan of Hirohito,* ed. Carol Gluck et al., pp. 1–26. New York: W. W. Norton, 1992.

———. "The Past in the Present." In *Postwar Japan as History,* ed. Andrew Gordon, pp. 64–95. Berkeley and Los Angeles: University of California Press, 1993.

———. "The Rape of Nanking: How 'the Nazi Buddha' Resisted the Japanese." *Times Literary Supplement,* 17 June 1997, pp. 9–10.

Gong, Gerritt, ed. *Remembering and Forgetting: The Legacy of War and Peace in East Asia.* Washington, D.C.: Center for Strategic and International Studies, 1996.

Han Wenning 韩文宁. "Qin-Hua Rijun zai Nanjing de wenhua dajielüe" 侵华日军在南京的文化大劫掠 (The Great Cultural Plundering of Nanjing by Invading Japanese Troops). *Yangzi wanbao* 扬子晚报 (8 December 1994): 10.

Harris, Sheldon. *Factories of Death: Japanese Biological Warfare, 1932–45, and the American Cover-up*. New York: Routledge, 1994.

Hartman, Geoffrey, ed. *Bitburg in Moral and Political Perspective*. Bloomington: Indiana University Press, 1986.

Hata Ikuhiko 秦郁彦. *Nanjing datusha zhenxiang: Riben jiaoshou de lunshu* 南京大屠殺真相：日本教授的論述 (The Truth of the Nanjing Massacre: Explications of a Japanese Professor). Yang Wenxin 楊文信, translator. Hong Kong: Shangwu yinshudian, 1995.

———. "Nankin daigyakusatsu 'Rābe kōka' o sokutei suru" 南京大虐殺「ラーベ効果」を測定する (The Nanjing Massacre: Examining the "Rabe Effect"). *Shokun!* 諸君 30.2 (February 1998): 80–89.

———. "The Nanking Atrocities: Fact and Fable." *Japan Echo* 25.4 (August 1998): 47–57.

———. "Nankin gyakusatsu jiken: kazu no kōsatsu" 南京虐殺事件：数の考察 (The Nanjing Massacre: A Study of the Numbers). Paper presented at the Fourth International Symposium on Sino-Japanese Relations, Keiō University, 16 November 1997.

———. *Nankin jiken: "Gyakusatsu" no kōzō* 南京事件：「虐殺」の構造 (The Nanjing Incident: The Structure of the "Massacre"). Tokyo: Chūō kōronsha, 1986.

———. "A Numerical Study of the Nanjing Incident." Paper presented at the conference "Nanking 1937," Princeton University, 22 November 1997.

———. "Seiji no omocha ni sareru rekishi ninshiki" 政治のオモチャにされる歴史認識 (Historical Understanding, a Plaything of Politics). *Shokun!* 諸君 29.9 (September 1997): 36–43.

———. "Ronsōshi kara mita Nankin gyakusatsu jiken" 論争史から見た南京虐殺事件 (The Nanjing Atrocity Incident as Seen From The History of The Debate). *Seiron* 正論 198 (February 1989): 234–46.

———. *Shōwa shi no nazo o ou* 昭和史の謎を追う (The Pursuit of Riddles in the History of the Shōwa Period), vol. 1. Tokyo: Bungei shunjū, 1995.

Hata Kensuke 秦賢助. "Horyo no chi ni mamireta byakko butai" 捕虜の血にまみれた白虎部隊 (The White Tiger Battalion Which Was Covered with the Blood of Prisoners). *Nihon shūhō* 日本週報 38.9 (25 February 1957): 13–15.

Hayashi Fusao 林房雄. *Dai tō-A sensō kōteiron* 大東亜戦争肯定論 (The Affirmative Thesis on the Greater East Asian War). Tokyo: Banchō shobō, 1964.

———. *Zoku dai tō-A sensō kōteiron* 続大東亜戦争肯定論 (The Affirmative Thesis on the Greater East Asian War, Part II). Tokyo: Banchō shobō, 1965.

He Qifang 何其芳. "Ribenren de beiju" 日本人的悲剧 (The Japanese Tragedy). *Wenyi zhanxian* 文艺战线 2 (1939): 82–85.

Hein, Laura. "Doing the Really Hard Math." *Asian Studies Newsletter* 43.2 (spring 1998): 6.

"Heiwa ga miemasu ka" 平和が見えますか (Can You See Peace?). *Asahi shinbun* 朝日新聞, 15 August 1995, p. 8.

Herf, Jeffrey. *Divided Memory: The Nazi Past in the Two Germanies*. Cambridge, Mass.: Harvard University Press, 1997.

Higashinakano Osamichi 東中野修道."Aratamete 'Rabe no nikki' o tettei kenshō suru" 改めて「ラーベの日記」を徹底検証する (Thoroughly Investigating the "Rabe Diary" Again). *Seiron* 正論 308 (April 1998): 286–96.

———. *"Nankin gyakusatsu" no tettei kenshō* 「南京虐殺」の徹底検証 (A Thorough Investigation of the "Nanjing Massacre"). Tokyo: Tendensha, 1998.

———. "Rekishi no kenkyū ka rekishi no waikyoku ka: Nankin daigyakusatsuron no kansei" 歴史の研究か歴史の歪曲か：南京大虐殺論の陥穽 (The Study of History or the Distortion of History: A Pitfall in the Argument about the Nanjing Massacre). *"Kingendai shi" no jugyō kaikaku* 「近現代史」の授業改革 4 (June 1996): 37–45.

Hilberg, Raoul. "I Was Not There." In *Writing and the Holocaust*, ed. Berel Lang, pp. 17–25. New York: Holmes & Meier, 1988.

Hirayama Ikuo 平山郁夫. "Yūki o motte rekishi to mukiaou" 勇気をもって歴史と向き合おう (Confronting History Boldly). *Ronza* 論座 31 (November 1997): 196–97.

Hirsch, Herbert. *Genocide and the Politics of Memory: Studying Death to Preserve Life.* Chapel Hill: University of North Carolina Press, 1995.

Historikerstreit: Die Dokumentation der Kontroverse um die Einzigartigkeit der nationalsozialistischen Judenvernichtung. Munich: Piper Verlag, 1987.

Honda Katsuichi 本多勝一. *Chūgoku no Nihongun* 中国の日本軍 (The Japanese Army in China). Tokyo: Sōjusha, 1972.

———. *Chūgoku no tabi* 中国の旅 (Travels in China). Tokyo: Asahi shinbunsha, 1972.

———. "Gonin no taiken shi" 五人の体験史 (Oral Histories of Five People). In *Nankin daigyakusatsu no genba e* 南京大虐殺の現場へ (To the Scene of the Nanjing Massacre), ed. Hora Tomio 洞富雄, pp. 170–211. Tokyo: Asahi shinbunsha, 1988.

———. "Izaya Bendasan shi e no kōkaijō" イザヤベンダサン氏への公開状 (An Open Letter to Mr. Isaiah Bendasan). *Shokun!* 諸君 4:2 (February 1972): 208–17.

———. *The Nanjing Massacre: A Japanese Journalist Confronts Japan's National Shame.* Armonk, N.Y.: M. E. Sharpe, 1998.

———. *Nankin e no michi* 南京への道 (The Road to Nanjing). Tokyo: Asahi shinbunsha, 1987.

———. *Korosugawa no ronri* 殺す側の論理 (Logic from the Killer's Viewpoint). Tokyo: Asahi shinbunsha, 1984.

———. *Sabakareta Nankin daigyakusatsu* 裁かれた南京大虐殺 (The Nanjing Massacre on Trial). Tokyo: Banseisha, 1989.

———. "Zatsuon de ijimerareru gawa no me" 雑音でいじめられる側の眼 (From the Eyes of Those Who Were Made to Suffer by the Unpleasant Noise). *Shokun!* 諸君 4.4 (April 1972): 148–76.

Hong Guiji 洪桂己. *Riben zai Hua baoxing lu* 日本在华暴行录 (Account of the Atrocities Committed by Japan in China). Taibei: Guoshiguan, 1985.

———, ed. *Jindai Zhongguo waidie yu neijian shiliao huibian* 近代中国外谍与内奸史料汇编 (Edited History Materials on Modern China's Foreign Spies and Domestic Traitors). Taibei: Guoshiguan, 1979.

Hora Tomio 洞富雄. *Kindai senshi no nazo* 近代戦史の謎 (Riddles of Modern War History). Tokyo: Jinbutsu ōraisha, 1967.

———. *Nankin daigyakusatsu: "maboroshi" ka kōsaku hihan* 南京大虐殺：「まぼろし」化工作批判 (The Nanjing Massacre: Criticism of the Making of an Illusion). Tokyo: Gendaishi shuppankai, 1975.

———. *Nankin daigyakusatsu no genba e* 南京大虐殺の現場へ (To the Scene of the Nanjing Massacre). Tokyo: Asahi shinbunsha, 1988.

———. *Nankin daigyakusatsu no shōmei* 南京大虐殺の証明 (The Proof of the Nanjing Massacre). Tokyo: Asahi shinbunsha, 1986.

———. *Nankin jiken* 南京事件 (The Nanjing Incident). Tokyo: Shinjinbutsu ōraisha, 1972.

———. "Nankin jiken to shiryō hihan" 南京事件と史料批判 (The Nanjing Incident and Critique of the Historical Documents). *Rekishi hyōron* 歴史評論 6.277 (1973): part 1, 106–18.

———. *Nit Chū sensō: Nankin daigyakusatsu jiken shiryōshū* 日中戦争：南京大虐殺事件資料集 (The Sino-Japanese War: A Collection of Historical Materials on the Nanjing Massacre), vol. 1, *Kyokutō kokusai gunji saiban kankei shiryō hen* 極東国際軍事裁判関係資料編 (Historical Materials on the Tokyo War Crimes Trial). Tokyo: Aoki shoten, 1985.

———. *Nit-Chū sensō: Nankin daigyakusatsu jiken shiryōshū* 日中戦争：南京大虐殺事件資料集 (The Sino-Japanese War: A Collection of Historical Materials on The Nanjing Massacre), vol. 2, *Eibun shiryō hen* 英文資料編 (Historical Materials in English). Tokyo: Aoki shoten, 1985.

———. *Nit-Chū sensōshi shiryōshū 9: Nankin jiken II* 日中戦争史資料集史：南京事件 (A Collection of Historical Materials on the Sino-Japanese War: The Nanjing Incident). Tokyo: Kawade shobō shinsha, 1973.

Hora Tomio 洞富雄, Fujiwara Akira 藤原彰, and Honda Katsuichi 本多勝一, eds. *Nankin daigyakusatsu no kenkyū* 南京大虐殺の研究 (Studies of the Nanjing Massacre). Tokyo: Banseisha, 1992.

Hora Tomio 洞富雄 et al., eds. *Nankin jiken o kangaeru* 南京事件を考える (Consideration of the Nanjing Massacre). Tokyo: Ōtsuki shoten, 1987.

Hosaka Masayasu 保坂正康. *Bōkyaku sareta shiten* 忘却された視点 (A Forgotten Point of View). Tokyo: Chūō kōronsha, 1996.

Hosomi Kazuyuki 細見和之. "Dekigoto to kioku: 'Nankin daigyakusatsu' 60ka nen ni yosete" 出来事と記憶：「南京大虐殺」60カ年によせて (Event and Memory: On the 60th Anniversary of the "Nanjing Massacre"). *Hihyō kūkan* 批評空間 14 (July 1997): 66–77.

Howell, William Lee. "The Inheritance of War: Japan's Domestic Politics and International Ambitions." In *Remembering and Forgetting: The Legacy of War and Peace in East Asia,* ed. Gerritt W. Gong, pp. 82–102. Washington, D.C.: Center for Strategic and International Studies, 1996.

Hsu Shu-hsi 徐淑希. *A Digest of Japanese War Conduct* (日人战争行为集要). Shanghai: Kelly and Walsh, 1939.

———. *Documents of the Nanking Safety Zone* (南京安全区档案). Shanghai: Kelly and Walsh,1939.

———. *The War Conduct of the Japanese* (日人战争行为论要). Shanghai: Kelly and Walsh, 1938.

Ide Junji 井手純二. "Watashi ga mokugeki shita Nankin no sangeki" 私が目撃した南京の惨劇 (The Tragedy I Witnessed at Nanjing). *Zōkan rekishi to jinbutsu* 増刊歴史と人物 169 (1984): 272–76.

Ienaga Saburō 家永三郎. "The Historical Significance of the Tokyo Trial." In *The Tokyo War Crimes Trial: An International Symposium,* ed. C. Hosoya et al., pp. 165–70. Tokyo: Kodansha, 1986.

———. *The Pacific War, 1931–1945: A Critical Perspective on Japan's Role in World War II.* New York: Pantheon Books, 1978.

———. *Sensō sekinin* 戦争責任 (War Responsibility). Tokyo: Iwanami shoten, 1985.

———. *Taiheiyō sensō* 太平洋戦争 (The Pacific War). Tokyo: Iwanami shoten, 1986. Revised and expanded edition.

Ienaga Saburō 家永三郎 et al., eds. *Kyōkasho kara kesenai sensō no shinjitsu: rekishi o yugameru Fujioka Nobukatsu shi ra e no hihan* 教科書から消せない戦争の真実：歴史を歪める藤岡信勝氏らへの批判 (The Truth of the War That Cannot Be Erased from Textbooks: A Critique of the Fujioka Nobukatsu School and Its Distortion of History). Tokyo: Aoki shoten, 1996.

Iggers, George G. *Historiography in the Twentieth Century: From Scientific Objectivity to the Postmodern Challenge.* Hanover, N.H.: University of New England Press, 1997.

Iguchi Kazuki 井口和起 et al., eds. *Nankin jiken: Kyōto shidan kankei shiryōshū* 南京事件：京都師団関係資料集 (The Nanjing Incident: A Collection of Historical Materials of the Kyoto Division). Tokyō: Aoki shoten, 1989.

Ikei Masaru 池井優. *Nihon gaikō shi gaisetsu* 日本外交史概説 (An Outline of the History of Japanese Diplomacy). Tokyo: Keiō tsūshin, 1994.

Imai Masatake 今井正剛. "Nankin jōnai no tairyō satsujin" 南京城内の大量殺人 (Mass Executions within the City of Nanjing). *Bungei shunjū tokushū* 文芸春秋特集 (December 1956): 154–58.

Imai Seiichi 今井清一 et al., eds. *Shōwa shi* 昭和史 (History of the Shōwa Era). Tokyo: Iwanami shoten, 1994.

Inose Naoki 猪瀬直樹 et al., eds. *Mokugekisha ga kataru Shōwa shi: Nit-Chū sensō* 目撃者が語る昭和史：日中戦争 (Witnesses Discuss the History of the Shōwa Era: The Japan-China War), vol. 5. Tokyo: Shinjinbutsu ōraisha, 1989.

International Military Tribunal for the Far East. *The Tokyo War Crimes Trial.* Annotated, compiled, and edited by R. John Pritchard and Sonia Magbanau Zaide. New York: Garland, 1981.

International Society for Educational Information (ISEI). *Japan in Modern History: High School.* 2 vols. Tokyo: ISEI, 1995.

———. *Japan in Modern History: Junior High School.* Tokyo: ISEI, 1994.

———. *Japan in Modern History: Primary School.* Tokyo: ISEI, 1993.

In the Name of the Emperor. Videocassette. Dir. Christine Choy and Nancy Tong. New York: Film News Now Foundation, 1995.

Inumaru Giichi 犬丸義一. *Rekishi kagaku no kadai to Marukusushugi* 歴史科学の課題とマルクス主義 (The Task of Historical Science and Marxism). Tokyo: Azekura shobō, 1970.

———. "Sengo Nihon Marukusushugi shigaku ni kansuru oboegaki: 1945–50 nen o chūshin ni" 戦後日本マルクス主義史学に関

する覚書き: 1945–50 年を中心に (A Memorandum on the Issue of Marxist Historiography in Postwar Japan: Concerning 1945–50). In *Kōza Nihon shi* 講座日本史 (Kōza series: Japanese History, vol. 10), ed. Rekishigaku kenkyūkai 歴史学研究会, pp. 97–172. Tokyo: Tōdai shuppankai, 1971.

Ishihara Shintarō 石原慎太郎. "'Nankin daigyakusatsu' no kyokō: rekishi no kaizan o haisu" 「南京大虐殺」の虚構：歴史の改竄を排す (The Fiction of the "Nanjing Massacre": Driving away Revisions of History). *Shokun!* 諸君 26.7 (July 1994): 156–61.

Ishihara Shintarō 石原慎太郎, Watanabe Shōichi 渡辺昇一, and Ogawa Kazuhisa 小川和久. *Sore de mo "No" to ieru Nihon* それでも「NO」と言える日本 (A Japan That Can Still Say "No"). Tokyo: Kōbunsha, 1990.

Ishii Akira 石井明. "Sengo Nit-Chū kankei no kiseki" 戦後日中関係の軌跡 (A Path of Postwar Japan-China Relations). *Gaikō fōramu* 外交フォーラム 10, special issue (1997): 94–107.

Ishikawa Tatsuzō 石川達三. *Ikite iru heitai* 生きている兵隊 (Living Soldiers). *Chūō kōron, gekidō no Shōwa bungaku* 中央公論、激動の昭和文学 (November 1997): 274–350.

Ishiko Junzō 石子順造. "Nankin gyakusatsu jiken: hōdō sarenakatta jijitsu no imi" 南京虐殺事件：報道されなかった事実の意味 (The Nanjing Massacre: The Meaning of Unreported Facts). In *Kōza: Komyunikēshon 5: Jiken to hōdō* 講座：コミュニケーション5：事件と報道 (Communication, Five: Incidents and Reporting), ed. Etō Fumio 江藤文夫 et al., pp. 179–200. Tokyo: Kenkyūsha, 1972.

Itakura Yoshiaki 板倉由明. "Hata Ikuhiko shi e no chūkoku: 'Zangeya Sone Kazuo' e no shinkō" 秦郁彦氏への忠告：ザンゲ屋曽根一夫への信仰 (Fidelity to Mr. Hata Ikuhiko: Believing the Professional Confessor Sone Kazuo). *Getsuyō hyōron* 月曜評論 1331 (5 October 1997): 3–4.

———. "Matsui Iwane nikki no kaizan ni tsuite" 松井石根日記の改竄について (About the Distortion of Matsui Iwane's Diary). *Bungei shunjū* 文芸春秋 64.1 (January 1986): 186–94.

———. "'Nankin daigyakusatsu 20 man' setsu e no hanshō" 「南京大虐殺二十万」説への仮証 (Refuting the Theory of 200,000

Deaths of the Nanjing Massacre). *"Kingendai shi" no jugyō kaikaku* 「近現代史」の授業改革 1 (September 1995): 71–79.

———. "'Nankin gyakusatsu' no zangeya Sone Kazuo no shōtai" 「南京虐殺」のザンゲ屋曽根一夫の正体 (Unmasking Sone Kazuo, a Professional Confessor about the "Nanjing Massacre"). *Shokun!* 諸君 20.12 (December 1988): 126–46.

———. "Shinbun ga ōkiku sodateta chiisa na gohō" 新聞が大きく育てた小さな誤報 (A Small Erroneous Report That Was Made Big by the Newspapers). *Shokun!* 諸君 14.11 (November 1982): 48–59.

Jaspers, Karl. *The Question of German Guilt.* Trans. E. B. Ashton. New York: Dial, 1947.

Jay, Martin. "Of Plots, Witnesses, and Judgments." In *Probing the Limits of Representations: Nazism and the "Final Solution,"* ed. Saul Friedländer, pp. 97–107. Cambridge, Mass.: Harvard University Press, 1992.

"Jijitsu gonin o Eibun de shiteki" 事実誤認を英文で指摘 (Pointing Out Distortions in English). *Sankei shinbun* 産経新聞, evening edition, 13 April 1998.

Kaikosha 偕行社. *Nankin senshi* 南京戦史 (War History of Nanjing). 3 vols. Tokyo: Kaikōsha, 1989.

Kamata Sadao 鎌田定夫. "Genbaku shiryōkan de nani o manabu ka" 原爆資料館で何を学ぶか (What We Learn from the [Nagasaki] Atomic Bomb Museum). *Rekishi chiri kyōiku* 歴史地理教育 561 (April 1997): 62–67.

———. "Nagasaki genbaku shiryōkan no kagai tenji mondai" 長崎原爆資料館の加害展示問題 (The Issue of the Portrayal of Victimizers at the Nagasaki Atomic Bomb Museum). *Kikan sensō sekinin kenkyū* 季刊戦争責任研究 14 (winter 1996): 22–31.

Kammen, Michael. "Some Patterns and Meanings of Memory Distortion in American History." In *Memory Distortion: How Minds, Brains, and Societies Reconstruct the Past,* ed. Daniel L. Schacter, pp. 329–45. Cambridge, Mass.: Harvard University Press, 1995.

Kanda Fumihito 神田文人 *Shōwa shi nenpyō* 昭和史年表 (Chronology of the Shōwa Era). Tokyo: Shōgakkan, 1995.

Kariya Tetsu 雁屋哲. "Kōmori o ute!" 蝙蝠を撃て (Beat a Bat). *Shūkan kin'yōbi* 週刊金曜日 (14 March 1997): 46–49.

Kasahara Tokushi 笠原十九司. *Ajia no naka no Nihongun: sensō sekinin to rekishigaku, rekishi kyōiku* アジアの中の日本軍：戦争責任と歴史学、歴史教育 (The Japanese Military in Asia: War Responsibility, Historical Study, and Historical Education). Tokyo: Ōtsuki shoten, 1994.

———. "Nanjing datusha de quanmao" 南京大屠殺的全貌 (Overall View of the Nanjing Massacre). In *Qin-Hua Rijun Nanjing datusha shi guoji xueshu taolunhui lunwenji* 侵华日军南京大屠杀史国际学术讨论会论文集 (Essays from an International Symposium on the History of the Nanjing Massacre by the Japanese Army of Invasion into China), ed. Chen Anji 陈安吉, pp. 31–39. Hefei: Anhui daxue chubanshe, 1998.

———. "Nankin daigyakusatsu no zenbō wa naze hōdō sarenakatta ka" 南京大虐殺の全貌がなぜ報道されなかったか (Why Was the Nanjing Massacre Not Reported?). *Rekishi chiri kyōiku* 歴史地理教育 396 (April 1986): 56–63; 397 (May 1986): 50–57; 398 (June 1986): 56–63; 399 (July 1986): 52–59; 400 (August 1986): 70–76; 401 (September 1986): 52–59.

———. "'Nankin daigyakusatsu' to rekishi kenkyū" 「南京大虐殺」と歴史研究 (The Nanjing Massacre and Historical Research). *Rekishi chiri kyōiku* 歴史地理教育 376 (December 1984): 59–67.

———. "'Nankin daigyakusatsu' wa nakatta no ka" 「南京大虐殺」はなかったのか (Was the Nanjing Massacre a Fabrication?). *Rekishi chiri kyōiku* 歴史地理教育 395 (March 1986): 94–96.

———. *Nankin jiken* 南京事件 (The Nanjing Incident). Tokyo: Iwanami shoten, 1997.

———. *Nankin nanminku no hyakunichi: gyakusatsu o mita gaikokujin* 南京難民区の百日：虐殺を見た外国人 (One Hundred Days in the Nanjing Safety Zone: Foreigners Who Witnessed the Massacre). Tokyo: Iwanami shoten, 1995.

———. *Nit-Chū zenmen sensō to kaigun: Panai gō jiken no shinsō* 日中全面戦争と海軍：パナイ号事件の真相 (Total War between Japan and China and the Navy: The Truth of the USS Panay Incident). Tokyo: Aoki shoten, 1997.

———. "Saisho no Nankin daigyakusatsu hōdō" 最初の南京大虐殺報道 (The First Newspaper Accounts of the Nanjing Massacre). *Rekishi chiri kyōiku* 歴史地理教育 409 (March 1987): 52–59.

———. "Sensō kōteiron, menzairon no kiseki to genzai" 戦争肯定論、免罪論の軌跡と現在 (The Trajectory of the Argument That Affirms and Legitimizes the War). *Jinmin no rekishigaku* 人民の歴史学 128 (June 1996): 1–14.

Kasahara Tokushi 笠原十九司, Matsumura Takao 松村高夫, and Watanabe Harumi 渡辺春巳, eds. *Rekishi no jijitsu o dō nintei shi dō oshieru ka* 歴史の事実をどう認定し、どう教えるか (How Historical Facts Should Be Recognized and Taught). Tokyo: Kyōiku shiryō shuppankai, 1997.

Kasahara Tokushi 笠原十九司, Suzuki Tadaaki 鈴木忠明, and Watanabe Harumi 渡辺春巳. "Nankin gyakusatsu jiken" 南京虐殺事件 (The Incident of the Nanjing Massacre). In *Rekishi no jijitsu o dō nintei shi dō oshieru ka* 歴史の事実をどう認定しどう教えるか (How Historical Facts Should Be Recognized and Taught), ed. Kasahara Tokushi, Matsumura Takao 松村高夫, and Watanabe Harumi, pp. 64–147. Tokyo: Kyōiku shiryō shuppankai, 1997.

Kellner, Hans. "'Never Again' Is Now." *History and Theory* 33 (1994): 127–44.

Kikan sensō sekinin kenkyū 季刊戦争責任研究 1 (fall 1993); 2 (winter 1993); 3 (spring 1994); 4 (summer 1994); 5 (fall 1994); 6 (winter 1994); 7 (spring 1995); 8 (summer 1995); 9 (fall 1995); 10 (winter 1995); 11 (spring 1996); 12 (summer 1996); 13 (fall 1996); 14 (winter 1996); 15 (spring 1997); 16 (summer 1997); 17 (fall 1997); 18 (winter 1997); 19 (spring 1998); 20 (summer 1998); 21 (fall 1998); 22 (spring (1999).

Kimijima Kazuhiko 君島和彦. "Nankin jiken no gyakusatsu shashin" 南京事件の虐殺写真 (Photograph of the Massacre at the Nanjing Incident). In *Shiryō: kyōyō no Nihon shi* 史料、教養の日本史 (Historical Materials: Japanese History for Education), ed. Takeuchi Makoto 竹内誠 et al., p. 218. Tokyo: Tokyo University Press, 1991.

"Kingendai shi" no jugyō kaikaku 「近現代史」の授業改革 1 (September 1995).

"Kingendai shi" no jugyō kaikaku 「近現代史」の授業改革 4 (June 1996).

Kisaka Jun'ichirō 木坂順一郎. "Ajia, taiheiyō sensō no rekishiteki seikaku o megutte" アジア、太平洋戦争の歴史的性格をめぐって (Historical Characteristics of the Asia-Pacific War). *Nenpō Nihon gendai shi* 年報日本現代史 (1995): 1–43.

Kitsukawa Manabu 橘川学. *Nihon wa shinryaku koku de wa nai* 日本は侵略国ではない (Japan Was Not an Aggressive Nation). Tokyo: Akatsuki shobō, 1983.

Kobayashi, Yoshinori 小林よしのり. "Shin gomanizumu sengen" 新ゴマニズム宣言 (A Declaration of Arrogance, New Version). Chap. 37. *Sapio,* 12 March 1997, pp. 65–74.

———. "Shin gomanizumu sengen" 新ゴマニズム宣言 (A Declaration of Arrogance, New Version). Chap. 72. *Sapio,* 24 June 1998, pp. 69–76.

———. *Shin gomanizumu sengen 3* 新ゴマニズム宣言 3 (A Declaration of Arrogance, New Version), vol. 3. Cartoon. Tokyo: Shōgakkan, 1997.

Kobori Keiichirō 小堀桂一郎. *Kinjō tennō ron* 今上天皇論 (An Essay on the Current Emperor). Tokyo: Nihon kyōbunsha, 1986.

———. "Kyōkasho mondai, watashi no teigen" 教科書問題、私の提言 (My Suggestion on the Issue of the Textbook Controversy). *Shokun!* 諸君 14.10 (October 1982): 46–62.

Kobori Keiichirō 小堀桂一郎, Hasegawa Michiko 長谷川三千子, and Watanabe Shōichi 渡辺昇一. "Eiga 'Tōkyō saiban' ni monomōsu" 映画「東京裁判」にモノ申す (A Challenge to the Film *Tokyo War Crimes Trial*). *Shokun!* 諸君 15.8 (August 1983): 24–42.

Kojima Noboru 児島襄 et al. *Jinrui wa sensō o fusegeru ka* 人類は戦争を防げるか (Can Humanity Prevent Wars?). Tokyo: Bungei shunjūsha, 1996.

Kojima Reiitsu. "Accumulation, Technology, and China's Economic Development." In *The Transition to Socialism in China,* ed. Mark Seldon and Victor Lippit, pp. 238–65. New York: M. E. Sharpe, 1982.

Komagome Takeshi 駒込武. "'Jiyū shugi shikan' wa watashitachi o 'jiyū' ni suru no ka?" 「自由主義史観」は私達を「自由」にする

のか (Does the "Liberal Historical View" Liberate Us?). *Sekai* 世界 633 (April 1997): 59–73.

Komatsu Yutaka 小松豊. "Kagai no men o chūshin ne sueta 15 nen sensō no gakushū" 加害の面を中心にすえた十五年戦争の学習 (The Study of the Fifteen-Year War with Emphasis on [Japan's] Role as Victimizer). *Rekishi chiri kyōiku* 歴史地理教育 339 (August 1982): 14–23.

Koyama Hitoshi 小山仁示. "Piisu Ōsaka e no uyoku no kōgeki" ピースおおさかへの右翼の攻撃 (Right-wing Attacks on Peace Osaka). *Kikan sensō sekinin kenkyū* 季刊戦争責任研究 19 (spring 1998): 42–49.

Kristof, Nicholas D. "Many in Japan Oppose Apology to Asians for War." *New York Times*, 6 March 1995, p. A9.

Kusawake Kyōko 草分京子. "'Tannaka heiwa no hi' wa watashitachi no atarashii dai ippo" 「谷中平和の碑」は私たちの新しい第一歩 (The "Tannaka Peace Monument" Symbolizes Our New Step). *Rekishi chiri kyōiku* 歴史地理教育 557 (December 1996): 34–45.

Kyōkasho kentei soshō o shien suru zenkoku renrakukai 教科書検定、訴訟を支援する全国連絡会 (The National Liaison Conference Supporting [Ienaga's] Textbook Case). *Kyōkasho kara kesenai sensō no shinjitsu* 教科書から消せない戦争の真実 (Truth that Can't Be Erased from Textbooks). Tokyo: Aoki shoten, 1996.

Kyōkasho repōto '97 教科書レポート '97 (Textbook Report, 1997) 41 (February 1997).

"Kyōkasho sara ni 'senzen' fukken e; Monbusho kōkō shakai chūshin ni kentei kyōka; 'Shinryaku' hyōgen usumeru; kodai tennō ni mo keigo" 教科書さらに「戦前」復権へ；文部省高校社会中心に検定強化；「侵略」表現薄める；古代天皇にも敬語 (Textbooks Return Further "Toward Prewar" Position; The Ministry of Education Tightens the Standards of Textbook Authorization, Especially for High School History [Textbooks]; The Term "Aggression" Toned Down; Honorific Language Added to Descriptions of the Emperors in the Ancient Period). *Asahi shinbun* 朝日新聞, 26 June 1982, p. 1.

"Kyō no mondai" 今日の問題 (The Issue for Today). *Asahi shinbun* 朝日新聞, evening edition, 7 December 1963, p. 1.

LaCapra, Dominick. “Representing the Holocaust: Reflections on the Historian’s Debate.” In *Probing the Limits of Representation: Nazism and the “Final Solution,”* ed. Saul Friedländer, pp. 108–27. Cambridge, Mass.: Harvard University Press, 1992.

Li Enhan 李恩涵. “Nanjing datusha de tusha mingling wenti” 南京大屠殺的屠殺命令問題 (The Problem of Ordering a Massacre in the Nanjing Massacre). In *Ribenjun zhanzheng baoxing zhi yanjiu* 日本軍戰爭暴行之研究 (Researching the War Brutality of the Japanese Military), pp. 104–56. Taibei: Taiwan shangwu yinshuguan, 1994.

Li, Haibo. “Unforgettable Atrocity.” *Beijing Review* (14–20 August 1995): 14–22.

Lipstadt, Deborah. *Denying the Holocaust: The Growing Assault on Truth and Memory.* New York: Free Press, 1993.

Lozowick, Yaacov, and Rochelle L. Millen. “Pitfalls of Memory: Israeli-German Dialogues on the Shoah.” In *New Perspectives on the Holocaust,* ed. Rochelle L. Millen, pp. 265–74. New York: New York University Press, 1996.

Lübbe, Hermann. “Der Nationalsozialismus im politischen Bewußtsein der Gegenwart.” In *Deutschlands Weg in die Diktatur: Internationale Konferenze zur nationalsozialistischen Machtübernahme im Reichstagsgeväude in Berlin,* pp. 329–349. Berlin: Siedler Verlag, 1983.

Luo Changhong 罗昌洪. “Shenpan Riben zhanfan: junshi fating de zujian jingguo” 审判日本战犯：军事的组建经过 (Trials of Japanese War Criminals: Forming the Military Court). *Nanjing shizhi* 南京史志 5 (1992): 30–31.

Maier, Charles S. *The Unmasterable Past: History, Holocaust, and German National Identity.* Cambridge, Mass.: Harvard University Press, 1988.

Matsumoto Ken’ichi 松本健一. “Nankin daigyakusatsu no shinwateki kōzō” 南京大虐殺の神話的構造 (The Mythic Structure of the Nanjing Massacre). *Shokun!* 諸君 26.9 (September 1994): 96–105.

———. “Shinwa to shite no Nankin daigyakusatsu” 神話としての南京大虐殺 (The Nanjing Massacre as Myth). *Seiron* 正論 147 (March 1985): 110–22.

Mayer, Arno J. *Why Did the Heavens Not Darken: The "Final Solution" in History.* New York: Pantheon Books, 1988.

"Meiji 100 nen o iwau igi to riyū" 明治百年を祝う意義と理由 (The Reason to Celebrate the 100th Anniversary of the Meiji and Its Significance). *Rekishigaku kenkyū* 歴史学研究 320 (January 1967): 63–64.

Meng Guoxiang 孟国祥 and Cheng Tangfa 程堂发. "Chengzhi hanjian gongzuo gaishu" 惩治汉奸工作概述 (A General Account of Punishing Traitors). *Minguo dang'an* 国民档案 2 (1994): 105–12.

Milgram, Stanley. *Obedience to Authority: An Experimental View.* New York: Harper and Row, 1974.

Millen, Rochelle L., ed. *New Perspectives on the Holocaust.* New York: New York University Press, 1996.

Miller, Judith, *One, By One, By One. Facing the Holocaust.* New York: Touchstone/Simon Schuster, 1990.

Minear, Richard H. *Victor's Justice: The Tokyo War Crimes Trial.* Princeton, N.J.: Princeton University Press, 1971.

Ministry of Foreign Affairs, Japan. *Diplomatic Blue Book 1990: Japan's Diplomatic Activities.* Tokyo: Ministry of Foreign Affairs, 1991.

Miyata Eijirō 宮田栄二郎. "Reddo pāji" レッドパージ (Red Purge). In *Nihon kingendai shi jiten* 日本近現代史辞典 (Encyclopedia of Modern and Contemporary Japanese History). Tokyo: Tōyō keizai shinpōsha, 1978.

Miyazaki Yoshimasa 宮崎吉政 et al., eds. *Shinbun shūsei Shōwa shi no shōgen* 新聞集成昭和史の証言 (A Collection of Newspapers: Testimonies of the Shōwa Era), vols. 21, 22, and 25. Tokyo: SBB shuppankai, 1991.

Mori Masataka 森正孝. *Nihon no Chūgoku shinryaku* 日本の中国侵略 (Japanese Aggression in China). Tokyo: Akashi shoten, 1991.

Murakami Hatsuichi 村上初一. *Dokugasutō no rekishi* 毒ガス島の歴史 (History of the Poison Gas Island). Hiroshima: Murakami Hatsuichi, 1996.

Nakamura Akira 中村粲. *Dai tō-A sensō e no michi* 大東亜戦争への道 (En Route to the Greater East Asian War). Tokyo: Tendensha, 1990.

———. "Nankin jiken rokujūnenme no shinjitsu: 'Rābe nikki' no shinpyōsei o tou" 南京事件六十年目の真実：ラーベ日記の信憑性を問う (The Truth on the Sixtieth Anniversday of the Nanjing Massacre: Questioning the Reliability of the Rabe Diary). *Seiron* 正論 305 (January 1998): 90–101.

Nakamura Kikuji 中村紀久二. *Kyōkasho no hensan, hakkō kyōkasho seido no hensen ni kansuru chōsa kenkyū* 教科書の編纂・発行教科書制度の変遷に関する調査研究 (A Study of the Changes of Compilation and Publishing of Textbooks). Tokyo: Kyōkasho kenkyū sentā, 1997.

Nanjing datusha ziliao bianji weiyuanhui 南京大屠杀史料编辑委员会 (Committee for the Compilation of Sources on the Nanjing Massacre). *Qin-Hua Rijun Nanjing datusha shiliao* 侵华日军南京大屠杀史料 (Historical Materials on the Nanjing Massacre by the Japanese Troops Who Invaded China). Nanjing: Jiangsu guji chubanshe, 1985.

"Nanjing Students Forced to Visit Massacre Memorial Hall." In "NewsHound," *San Jose Mercury Press* (NewsHound@sjmercury.com), 6 November 1996.

"'Nankin daigyakusatsu' no kakushin" 「南京大虐殺」の核心 (The Core of the "Nanjing Massacre"). *Shokun!* 諸君 17.4 (April 1985): 68–87.

"'Nankin gyakusatsu' jiken" 南京虐殺事件 (The Nanjing Massacre Incident). In *Rekishi no jijitsu o dō nintei shi dō oshieru ka* 歴史の事実をどう認定しどう教えるか (How Historical Facts Should Be Recognized and Taught), ed. Kasahara Tokushi 笠原十九司 et al., pp. 64–147. Tokyo: Kyōiku shiryō shuppankai, 1997.

"Nankin gyakusatsu sansensha no shōgen" 南京虐殺参戦者の証言 (Eyewitness Evidence of Those Who Participated in the Nanjing Massacre). *Bungei shunjū* 文芸春秋 62.12 (December 1984): 214–36.

Nankin jiken chōsa kenkyūkai 南京事件調査研究会 (The Study Group on the Nanjing Incident). *Nankin jiken shiryōshū* 南京事件資料集 (A Collection of Historical Materials on the Nanjing Incident), vol. 1, *America kankei shiryō hen* アメリカ関係

資料編 (Historical Materials with Regard to the United States). Tokyo: Aoki shoten, 1992.

———. *Nankin jiken shiryōshū* 南京事件資料集 (A Collection of Historical Materials on the Nanjing Incident), vol. 2, *Chūgoku kankei shiryō hen* 中国関係資料編 (Historical Materials with Regard to China). Tokyo: Aoki shoten, 1992.

Nankin shi bunshi shiryō kenkyūkai 南京市文史資料研究会, comp. *Shōgen: Nankin daigyakusatsu* 証言：南京大虐殺 (Evidence: The Nanjing Massacre). Trans. Kagami Mitsuyuki 加加美光行 and Himeta Mitsuyoshi 姫田光義. Tokyo: Aoki shoten, 1984.

"News Reported in Japan." On h-asia@h-net.msu.edu, 6 May 1997.

NHK hōsō seron chōsajo NHK 放送世論調査所. *Zusetsu sengo seron shi* 図説戦後世論史 (A Diagrammatic Chart of Public Opinion in the Postwar Period). Tokyo: Nihon hōsō shuppan kyōkai, 1983.

"Nihon bōeijō no seiyaku, Beigun kakunin, enjo o yakusu" 日本防衛上の制約、米軍確認、援助を約す (The American Military Acknowleges Japan's Limitation on Its Defense and Promises Its Help). *Asahi shinbun* 朝日新聞, 25 October 1953, p. 1.

Nihon minshutō 日本民主党 (The Japanese Democratic Party). *Ureubeki kyōkasho no mondai* うれうべき教科書の問題 (Deplorable Problems in School Textbooks). Tokyo: Nihon minshutō, 1955.

Nihon no sensō sekinin shiryō sentā 日本の戦争責任資料センター(The Center for Research and Documentation on Japan's War Responsibility). *Kikan sensō sekinin kenkyū* 季刊戦争責任研究, nos. 1–22.

"Nihon o yurugashita 100 yo nichi" 日本を揺るがした百余日(100 Days That Shook Japan). *Shūkan asahi* 週刊朝日, 25 January 1989, pp. 2–7.

"Nihon seifu e no hoshō motomeru hōan o shiji" 日本政府への補償求める方案を支持 (Support for a Plan to Seek Reparations from the Japanese Government). *Sankei shinbun* 産経新聞, 9 May 1998.

Nik-Kan rekishi kyōkasho kenkyūkai 日韓歴史教科書研究会 (Japan-Korea History Textbook Study Group), ed. *Kyōkasho o*

Nik-Kan kyōryoku de kangaeru 教科書を日韓協力で考える (Considering Textbooks with Japanese-Korean Cooperation). Tokyo: Ōtsuki shoten, 1993.

Novick, Peter. *That Noble Dream: The "Objectivity Question" and the American Historical Profession.* New York: Cambridge University Press, 1988.

Oda Baku 小田莫. "Jūgonen sensō o dō oshieru ka" 十五年戦争をどう教えるか (How to Teach the Fifteen-Year War). *Rekishi chiri kyōiku* 歴史地理教育 219 (December 1973): 28–33.

Ōkuma Nobuyuki 大熊信行. "Nihon minzoku ni tsuite" 日本民族について (About the Japanese People). *Sekai* 世界 217 (January 1964): 66–76.

Okuno Seisuke 奥野誠亮. "'Shinryaku hatsugen' doko ga warui" 侵略発言どこが悪い (What's Wrong with My Comment on Japan's "Aggression"?). *Bungei shunjū* 文芸春秋 66.7 (July 1988): 112–26.

Ono Kenji 小野賢二. "Kagai no kiroku: Nankin daigyakusatsu nikki" 加害の記録：南京大虐殺日記 (Account of a Victimizer: Diary of the Nanjing Massacre). *Shūkan kin'yōbi* 週刊金曜日 1.6 (10 December 1993): 7–23.

Ono Kenji 小野賢二 et al., eds. *Nankin daigyakusatsu o kiroku shita kōgun heishitachi* 南京大虐殺を記録した皇軍兵士たち (The Soldiers Who Recorded the Nanjing Massacre). Tokyo: Ōtsuki shoten, 1996.

Onodera Toshitaka 小野寺利孝. "Sengo hoshō saiban tōsō no kadai to tenbō" 戦後補償裁判闘争の課題と展望 (Problems and Prospects in Postwar Legal Struggles over Government Reparations). *Hō to minshushugi* 法と民主主義, 328 (May 1998): 12–15.

"Osanago ni mo bōkō, Nankin daigyakusatsu o bakuro" 幼な子にも暴行、南京大虐殺を暴露 (Children, Too, Were Massacred; Revealing the Massacre at Nanjing). *Asahi shinbun* 朝日新聞, 26 July 1946, p. 2.

Ōta Katsuhiro 太田勝洪. "Dai niji sekai taisen go no Nit-Chū kankei" 第二次世界大戦後の日中関係 (Sino-Japanese Relations since World War II). In *Kindai Nit-Chū kankei shi nyūmon* 近代日中関係史入門 (An Introduction to the History of Modern Sino-Japanese Relations), ed. Yamane Yukio 山根幸夫, Fujii

Shōzō 藤井昇三, Nakamura Tadashi 中村義, and Ōta Katsuhiro, pp. 363–404. Tokyo: Kenbun shuppan, 1992.

Pepper, Suzanne. *Civil War in China: The Political Struggle, 1945–1949.* Berkeley and Los Angeles: University of California Press, 1978.

Piccigallo, Philip R. *The Japanese on Trial: Allied War Crimes Operations in the East, 1945–1951.* Austin: University of Texas Press, 1979.

Pritchard, John R. *The Tokyo War Crimes Trial.* 22 vols. New York: Garland Publishing, 1981.

Rabe, John. *Nankin no shinjitsu* 南京の真実 (The Truth about Nanjing). Trans. Hirano Kyōko 平野卿子. Tokyo: Kōdansha, 1997.

"'Reipu obu Nankin' 2 nen mae, dō taitoru shashinshū" 「レイプ・オブ・南京」2年前、同タイトル写真集 (A Collection of Photographs with the Same Title as [Iris Chang's] *Rape of Nanking* Was Published Two Years Ago). *Sankei shinbun* 産経新聞, evening edition, 25 May 1998.

"'Reipu obu Nankin' . . . shōko nashi? sōsaku? arata ni 3 mai giwaku shashin" 「レイプ・オブ南京」。。。証拠なし？創作？新たに3枚疑惑写真 (No Proof? Fabrication? Three Additional Doubtful Photographs in [Iris Chang's] *Rape of Nanking*). *Sankei shinbun* 産経新聞, 15 May 1998.

Reischauer, Edwin. *Japan: The Story of a Nation.* Tokyo: Tuttle, 1988.

Rekishi chiri kyōiku 歴史地理教育. *Shiryō Nihon kingendai shi III* 史料日本近現代史 III (Historical Materials: Modern and Contemporary Japanese History, III). Tokyo: Sanseidō, 1985.

Rekishi kentō iinkai 歴史検討委員会 (Committee to Examine History). *Dai tō-A sensō no sōkatsu* 大東亜戦争の総括 (An Outline of the Greater East Asia War). Tokyo: Tendensha, 1995.

Rekishi kyōikusha kyōgikai 歴史教育者協議会. *Heiwa hakubutsukan, sensō shiryōkan handobukku* 平和博物館・戦争資料館ハンドブック (Handbook for Peace and War Museums). Tokyo: Aoki shoten, 1995.

Roling, B. V. A. *The Tokyo Trial and Beyond: Reflections of a Peacemonger.* Cambridge, Eng.: Polity Press, 1993.

Rosenbaum, Alan, ed. *Is the Holocaust Unique? Perspectives on Comparative Genocide.* Boulder, Colo.: Westview Press, 1996.

Rummel, R. J. *China's Bloody Century: Genocide and Mass Murder since 1900.* New Brunswick, N.J.: Transaction Publishers, 1991.

"Saki no sensō 'shinryaku sensō' to meigen" 先の戦争「侵略戦争」と明言 (Assertion of the Last War as an "Aggressive War"). *Asahi shinbun* 朝日新聞, 11 August 1993, p. 1.

Sase Masamori 佐瀬昌盛. "Nagano hatsugen to kokusai kankaku" 永野発言と国際感覚 (The Nagano Speech and International Feelings). *Shokun!* 諸君 26.7 (July 1994): 162–70.

Satō Kazuo 佐藤和男. *Kenpō kyūjō, shinryaku sensō, Tōkyō saiban* 憲法九条・侵略戦争・東京裁判 (Article 9 of the Constitution, Aggressive War, and the Tokyo War Crimes Trial). Tokyo: Hara shobō, 1985.

———. "Rekishi no naka no kokusaihō: 'shinryaku' 'shinryaku sensō'" 歴史の中の国際法：「侵略」「侵略戦争」 (International Law in History: 'Aggression' and 'Aggressive War'). *"Kingendai shi" no jugyō kaikaku* 「近現代史」の授業改革 1 (September 1995): 66–70.

Schacter, Daniel L., ed. *Memory Distortion: How Minds, Brains, and Societies Reconstruct the Past.* Cambridge, Mass.: Harvard University Press, 1995.

Schilling, Donald G. "The Dead End of Demonizing: Dealing with the Perpetrators in Teaching the Holocaust." In *New Perspectives on the Holocaust,* ed. Rochelle L. Millen, pp. 196–211. New York: New York University Press, 1996.

Schudson, Michael. "Dynamics of Distortion in Collective Memory." In *Memory Distortion: How Minds, Brains, and Societies Reconstruct the Past,* ed. Daniel L. Schacter, pp. 346–64. Cambridge, Mass.: Harvard University Press, 1995.

Sensō giseisha o kokoro ni kizamu kai 戦争犠牲者を心に刻む会 (A Group That Keeps War Victims in Their Memory). *Ajia no koe* アジアの声 (Voice of Asia). Ōsaka: Tōhō Shuppan, 1987.

Shimada Katsumi 島田勝巳. "Nankin kōryakusen to gyakusatsu jiken" 南京攻略戦と虐殺事件 (The Battle of Aggression at Nanjing and the Massacre). *Tokushū jinbutsu ōrai* 特集人物往来 1.3 (June 1956): 106–11.

Shimono Ikkaku 下野一霍 and Gotō Kōsaku 五島広作. *Nankin sakusen no shinsō* 南京作戦の真相 (The Truth about the Nanjing Operation). Tokyo: Tōkyō jōhōsha, 1966.

"Shinpojiumu: Atarashii rekishizō o motome" シンポジウム：新しい歴史像を求め (Symposium: Toward a New View of History). *Seiron* 正論 (August 1997): 46–91.

Shirota Tsuyoshi 代田毅. "Sensō taiken o dō oshieru ka" 戦争体験をどう教えるか (How to Teach the Wartime Experience). *Rekishi chiri kyōiku* 歴史地理教育158 (August 1969): 32–36.

Shōgen: Nankin daigyakusatsu 証言: 南京大虐殺 (Evidence: The Nanjing Massacre). Trans. Kagami Mitsuyuki 加加美光行 and Himeta Mitsuyoshi 姫田光義. Tokyo: Aoki shoten, 1984.

Shōji Akira 庄司章. "Senjika no Nihon wa 'fashizumu?'" 戦時下の日本は「ファシズム」(Was Japan "Fascist" during the War?). *"Kingendai shi" no jugyō kaikaku* 「近現代史」の授業改革 1 (September 1995): 60–65.

Shōwa niman nichi no zen kiroku 昭和二万日の全記録 (All Records of 20,000 Days of the Shōwa Era), vol 15. Tokyo: Kōdansha, 1990.

Smalley, Martha Lund, ed. *American Missionary Eyewitnesses to the Nanking Massacre, 1937–38.* New Haven: Yale Divinity School Library, 1997.

Smith, Charles. "One Man's crusade: Kenji Ono lifts the veil on the Nanjing Massacre." *Far Eastern Economic Review* 157.34 (25 August 1994): 24–25.

Smythe, Lewis S. C. *War Damage in the Nanking Area, December 1937 to March 1938: Urban and Rural Surveys.* Shanghai: Mercury Press, 1938.

———. "What Happened in Nanking." *China Forum* (1 October 1938): 380–89.

Sone Kazuo 曽根一夫. *Moto kakyū heishi ga taiken kenbun shita jūgun ianfu* 元下級兵士が体験見聞した従軍慰安婦 (Comfort Women Whom the Former Rank-and-File Soldier Experienced). Tokyo: Shiraishi shoten, 1993.

———. *Nankin gyakusatsu to sensō* 南京虐殺と戦争 (The Nanjing Massacre and the War). Tokyo: Tairyūsha, 1988.

———. *Shiki Nankin gyakusatsu* 私記南京虐殺 (A Private Narrative of the Nanjing Massacre). Tokyo: Sairyūsha, 1984.

———. *Zoku shiki Nankin gyakusatsu* 続私記南京虐殺 (A Private Narrative of the Nanjing Massacre, Part II). Tokyo: Sairyūsha, 1984.

Song Shutong 宋书同. "Shenpan Nanjing datusha an zhufan Gu Shoufu de huiyi" 审判南京大屠杀案主犯谷寿夫的回忆 (Recollections of a Leading Nanjing Massacre War Criminal, Tani Hisao). Xuewen jizhuan 學文記傳 12:2 (February 1968): 17–20.

Stanford, Michael. *The Nature of Historical Knowledge.* Oxford: Basil Blackwell, 1986.

Sun Zhaiwei 孙宅巍, ed. *Nanjing datusha* 南京大屠杀 (The Nanjing Massacre). Beijing: Beijing chubanshe, 1997.

Suzuki Akira 鈴木明. "Mukai shōi wa naze korosareta ka: Nankin '100 nin giri' no maboroshi" 向井少尉はなぜ殺されたか南京「百人斬り」のまぼろし (Why Was Second Lieutenant Mukai Killed?: The Illusion of "Killing Competitions" in Nanjing). *Shokun!* 諸君 4.8 (August 1972): 178–203.

———. *"Nankin daigyakusatsu" no maboroshi* 「南京大虐殺」のまぼろし (The Illusion of the "Nanjing Massacre"). Tokyo: Bungei shunjū, 1973.

———. "'Nankin daigyakusatsu' no maboroshi" 「南京大虐殺」のまぼろし (The Illusion of the "Nanjing Massacre"). *Shokun!* 諸君 4.4 (April 1972): 177–91.

"Taisen no kōi 'kibishiku hansei'" 大戦の行為「厳しく反省」("Stern Reflection" on Behavior during the War). *Asahi shinbun* 朝日新聞, 4 May 1991, p. 1.

Takahashi Shirō 高橋史朗. *Tennō to sengo kyōiku* 天皇と戦後教育 (The Emperor and Postwar Education). Tokyo: Hyūman dokyumento sha, 1989.

Takahashi Tetsuya 高橋哲哉. "Tasha no sensō no kioku o mizukara no kakushinbu ni kizamu" 他者の戦争の記憶を自らの核心部に刻む (Engraving the Memory of Others' War in One's Own Inner Self). *Ronza* 論座 32 (December 1997): 181–91.

Tanaka Masaaki 田中正明. *Matsui Iwane taishō no jinchū nisshi*

松井石根大将の陣中日誌 (The Field Diary of General Matsui Iwane). Tokyo: Fuyō shobō, 1985.

———. *"Nanjing datusha" zhi xugou* 《南京大屠杀》之虚构 (The Illusion of the "Nanjing Massacre"). Beijing: Shijie zhishi chubanshe, 1985.

———. "'Nankin daigyakusatsu kinenkan' ni monomōsu" 「南京大虐殺記念館」に物申す (A Challenge to the "Nanjing Memorial Hall"). *Seiron* 正論 159 (December 1985): 102–15.

———. *"Nankin gyakusatsu" no kyokō* 「南京虐殺」の虚構 (The Fabrication of the "Nanjing Massacre"). With a foreword by Watanabe Shōichi 渡辺昇一. Tokyo: Nihon kyōbunsha, 1984.

———. "'Nankin gyakusatsu' Matsui Iwane no jinchū nisshi" 「南京虐殺」松井石根の陣中日誌 (The "Nanjing Massacre": The Field Diary of General Matsui Iwane). *Shokun!* 諸君 15.9 (September 1983): 64–79.

———. *Nankin jiken no sōkatsu: gyakusatsu hitei 15 no ronkyo* 南京事件の総括：虐殺否定十五の論拠 (An Outline of the Nanjing Incident: Fifteen Grounds for the Denial of the Massacre). Tokyo: Kenkōsha, 1987.

———. *Tōkyō saiban to wa nani ka* 東京裁判とは何か (What Was the Tokyo War Crimes Trial?). Tokyo: Nihon kōgyō shinbunsha, 1983.

Tanaka Satoshi 田中敏. "Nachisu no bōrei ga sasayaku 'Nihon akudama ron'" ナチスの亡霊が囁く「日本悪玉論」 (Murmurs of a Nazi Ghost: On the Evil Character of Japan). *Shokun!* 諸君 30.2 (February 1998): 242–51.

Tanaka Yuki. *Hidden Horrors: Japanese War Crimes in World War II*. Boulder, Colo.: Westview Press, 1996.

Tang Meiru 湯美如 and Zhang Kaiyuan 章開沅, eds. *Nanjing: 1937 nian 11yue zhi 1938 nian 5yue* 南京1937年11月至1938年5月 (Nanjing: November 1937 to May 1938). Hong Kong: Sanlian shudian, 1995.

Tawara Yoshifumi 俵義文. *Dokyumento "ianfu" mondai to kyōkasho kōgeki* ドキュメント「慰安婦」問題と教科書攻撃 (Documentary: The Issue of "Comfort Women" and Attacks on School Textbooks). Tokyo: Kōbunken, 1997.

———. *Kenshō, 15nen sensō to chūkō rekishi kyōkasho* 検証15年

戦争と中高歴史教科書 (Examination: The 15-Year War and Junior High and High School Textbooks). Tokyo: Gakushū no tomo sha, 1994.

———. *Kyōkasho kōgeki no shinsō* 教科書攻撃の深層 (The Depth of Attacks on School Textbooks). Tokyo: Gakushū no tomo sha, 1997.

———. "Kyōkasho no 'Nankin daigyakusatsu' kijutsu wa dō kawatta ka: 'Nankin daigyakusatsu' no kyōkasho kijutsu no suii" 教科書の「南京大虐殺」記述はどう変ったか：「南京大虐殺」の教科書記述の推移 (How the Description of the "Nanjing Massacre" Changed: The Changes of the Description in the Textbooks). In *Kyōkasho kōgeki no shinsō* 教科書攻撃の深層 (The Depth of Attacks of School Textbooks), pp. 158–70. Tokyo: Gakushū no tomo sha, 1997.

Terada Hideo 寺田英夫. "Chūgoku kingendai shi de nani o oshieru ka" 中国近現代史でなにを教えるか (What Should Be Taught in Modern and Contemporary Chinese History). *Rekishi chiri kyōiku* 歴史地理教育 216 (October 1973): 5–15.

Thomas, Gina, ed. *The Unresolved Past: A Debate in German History.* London: Weidenfeld and Nicolson, 1990.

Thomas, Julia A. "Photography, National Identity and the 'Cataract of Times': Wartime Images and the Case of Japan." *American Historical Review* 103.5 (December 1998): 1475–1501.

Timperley, H. J. *Japanese Terror in China.* New York: Modern Age Books, 1938.

———. *What War Means: The Japanese Terror in China, A Documentary Record.* London: Victor Gollancz, 1938.

Ting, Y. L. "Nanjing Massacre: A Dark Page in History." *Beijing Review* 28, no. 35 (September 2, 1985): 15–21.

Tokutake Toshio 徳武敏夫. *Kyōkasho no sengo shi* 教科書の戦後史 (Postwar History of School Textbooks). Tokyo: Shin Nihon shuppansha, 1995.

Tōkyō saiban 東京裁判 (The Tokyo War Crimes Trial). Videocassette. Dir. Kobayashi Masaki 小林正樹. Tokyo: Pony Canyon, 1983.

Tōkyō saiban kenkyūkai 東京裁判研究会 (The Study Group on the Tokyo War Crimes Trial). *Paru hanketsusho* パル判決書

(Pal's Judgment). 2 vols. Tokyo: Kōdansha gakujutsu bunko, 1984.

"The Tokyo Trial in Historic Perspective: Question and Answer Period." In *The Tokyo War Crimes Trial: An International Symposium,* ed. Hosoya Chihiro et al., pp. 105–21. Tokyo: Kodansha, 1986.

Tōyama Shigeki 遠山茂樹. *Kyōkasho kentei no shisō to rekishi kyōiku* 教科書検定の思想と歴史教育 (Theory of Textbook Authorization and Historical Education). Tokyo: Ayumi shuppan, 1983.

———. "Sengo no rekishigaku to rekishi ishiki" 戦後の歴史学と歴史意識 (Postwar Historical Study and Historical Consciousness). In *Tōyama Shigeki chosakushū* 遠山茂樹著作集 (The Works of Tōyama Shigeki), vol. 8. Tokyo: Iwanami shoten, 1991.

Tsuda Michio 津田道夫. *Nankin daigyakusatsu to Nihonjin no seishin kōzō* 南京大虐殺と日本人の精神構造 (The Nanjing Massacre and the Spiritual Structure of the Japanese). Tokyo: Shakai hyōronsha, 1995.

Ueno Chizuko 上野千鶴子. "Kioku no seijigaku: Kokumin, kojin, watashi" 記憶の政治学：国民・個人・私 (The Political Science of Memory: The Nation, the Individual, and the Self). *Inpakushon* インパクション 103 (30 June 1997): 154–74.

———. "Posuto reisen to 'Nihonban rekishi shūseishugi'" ポスト冷戦と「日本版歴史修正主義」(Japanese Historical Revisionism in the Post–Cold War Era). *Ronza* 論座 35 (March 1998): 62–74.

Uesugi Chitoshi 上杉千年. "Nagasaki genbaku shiryōkan no mondai bubun" 長崎原爆資料館の問題部分 (Controversial Photos Exhibited at the Nagasaki Atomic Bomb Museum). *Seiron* 正論 287 (July 1996): 238–46.

———. "'Waga Nankin puratōn' o kokuhatsu" 「わが南京プラトーンを告発」 (An Indictment of "Our Nanjing Platoon"). *Jiyū* 自由 35.6 (June 1993): 86–98.

Uesugi Satoshi 上杉聰. "'Ianfu' mondai no shinkyokumen" 「慰安婦」問題の新局面 (A New Aspect of the Problem of "Comfort Women"). *Kikan sensō sekinin kenkyū* 季刊戦争責任研究17 (fall 1997): 32–37.

Ueyama Shunpei 上山春平. "Dai tō-A sensō no isan" 大東亜戦争の遺産 (The Legacy of the Greater East Asian War). In *Ueyama Shunpei chosakushū* 上山春平著作集 (The Works of Ueyama Shunpei), 3:342–523. Kyōto: Hōzōkan, 1995.

———. "Dai tō-A sensō no shisō shiteki igi" 大東亜戦争の思想史的意義 (The Significance of the Greater East Asian War in Intellectual History). *Chūō kōron* 中央公論 76.9 (September 1961): 98–107.

United States Department of State. *Papers Relating to the Foreign Relations of the United States: Japan 1931–1941,* vol. 1. Washington, D.C.: Government Printing Office, 1943.

———. *Foreign Relations of the United States: Diplomatic Papers 1937,* vol. 3. Washington, D.C.: Government Printing Office, 1954.

———. *Foreign Relations of the United States: Diplomatic Papers 1938,* vol. 3. Washington, D.C.: Government Printing Office, 1954.

United States Strategic Bombing Survey, Morale Division. *The Effects of Strategic Bombing on Japanese Morale.* Washington, D.C.: Government Printing Office, 1947.

Varg, Paul A. *Missionaries, Chinese, and Diplomats: The American Protestant Missionary Movement in China, 1890–1952.* Princeton, N.J.: Princeton University Press, 1958.

Vautrin, Minnie. Diary, 1937–40. Yale Divinity School Library, Yale University, New Haven, Connecticut.

Wakatsuki Yasuo 若槻康雄. *Nihon no sensō sekinin* 日本の戦争責任 (Japan's War Responsibility). Tokyo: Hara shobō, 1995.

Watanabe Noboru 渡辺登. "Sensō, sengo sekinin o tou 731 butaiten o kaisai shite" 戦争・戦後責任を問う 731 部隊展を開催して (In the Wake of the Unit 731 Exhibition: Questions about War and Postwar Responsibility). *Kikan sensō sekinin kenkyū* 季刊戦争責任研究 2 (winter 1993): 57–62.

Watanabe Shōichi 渡辺昇一. "The Emperor and the Militarists." *Japan Echo* 18.2 (1991): 90–97.

———. "Higeki no shōchō: Shōwa tennō" 悲劇の象徴：昭和天皇 (Tragic Symbol: The Shōwa Emperor). *Shokun!* 諸君 23.2 (February 1991): 26–40.

———. "Manken kyo ni hoeta kyōkasho mondai" 万犬虚に吠えた教科書問題 (Ten Thousand Dogs Barked at the Textbook Controversy). *Shokun!* 諸君 14.10 (October 1982): 23–44.

———. "Nankin daigyakusatsu wa nakatta" 南京大虐殺はなかった (There Was No Nanjing Massacre). In *Soredemo "No" to ieru Nihon* それでも「NO」と言える日本 (A Japan That Can Still Say "No"), ed. Ishihara Shintarō 石原慎太郎, Watanabe Shōichi, and Ogawa Kazuhisa 小川和久, pp. 177–85. Tokyo: Kōbunsha, 1990.

"We Were in Nanjing." *Reader's Digest* 33.198 (October 1938): 41–44.

White, Hayden. *Content of the Form: Narrative Discourse and Historical Representation.* Baltimore: Johns Hopkins University Press, 1987.

———. "Historical Emplotments and the Problem of Truth." In *Probing the Limits of Representations: Nazism and the "Final Solution,"* ed. Saul Friedländer, pp. 37–53. Cambridge, Mass.: Harvard University Press, 1992.

Wray, Harry. "China in Japanese Textbooks." In *China and Japan: A Search for Balance since World War I,* ed. Alvin D. Cox and Hillary Conroy, pp. 115–31. Santa Barbara: ABC-CLIO, 1978.

Wu Tianwei 吴天威. "Nanjing datusha shijian zhi zaiyanjiu" 南京大屠杀事件之再研究 (A Re-examination of the Nanjing Massacre). *Xin-Hua wenzhai* 新华文摘 2 (1985): 61–68.

Xu Zhigeng 徐志耕. *Xueji: qin-Hua Rijun Nanjing datusha shilu* 血祭. 侵华日军南京大屠杀实录 (Blood Sacrifice: An Accurate Record of the Invading Japanese Army and the Nanjing Massacre). Beijing: Zhongguo renshi chubanshe, 1994.

Yamada Akira 山田朗. "Arata na kyōkasho kōgeki no haikei ni aru mono" 新たな教科書攻撃の背景にあるもの (Behind the Revised Attacks on Textbooks). *Kyōkasho repōto '98* 教科書レポート 42 (February 1998): 27–30.

Yamamoto Shichihei 山本七平. "Asahi shinbun no 'gomen nasai'" 朝日新聞の「ごめんなさい」 ("Apology" from the *Asahi shinbun*). *Shokun!* 諸君 4.1 (January 1972): 166–79.

———. "Honda Katsuichi sama e no hensho" 本多勝一様への返書 (Response to Mr. Honda Katsuichi). *Shokun!* 諸君 4.3 (March 1972): 40–60.

———. "Honda Katsuichi sama e no tsuishin" 本多勝一様への追伸 (Another Response to Mr. Honda Katsuichi). *Shokun!* 諸君 4.4 (April 1972): 132–43.

———. *Watashi no naka no Nihongun* 私の中の日本軍 (The Japanese Military through My Eyes). 2 vols. Tokyo: Bungei shunjū, 1975.

Yang Daqing 楊大慶. "Contested History: Re-presenting the Nanjing Massacre in Postwar Japan and China." In *Perilous Memories: The Asia-Pacific Wars,* ed. T. Fujitani et al. Durham, N.C.: Duke University Press, forthcoming.

———. "Convergence or Divergence? Recent Historical Writings on the Rape of Nanjing," *American Historical Review* 104.3 (June 1999): 842–65.

———. "The Making of a 20th Century *Rashomon:* The Nanjing Massacre." M.A. thesis, University of Hawai'i, 1989.

———. "Rekishika e no chōsen: 'Nankin atoroshitisu' kenkyū o megutte" 歴史家への挑戦：「南京アトロシティス」研究をめぐって (A Challenge to Historians: Studying the Nanjing Atrocity). *Shisō* 思想 890 (August 1998): 83–109.

———. "A Sino-Japanese Controversy: The Nanjing Atrocity as History." *Sino-Japanese Studies* 3.1 (November 1990): 14–35.

Yin, James, and Shi Young. *The Rape of Nanking: An Undeniable History in Photographs.* Chicago: Innovative Publishing Group, 1996.

Yokoyama Hiroaki 横山宏章. "Kaisetsu: Nankin no sanji to Rābe no nikki" 解説・南京の惨事とラーベの日記 (Explanation: The Nanjing Tragedy and the Rabe Diary). In *Nankin no shinjitsu* 南京の真実 (The Truth about Nanjing), by John Rabe, trans. Hirano Kyōko 平野卿子, pp. 323–33. Tokyo: Kōdansha, 1997.

Yoneyama, Lisa リサ米山. "'Hikokumin' no kioku to kioku no hikokuminka" 「非国民」の記憶と記憶の非国民化 (The Memory of the Unpatriotic and the Denationalizing of Memory). *Sekai* 世界 641 (October 1997): 266–68.

Yoshida Yutaka 吉田裕. *Gendai rekishigaku to sensō sekinin* 現代歴史学と戦争責任 (Modern Japanese History and War Responsibility). Tokyo: Aoki shoten, 1997.

———. "Heisoku suru nashonarizumu" 閉塞するナショナリズム (Blocked-up Nationalism). *Sekai* 世界 633 (April 1997): 74–82.

———. *Nihonjin no sensō kan: sengo shi no naka no henyō* 日本人の戦争観：戦後史の中の変容 (Japanese Views of the War: The Shifts in the Postwar History). Tokyo: Iwanami shoten, 1995.

———. *Tennō no guntai to Nankin jiken* 天皇の軍隊と南京事件(The Emperor's Military and the Nanjing Incident). Tokyo: Aoki shoten, 1986.

Yoshida Yutaka 吉田裕 et al., eds. *Haisen zengo: Shōwa tennō to gonin no shidōsha* 敗戦前後：昭和天皇と五人の指導者 (The Shōwa Emperor and Five Leaders at the Time of the Defeat). Tokyo: Aoki shoten, 1995.

Yoshimi Yoshiaki 吉見義明. *Kusa no ne no fashizumu* 草の根のファシズム (Grass Roots Fascism). Tokyo: Tōkyō daigaku shuppankai, 1990.

Yoshimi Yoshiaki 吉見義明 and Suzuki Yūko 鈴木祐子. "Kōshōron ni hantai suru: Nihongun 'ianfu' mondai no honshitsu to wa" 公娼論に反対する日本軍「慰安婦」問題の本質とは (Refuting Public Prostitution: The Essence of the Problem of the "Comfort Women"). *Sekai* 世界 632 (March 1997): 40–53.

Young, James E. "Toward a Received History of the Holocaust." *History and Theory* 35.4 (December 1997): 21–43.

Yu Xinchun. "Comments." In *The Tokyo War Crimes Trial: An International Symposium*, ed. Hosoya Chihiro et al., pp. 98–101. Tokyo: Kodansha, 1986.

"Zadankai: Nankin daigyakusatsu 'nakatta' koto ni shita seiryoku ga, hisshi de riyō suru saiban no hanketsu" 座談会：南京大虐殺「なかった」ことにした勢力が、必死で利用する裁判の判決 (Discussion: The Decision of the Court That Forces Claiming That the Nanjing Massacre Did Not Occur Desperately Use). *Shukan kin'yōbi* 週刊金曜日 4.31 (23 August 1996): 21–25.

"Zadankai II: Nyūginia kōchi kara Nankin e" 座談会II：ニューギニア高地から南京へ (Discussion: From the New Guinea Plains to Nanjing). *Rekishigaku kenkyū* 歴史学研究 568 (June 1987): 51–72.

Zhang Kaiyuan 章開源. *Nanjing datusha de lishi de jianzheng* 南京大屠殺的历史的见证 (An Eyewitness's Historical Records of the Nanjing Massacre). Wuhan: Huazhong shifan daxue chubanshe, 1995.

Zhang Li 张力. "'1937 nian zhi 1945 nian Zhong-Ri zhanzheng zhi zai jiantao: xin ziliao yu xin jieshi' guoji yantaohui" 1937年至1945年中日战争之再检讨: 新资料与新解释 (The International Symposium "Reassessing the Sino-Japanese War, 1937–1945: New Sources and Interpretations"). *Jindai Zhongguo shi yanjiu tongxun* 近代中国史研究通讯 21 (March 1996): 25–35.

Zhang Xianwen 张宪文. "Guizai chuangxin" 贵在创新 (Valuable Innovations). *Kang-Ri zhanzheng yanjiu* 抗日战争研究 26 (November 1997): 196–205.

Zhongguo dier lishi dang'anguan 中国第二历史档案馆 (Number Two China Historical Archives) et al., eds. *Qin-Hua Rijun Nanjing datusha dang'an* 侵华日军南京大屠杀档案 (Archival Materials on the Nanjing Massacre by the Japanese Troops Who Invaded China). Jiangsu: Jiangsu guji chubanshe, 1987.

Zhu Chengshan 朱成山, ed. *Qin-Hua Rijun Nanjing datusha xinchunzhe zhengyanji* 侵华日军南京大屠杀幸存者证言集 (Collection of Testimonies by Survivors of the Nanjing Massacre of the Japanese Army of Invasion). Nanjing: Nanjing daxue chubanshe, 1994.

"Zhuiyi Rikou Nanjing datusha" 追忆日寇南京大屠杀 (Remembering the Nanjing Massacre Committed by the Japanese Invaders). *Xinhua yuebao* 新华月报 3 (1951): 988–91.

Zoku gendaishi shiryō (6): Gunji keisatsu 続現代史資料6: 軍事警察 (Materials in Contemporary History, Continued, 6: The Military Police). Tokyo: Misuzu shobō, 1982.

Zou Mingde 邹明德 et al. "Nanjing datusha de lishi shishi burong cuangai" 南京大屠杀的历史事实不容篡改 (The Historical Facts of the Nanjing Massacre Will Not Permit Tampering). *Lishi dang'an* 历史档案 4 (1982): 85–88.

Contributors

MARK S. EYKHOLT is the Director of Intern Programs for the Japan Program and China Program at the Massachusetts Institute of Technology. He received his Ph.D. in Modern Chinese History in June of 1998 from the University of California, San Diego. His dissertation was titled "Living the Limits of Occupation in Nanjing, China, 1937–1945." His research interest is Sino-Japanese relations in the twentieth century.

JOSHUA A. FOGEL is professor of comparative East Asian history at the University of California, Santa Barbara. He received his Ph.D. in history from Columbia University in 1980. His recent publications include *The Literature of Travel in the Japanese Rediscovery of China* (1996) and *Imagining the People: Chinese Intellectuals and the Concept of Citizenship, 1890–1920* (co-editor with M. E. Sharpe, 1997). He is presently researching the Japanese community of Shanghai from the 1860s until the first Sino-Japanese War.

CHARLES MAIER teaches modern European history at Harvard University and is director of its Minda de Gunzburg Center for European Studies. He is the author of, among other works, *Recasting Bourgeois Europe* (1975), *The Unmasterable Past: History, Holocaust, and German National Identity* (1988), and *Dissolu-*

tion: The Crisis of Communism and the End of East Germany (1997). Among his recent scholarly concerns has been the relationship of historical narrative to the work of "truth commissions" after human-rights abuses.

DAQING YANG is assistant professor of history and international affairs at George Washington University, where he teaches modern Japanese history. Educated in Nanjing, Hawaii, and Chicago, he received his Ph.D. from Harvard University in 1996. His recent publications include a review article, "Convergence or Divergence: Recent Historical Writings on the Rape of Nanjing," which appeared in the June 1999 issue of *American Historical Review.* He is currently completing a book manuscript on the role of telecommunications networks in Japan's empire-building efforts between 1931 and 1945.

TAKASHI YOSHIDA is a Ph.D. candidate in the History Department, Columbia University, where he completed his masters thesis in 1996. He has taught modern Japanese history at Marymount Manhattan College and Pace University in New York. He is currently in Japan where he is finishing his dissertation, tentatively titled "Refighting the Nanjing Massacre: Internationalization of History and Memory."

Index

Text: 10/13 Aster
Display: Aster
Composition: Integrated Composition Systems, Inc.
Printing and binding: Haddon Craftsmen
Index: Barbara Roos